House Life

House Life

Space, Place and Family in Europe

**Edited by
Donna Birdwell-Pheasant
and
Denise Lawrence-Zúñiga**

BERG

Oxford • New York

First published in 1999 by
Berg
Editorial offices:
150 Cowley Road, Oxford, OX4 1JJ, UK
70 Washington Square South, New York, NY 10012, USA

Berg is the imprint of Oxford International Publishers Ltd.

Library of Congress Cataloging-in-Publication Data

A catalogue record for this book is available from the Library of Congress.

British Library Cataloguing-in-Publication Data

A catalogue record for this book is available from the British Library.

ISBN 1 85973 230 5 (Cloth)
1 85973 235 6 (Paper)

Typeset by JS Typesetting, Wellingborough, Northants.
Printed and bound in Great Britain by
Biddles Ltd, Guildford and King's Lynn

"Like the house builder, old breaker of stones and splitter of trees, we must destroy, but not to leave the world in disarray, shattered into millions of little cards, sealed in hermetic typologies. In the spirit of the builder, we break reality apart to rebuild it . . . He makes houses out of smashed scraps of nature. We make meaning out of ruined houses, moving from pattern to change, logic to will, culture to history . . ."

—Henry Glassie
Passing the Time in Ballymenone

Contents

Notes on Contributors

Joëlle Bahloul is associate professor of anthropology and Jewish studies at Indiana University (Bloomington). She received the doctoral degree in social and cultural anthropology from the École des Hautes Études en Sciences Sociales (University of Paris) in 1981. She has conducted research on Jewish minorities in France and in Italy. She is the author of *The Architecture of Memory* (Cambridge University Press, 1996).

Donna Birdwell-Pheasant is professor of anthropology at Lamar University in Beaumont, Texas, and holds a Ph.D. in anthropology from Southern Methodist University. Her research in Central America and Ireland has focused on family systems and the historical development of inequality. She has published two book chapters and several articles in journals (including *Journal of Family History* and *American Ethnologist*). She most recently authored "Family Systems and the Foundations of Class in Ireland and England" for *History of the Family: An International Quarterly* (1998).

Sally S. Booth teaches at the Friends World College of Long Island University in Southampton, New York. In her research in Sicily and the United States, she addresses the culture and political economy of land use and architecture, especially in the context of reconstruction and resettlement. Her current work involves the changing culture and politics of land use and open space preservation efforts in eastern Long Island.

Caroline B. Brettell is professor and Chair of the Department of Anthropology at Southern Methodist University. Her major areas of research interest are the anthropology of Europe, the anthropology of gender and family, the anthropology of religion, ethnicity and immigration, and the intersections of anthropology and history. In addition to numerous book chapters and articles, she has written several books, including *Men Who Migrate, Women Who Wait: Population and History in a Portuguese Parish* (Princeton, 1986) and *We Have Already Cried Many Tears: The Stories of Three Portuguese Migrant Women* (Waveland, 1995). She is editor of *When They Read What We Write: The Politics of Ethnography* (Bergin and Garvey, 1993).

Vladimir Ilić is a Project Architect at the architectural firm HOK, Inc., San Francisco, specializing in hotels, resorts, and housing. He has conducted research on industrialized housing in Delft, Holland.

Alice V. James is associate professor of anthropology at Shippensburg University, a senior research associate at the Population Research Institute at Pennsylvania State University, and recently a visiting scholar at the National Center for Social Science Research in Athens, Greece. Her research interests include household formation and process. Among her recent publications are "Fertility Patterns in a Bastardy Prone Sub-Society" (with W. T. Morrill) in *Journal of Quantitative Anthropology* (1991) and "Household Formation on St. Bart, F.W.I.: Continuity and Change," (with W. T. Morrill) in *Human Ecology* (1990).

Loukas Kalisperis is associate professor of architecture and Director of the Stuckeman CAD Laboratory at Pennsylvania State University. He received the Ph.D. in the Interdisciplinary Graduate Program in the Humanities in 1989. He is a registered architect in Greece and a member of the Technical Chamber of Greece.

Denise Lawrence-Zúñiga is professor of environmental studies in the College of Environmental Design at the California State Polytechnic University – Pomona. Her doctoral degree in cultural anthropology is from the University of California – Riverside. Her research focuses on anthropological approaches to the built environment. She is co-author with Setha Low of "The Built Environment and Spatial Form," *Annual Review of Anthropology* (1990) and author of "Transcendence of Place: The Role of *La Placeta* in Valencia's *Las Fallas*" in *Place Attachment* (1992).

Judith A. Rasson is research associate at the University of California – Los Angeles, Institute of Archaeology, where she edits the *Archaeological Research Tools* series. She worked as an archaeologist in Yugoslavia between 1968 and 1982 and served as an interpreter for Project Joint Endeavor in Bosnia in 1996–7. She is currently excavating with a Hungarian team at the Bronze Age tell Százhalombatta-Földvár. Rasson published an article entitled "Ex Balcanis Lux" with Robert K. Evans in *American Antiquity* and an article in Ruth Tringham and Dusan Krstic's volume entitled *Selevac: A Neolithic Village in Yugoslavia* (1990).

Mirjana Stevanović is a research associate in the Department of Anthropology, University of California at Berkeley, currently excavating at the site of Çatal Höyük in Turkey. She specializes in reconstructing ancient architecture. Her publications include "The Age of Clay: The Social Dynamics of House Destruction" in the *Journal of Anthropological Archaeology*.

Susan Buck Sutton is professor of anthropology at Indiana University – Purdue University at Indianapolis. Her research focuses on issues of migration, settlement, and understandings of the "traditional" in recent Greek history. She is author or editor of three volumes: *A Contingent Countryside: Settlement, Economy and Land Use in the Southern Argolid Since 1700* (Stanford University Press, forthcoming), *Constructed Meanings: Form and Process in Greek Architecture* (special edition of the *Yearbook of Modern Greek Studies*, 1995), and *The Landscape and People of the Franchthi Region* (Indiana University Press, 1987).

Lawrence J. Taylor is professor of anthropology at the National University of Ireland, Maynooth. He is author of *Dutchmen on the Bay* and *Occasions of Faith* (both University of Pennsylvania Press) and of *The Road to Mexico* (with photographer Maeve Hickey, University of Arizona Press). He has also published more than two dozen articles on a wide variety of cultural topics.

Preface

This book began as a panel for the 1992 meeting of the American Anthropological Association. The panel was organized by the two editors, who had met one another a year previously at a business meeting of the Society for the Anthropology of Europe. It was SAE that sponsored the ensuing panel as an invited session – or, rather, as two invited sessions, one for oral papers and a second for poster papers. Two of those poster papers developed into contributions to the present book, and all but one of the original oral papers are also included.

Lawrence-Zúñiga's and Birdwell-Pheasant's encounter was a fortuitous one, for we have learned much from one another – and from our contributing authors – through this shared project. In 1992, Lawrence-Zúñiga's scholarly involvement with issues of the built environment was already one of long standing, while Birdwell-Pheasant's involvement had been more casual, entailing only a brief foray into the study of houses during fieldwork in Belize, Central America, during the 1970s. Birdwell-Pheasant was most deeply concerned with issues of the family.

Birdwell-Pheasant extends her thanks to Robert Moulton and Lamar University for assistance in defraying some of the costs of production of this manuscript. She also thanks her children, Brendan and Rebecca, for their patience and support when deadlines loomed and Mom had to post "Do Not Disturb" signs on the door.

Lawrence-Zúñiga gratefully acknowledges the infectious enthusiasm of California Polytechnic-Pomona architecture students committed to the exercise of three-dimensional thinking and skillful rendering of the built environment in two dimensions. In particular, the contributions of Dana Hendrix, Carmen Manriquez, Silke Metzler, Lisa Teichgraeber, and Chunni Thai were indispensable to the task of making house forms a visual reality. Thanks also go to Dan Lawrence for the continuing education in architecture, and to husband, Richard, and son, Scott, for their patience and moral support.

We would like to thank all our authors for their scholarship and insights, which gave this book life. Their diligent efforts in undertaking several rewrites and their supreme patience in dealing with two editors – one in Texas, one in California – are also to be commended. The present work also benefited from the helpful comments of Tamara Hareven, who was a discussant on the original panel at the AAA, and anonymous reviewers. Finally, we would like to thank all those wonderful people who brought us email and the FAX machine, two inventions that make collaborative scholarship across considerable geographical distance a feasible project.

Introduction: Houses and Families in Europe
Donna Birdwell-Pheasant and *Denise Lawrence-Zúñiga*

Humans require shelter, and for hundreds of millennia we have built such shelters for ourselves and our families when and where we have needed them. The shelters we build have become one of the several symbols of our very humanity, in which our vulnerability, sociality, ingenuity, and creativity contend and coalesce and find expression in material form. Our lives and our houses intertwine in a thousand ways.

Exactly when humans began to construct shelters and conceive of them as "home" is impossible to tell. The tendency for the same group of individuals to return repeatedly to a favored spot for activities such as food sharing dates back probably to the earliest ancestral species of our genus, *Homo habilis* (Potts 1984, 1988). It was *habilis'* descendant *Homo erectus* who likely mastered the use of fire more than a million years ago, thereby transforming the habituation of a space into a place of habitation. With fire there was security and warmth and light (Fisher 1983: 198–9; Clark and Harris 1985), and a fuller range of human activities could be safely conducted in and around one central place. Some of the earliest built shelters known to archaeologists are found in Europe, at Terra Amata, France (de Lumley 1969; Binford 1981; Stringer and Gamble 1993).

Houses and Anthropology

Anthropologists have generally tended to treat houses as a backdrop, a setting with props where presumably more interesting and important aspects of the drama of human cultural and social life are played out. The implicit definition of "house" – alternatively known as "dwelling" (e.g. Oliver 1987) or subsumed under "domestic architecture" (e.g. Kent 1990b) – that emerges from the anthropological and archaeological literature refers to a built form where people sleep, eat, socialize, and engage in a variety of economic, symbolic, and other activities that sustain the people who use it. The house shelters from the elements both people and their resources, including equipment, furnishings, food stores, and animals, as well as sacred paraphernalia and symbolic goods.

Clark Wissler (1923) included houses under the rubric of "shelter" as a critical component of the universal cultural inventory of human beings, and Murdock listed "housing" in his 1945 "partial list" of human universals. The latest treatment of human universals (Brown 1991), contains exactly one sentence about houses: "The UP [Universal People] always have some form of shelter from the elements" (1991: 136). Brown does not even mention that this shelter is built, much less refer to the rich range of meanings with which these "Universal People" are wont to endow even the simplest "shelter from the elements," nor the deep emotions that emerge as they make it their home.

Lewis Henry Morgan's *Houses and House-life of the American Aborigines* (1981 [1881]) was one of the first anthropological works to address the role of the house in domestic social organization. Malinowski's 1913 definition of family specified a group of kin occupying "a definite physical space, a hearth and home" (Collier, Rosaldo and Yanagisako 1987). Subsequent definitions of other kinship groups have also emphasized the salience of co-residence (see Parkin 1997: 146), implying thereby some sort of residence or house.

In recent years, archaeologists, historians, and ethnographers alike have gravitated toward the household rather than the family or other kin group as their preferred unit of analysis, accentuating the need for a deeper understanding of the house in anthropological analysis. Archaeologists' partiality to the concept of household is easily explained by the materiality of the house as a recoverable feature in excavations and the identity of households with activities that have clear material products and correlates (Rathje 1981, cited in Netting, Wilk and Arnould 1984; Collier, Rosaldo and Yanagisako 1987). Historians have found census records conveniently organized into households, while ties of kinship and family more often must be inferred from disparate records of births, marriages, deaths, and legal transactions. Many ethnographers, too, have come to favor the concept of household. At its best, "household" describes an economically and socially important unit that – to the extent that its members are associated with (if not consistently co-resident within) a specific dwelling – can be successfully and usefully bounded in space and (somewhat less successfully) in time as well. The difficulty in defining temporal boundaries for households was alleviated somewhat through the development of the notion of developmental cycles in domestic groups (Fortes 1971 [1958]; Goody 1971 [1958]). Anthropologists have also sought to generate typologies of households in terms of morphology and function (Netting, Wilk and Arnould 1984).

Some anthropologists have seen a conceptual opposition of "household versus family." Netting, Wilk and Arnould state: "While both households and families are culturally defined, the former are task-oriented residence units and the latter are conceived of as kinship groupings that need not be localized" (1984: xix–xx). Wilk then argues for the priority of task-orientation over co-residence by observing that the Kekchi households he studied in Belize cannot be defined on the basis of co-residence, but rather "on the basis of the activities of production and distribution"

(1984: 224). Wallerstein and Smith define the household as "the social unit that effectively over long periods of time enables individuals, of varying ages and of both sexes, to pool income coming from multiple sources in order to ensure their individual and collective reproduction and well-being" (1992: 13). Laslett's operational definition of co-residence includes not only elements of economic cooperation, but also procreation and child-rearing (Laslett and Wall 1972).

Writing on the Balearic Island community of Formentera, Bestard-Camps found that it was "necessary to make an analytical distinction" between household and family, since this distinction "can be observed in the everyday discourse of Formentera, where a universe of kinship and a universe of locality are quite evident" (1991: 75). He goes on to insist that family and household must be treated as "two principles of social classification and organization that do not belong to the same universe of discourse" (Bestard-Camps 1991: 75).

But family and household are impossible to keep separate. Even studies that take the family as the ostensible unit of analysis include implicit consideration of the house and household. Families must be housed. Donald Pitkin, for example, found the question of house-building to be an integral element in the life of a Calabrian family, whose history he recounts in his monograph, *The House that Giacomo Built* (1985). Furthermore, our anthropological definitions of the family still sometimes include – either explicitly or implicitly – a criterion of co-residence, even though family life is not completely contained within residences, and households may even include key members who are not regularly co-resident (Brettell 1986, 1988; Wilk 1990). Laslett introduced the concept of "houseful" to separate mere co-residence from the functions of mutual support and domestic cooperation that are essential to households and/or families (1983: 514).

Our anthropological concepts of household and family are not in opposition; they do not define separate realms of discourse. Family (for which the primary reference is kinship) and household (where the primary reference is locality) not only belong to the same universe, they are mutually constituting, with the house itself often serving as the mediating element. It is most often the house that permits us to define households; it is the indispensable reproductive and social reproductive role of family that makes such definition worthwhile. The two concepts are neither congruent nor interchangeable, but they are, at every level beyond the merely anecdotal, absolutely inseparable. They are not alternative mechanisms for the classification of social life.

Both households and families use houses more than as settings for "activities of production and distribution" (Wilk 1984: 224) or as consumer goods (Wilk 1990). They are also mechanisms of communication (Blanton 1994), which channel and regulate social interaction among family members and between separate households (Segalen 1983). Houses are as much cultural constructions as they are built forms. The house defines a place that "belongs to" a particular set of people and also defines, through co-residence and shared usage, the set of people that "belong to" a particular place. The propensity of some Europeans to identify people by their house names rather than the other way around highlights this point (Bestard-Camps 1991; Pine 1996; Gaffin 1996: 95–7).

Architectural scholar Amos Rapoport credits anthropological research with focusing attention on the power of built forms to carry meaning and evoke sentiment (Rapoport 1982). Wilson has described the house as "a technical and cognitive instrument, a tool for thought as well as a technology of shelter" (1988: 5). Through their capacity both to signify appropriate behaviors and to accommodate them, house forms and their resident social groups are mutually constituting. Furthermore, as the built environment accumulates more significations through its historical associations with human occupation over time, understanding their meaning must be approached via the total cultural context of which they are a part.

Among the most fundamental symbolic messages found in houses is the coded distinction between public and private space. Wilson notes that "domestic walls divide space between the public and private, a division that is most important for the development of both the avoidance and the enhancement of human attention" (1988: 5). This division, he notes further, entails "possibilities for concealment" as well as "opportunities for display" (1988: 5). All physically bounded domestic spaces are private to the extent that they allow household members to control access to themselves, perhaps to conceal or hide behavior from the view of others or manage the knowledge others have about them; public spaces, in contrast, are those located beyond the boundaries of home where residents have little or no control. Within the home itself, however, spaces are further differentiated by control of access, often relegating some spaces to group activities or hospitality while others accommodate individual and intimate activities. The "front stage" refers to spaces where the family presents or displays itself and entertains outsiders, while the "back stage" indicates areas of presumably greater individual control where household members prepare, rest and seek solitude. Archaeologist Richard Blanton classifies features of house form (including size, number of specialized rooms, hierarchical layout, spatial complexity, elaboration of symbolic content and external decoration) in terms of two general dimensions – canonical and indexical communication. While canonical elements refer to "back region" and interior elaborations of gender, generation and rank that communicate primarily to residents, indexical elements are "front region," exterior elaborations that indicate status and wealth to those outside the household (Blanton 1994: 10).

While anthropologists may have cued scholars in other fields to the capacity of houses to convey meaning, we still have much to learn from them about the physicality of the house itself. Taylor (Chapter 9) explores the role of ideas about the built environment in the development of general anthropological theory, accessing works of philosophy and literature as well as social theory. He observes that in both England and America, social science developed "in disregard of things (and bodies)".

Other anthropologists (e.g. Kent 1990a; D. Lawrence and Low 1990) have recently turned toward scholars in architecture and history, as well as other social and behavioral sciences such as environmental psychology, sociology, and geography, who have devised various approaches in an effort to place the immense physical diversity, social complexity, and cultural and emotional content of houses within a comparative and/or evolutionary context. Architectural approaches seek to identify the multiple factors responsible for the production of particular built forms distinguished by size, scale, volume, massing, proportion, solid–void relations, level changes, plan, materials, color, decoration, placement of permeable elements, and so on. These explanations typically concentrate on materials and methods of construction, adaptation to climate and environment, expertise of designers/builders, accommodation of organized social groups, and symbolic expression (see Oliver 1987, 1997).

Rapoport's voluminous and encyclopedic writings include one of the earliest comparative discussions of domestic architecture, *House Form and Culture* (1969). Resisting the notion that house form could be explained exclusively or simplistically in terms of environment, availability of materials, or "tradition," Rapoport articulates an explicit but unfortunately linear scheme linking house form and culture, one that emphasizes sociocultural factors modified by environmental and technological constraints. Rapoport argues: "What finally decides the form of a dwelling, and moulds the spaces and their relationships, is the vision that people have of the ideal life" (1969: 47). This vision, rooted in culture, finds expression in world view and then lifestyle, which are the direct generators of the patterned activities people attempt to accommodate in the construction of built forms. In addition to viewing built forms as the products of human activities, or "activity systems,"[1] modified by world view, Rapoport argues that built forms are a communicative device, that they are encoded with meaning as a result of humans' interactions with them, and that they act as a mnemonic for cuing appropriate behavior (1982). The meanings encoded in houses may be mundane ones providing instrumental cues for human behavior – a staircase indicating uses of ascent and descent, or a chair indicating the possibility of repose (Eco 1972). Beyond these utilitarian meanings of architectural features, however, is a system of spatial meanings that interacts with the social system with which it is in contact.

European Cultures and Anthropological Concepts

While anthropologists have sought diligently to differentiate concepts of "house" and "home," "household" and "family," the unity (or mutuality) of these concepts is embedded in many European cultural traditions. Indeed, the anthropological approach to households, family, and house is likely rooted in "folk models" of domestic society derived from European experience (Parkin 1997: 137; Bouquet 1996). If so, it would seem that our concepts tap into several cultural and historical traditions. Contemporary English alternatives for "house" – dwelling, residence, abode – reverberate with the ancient notion of stopping or staying in a place or a habitual returning to a place. The term "house" comes from the Old English *hus* and related *huden*, meaning "to hide" and yielding also "hut," "huddle," and "hoard." This northern European term conveys the fragile and exposed side of the dwellers. The Latin term *domus*, on the other hand, gives us "domicile" (used more often in legal writings than in conversation), as well as "domesticate," "dominate," and "dominion" (Danto 1982). This Mediterranean construction of the house produces a symbol of power, rulership and ownership, with rights and privileges enabling the dweller to impose through possession and transform through habitation (Danto 1982: 8; Rykwert 1991: 52). German philosopher Heidegger went back to Old English and High German roots to derive his concept of "building as dwelling, that is, as being on the earth" (quoted in Bourdier 1989: 40).

The term "house" is often paired with (or interchanged with) "home" (German: *Haus und Heim*). These two terms describe distinct cultural constructions (Rykwert 1991: 52). While "house" implies a physical structure or shelter, "home" defines a place of origin and retreat, such as one's natal village or birthplace, one's country or other native place. Home is a concept of place rather than space, implying emotional attachment and meaning beyond the constraints of the physicality of any particular dwelling house (cf. R. Lawrence 1987). "Home," thus, may take on the meaning of a territory, a physical reference point, a symbol of self, or a manifestation of family identity (Hayward 1975). When Robert Frost wrote that "Home is the place where, when you have to go there, They have to take you in,"[2] the implication was clear. At home, I can count on the welcoming presence of a persistent "they" who are really "us" – caring others, my people, my family (Hollander 1991: 31–3). The idea of attachment, of mooring and roots, is made clear in Hobsbawm's observation that home is "not the destiny of our journeys but the place from which we set out and to which we return, at least in spirit" (1991: 65).

There is more. In classical Latin, a *familia* referred to "everything and everybody under the authority of the household head" (Herlihy 1985: 2), a definition that encompassed not only persons (kin or not) but also the economic resources necessary for their support, including their dwellings.[3] The Greek *oikos* embraced the entire "domestic economy," including inhabitants as well as their material base of operations – house as well as household (Jameson 1990: 109). In the Catalonian *casa*, "the family and property are identified as a single reality" (d'Argemir 1988: 144). Pina-Cabral's definition of *casa* for the Portuguese case (cited by Brettell in Chapter 2) refers to "a compound of land, buildings, animals, people, absent relatives, and even the dead of the household" (1986: 38). In Serbia, the term *kuća* means both house and the extended family (see Rasson *et al.*, Chapter 7). In all these cases, the physical structure of the house, with its contents, and the family conceptually form a single, enduring unit of society that combines social, economic, and ritual practices in its own biological and social reproduction.[4]

In Europe, "house" and "family" sometimes become indistinguishable. When we hear of the "House of Windsor," we know that the reference is not to an architectural form, but rather to a constructed family line extending across many generations. Such a concept is often extended to business enterprises ("*Maison de . . .*") or political entities (House of Lords, House of Representatives). In each case, "house" implies corporate longevity, transcending the human life-span, often many times over.

It is this usage that Lévi-Strauss sought to elaborate in his concept of the "house society," developed in the 1980s. Lévi-Strauss derived his concept from comparisons of certain North American Indian societies (Yurok, Kwakiutl) with medieval European ones, bringing Europe more clearly into the purview of anthropology's comparative kinship studies. When Lévi-Strauss describes the house, he denotes far more than a constructed shelter. A house is "a corporate body holding an estate made up of both material and immaterial wealth, which perpetuates itself through the transmission of its name, its goods and its titles down a real or imaginary line, considered legitimate as long as this continuity can express itself in the language of kinship or of affinity and, most often, of both" (1982: 174; also 1991: 435).[5] He emphasizes further the ability of the house to reunify and transcend the contradictory forces of "patrilineal descent and matrilineal descent, filiation and residence, hypergamy and hypogamy, close marriage and distant marriage, heredity and election" (1982: 184).

This recognition that contradictory forces are at work within the institution of the house is a significant contribution, but not satisfactorily explained by Lévi-Strauss' theory, which is complicated by the vague assertion that house society is somehow transitional between kin-based and class-based societies[6] (Lévi-Strauss 1987: 151). Carsten and Hugh-Jones called it a "hybrid" form (1995: 10). Because the mechanisms of this transition or hybridization are left unexplained, efforts to apply the house society model ethnographically have met with inconsistent success. Macdonald cautions that "the question needing an answer is if what the ethnologists, on the one hand, and the native peoples, on the other, call 'house' corresponds well to that which Lévi-Strauss thus defined" (author's translation, 1987: 4). Headley, who applied the concept of "house society" to an array of Southeast Asian locales, refers to the house as "a technique or strategy for extending the idiom of the family" and as "a strategy for accumulating and installing family identity even beyond the loosely classificatory family limits" (1987: 210). This is a useful observation and more pertinent to the kinds of questions posed here than the more knotty theoretical construct Lévi-Strauss termed "house society."

Questions of Agency

To argue, as we do here, that houses and families are mutually constituting, inevitably raises questions of agency. Though often credited with corporate agency (Parkin 1997; Lévi-Strauss 1991), families, households, and houses are composed of and/or constructed by individuals, whose personal agency may at times be compromised but never canceled. Eugene Hammel argues that the household is "simply not a very good unit of observation," advising that "we would do well to observe not households but the important behaviors and norms of persons interacting by virtue of comembership" (1984: 40). Laslett goes even farther, describing the household as a "knot of individual interests" (1984). Focusing exclusively on the agency of individuals, however, compromises our ability to account for the power of houses to structure and constrain the lives of these individual agents.

Material dimensions of family life are evident in the work of several scholars who have endeavored to re-situate social theory in space as well as time (Agnew 1989; Richardson 1989; Soja 1989). Giddens' notion of *structuration* (1984) and Bourdieu's concept of *habitus* (1976) both show great sensitivity to the incorporation of material and spatial dimensions of social action and their linkage to actors' conceptual frameworks. Bourdieu specifically focuses on *habitus* as a "system of predispositions inculcated by the material circumstances of life and by family upbringing" (1976: 118). The materiality of domestic life is a central factor in forming and reproducing the family biologically, socially, economically and morally. Bourdieu's notion of "double structuration" is also relevant, with its focus on the manner in which separate entities become embedded in one another (Barnard 1990: 203).

"Agency," according to Alfred Gell, "is attributable to those persons (and things. . .) who/which are seen as initiating causal sequences of a particular type, that is, events caused by acts of mind or will or intention, rather than the mere concatenation of physical events" (1998: 16). Gell's definition is particularly pertinent to the present work, as it extends agency to works of art and other artifacts, including houses (1998: 252). Artifacts are not merely the products or "patients" of social agents, but embody the "distributed personhood" of their makers, and thus truly exercise agency in their own right and serve as vehicles of social relations (1998: 18–21).

Gell describes houses as "artefacts with very special characteristics all their own," which have an "organic plan and capacity for disassembly and reassembly, remodelling and redecoration" that "allows them to objectify the organic connectedness of historical processes" (1998: 252). The acts involved in building and remodeling houses; in family formation, sustenance and dissolution; in daily living in a house, passing a house on to the next generation, or selectively using a house to include or exclude family members all index agency. By such acts, individuals participate in routines or make conscious choices and plans, but also employ strategies involving principles and objectives consistent with the collective interests of family and household groups of which they are members. Although agency entails intent, actors need not be conscious or even aware of the strategies of family reproduction that they implement.

The production and use of houses, then, are not just exercises in the practical generation of cultural forms; they entail the reciprocal influence of the domestic environment on actors who find their daily activities both enabled and constrained by the physical character of the house and its contents. Houses are encoded with practical meanings denoting proper spaces for preparing food and eating, sleeping, storing possessions, and the like, but tensions often develop between meaning and praxis. The search for a solution or accommodation involves family and household members in producing and reproducing an objective domestic structure that embodies its own generative principles. Houses are also encoded with complex symbolic meanings, expressing identity, status and the good life, which, coupled with their practical dimensions, endow houses with the power to communicate, represent, influence and teach. This power is reinforced by the conservative character of durable European house forms, which by their solidity and fixed physicality discourage questioning while lending legitimacy to the practical and moral orders they represent. They often operate as unobtrusive, "natural" and self-evident containers of human activity, and frequently appear to be taken for granted by their occupants.

Much of what family and household members experience as the physical structure of the house is in fact the collective outcome of the agency of others, especially in the past, even the remote past. As Illich has stated, "To dwell means to live in the traces that past living has left" (1982, quoted in Bourdier 1989: 40). Studying the European house provides a uniquely clear case: Europeans live within and act in terms of physical structures whose siting, size, arrangement, and very substance are the residue of others' choices and strategies. Wilson associates the emergence of "relatively permanent dwellings" as a key element in the domestication of the human species (1988: 3). It may also be an element in the emergence of patriarchy and status or class differentiation. Less durable structures are more amenable to self-construction by women in non-stratified societies and by the poor and younger generations in all societies.[7] Because of the unique role that the house plays as a fixed and limited resource essential for biological and social reproduction, it readily becomes an agent of differentiation and hierarchization within societies. Bourdier and AlSayyad devised "an understanding of dwelling as the materialization of the bond between people and the means by which they choose to transmit 'handed-down' knowledge and social practices" (1989b: 11).

Sometimes the structure that houses impose upon family life and individuals within families is ingenuous and readily received and reproduced as "tradition."

This is not to say that the effects are entirely benign, as houses often can be seen as instruments in the hegemony of gender, generation, and class within even the most "traditional" systems. In other times and places – and especially since the nineteenth century in Europe – the imposition of houses with a given structure has been by design, with clear intent to change the lives of the people who inhabit them. In Europe, the hegemony of bourgeois culture, of scientific and rationally enlightened planning, and of the market began to contend vigorously with "tradition" in the generation of families and houses. By the late twentieth century, the success of modern housing in Europe (and North America) had reached beyond its originating locus to find increasingly global acceptance. With much of the world now experiencing the influx of Western housing, it is important to understand the historical and cultural origins of these forms and their mutually constituting relations with the families that occupy them.

The process of materializing social relations in built forms began a long time ago in Europe. An insightful study by archaeologist Matthew Johnson documents changing house forms in rural Suffolk, England, in the fourteenth to sixteenth centuries. Johnson argues that these changes were a precursor to eighteenth- and nineteenth-century housing alterations expressing privacy and class differentiation (1993). The fourteenth-century medieval open hall, with its multifunctional central hearth plus storage and parlor attached to either side, was a space jointly used by both the landowning family and their dependents, including servants, whose interactions were based on mutual understandings of proper relations of status and deference. This open hall plan gave way by the sixteenth century to a closed house form, in which a lobby entry bisected the house and the hearth, dividing the functions of the hall into two parts, spatially segregating the two classes, and stimulating the development of a class consciousness that began to separate the landowning class itself "for itself" from all others (1993: 107).

Johnson links the architectural expression of this precipitating class structure to larger economic and cultural changes, including an emphasis on physical division and enclosure as a means of control, the rise of the concept of privacy, and the idealization of rational thinking, which placed a high value on designating space according to use. But architectural forms were more than mere expressions of change; they promoted the changes in society themselves by physically reorganizing social groups and channeling their activities and interactions. By the seventeenth century, the growing rural adoption of "polite architecture" – a codified, international, formal architecture – had firmly and irrevocably come to establish, reinforce and symbolize the separation and domination of the landed classes (1993: 140). Building social relations into the physical structure of houses and house systems made them more easily separable from their original social context and even permitted the export and imposition of social forms favored by dominant classes, cultures and nations.

By the nineteenth century, the growing European bourgeois classes popularized more modest and technologically sophisticated versions of the landed estate and urban mansion, encoding into the physical structure of the house elaborated concepts of family and individual privacy and a rational order compartmentalizing activities and individualizing spaces. Although this form of housing was copied and adapted and later imposed by governments across Europe, homogeneity has not ensued. This is, in part, because people selectively appropriate or subversively modify elements of the modern house, or else find new value in the retention of older vernacular houses, such that multiple forms of housing exist today. In fact, new hegemonic influences of industrialized production, mass marketing and advertising have begun to commodify housing, shifting the meaning of the house yet again.

The chapters in this volume explore the materiality and meanings of European houses from a number of perspectives. We have arrayed the contributions into three sets: In Part I, Brettell, Sutton and Birdwell-Pheasant examine the interaction of houses and families (in Portugal, Greece, and Ireland, respectively) over multiple generations and in historical context. In Part II, Booth; Lawrence-Zúñiga; Rasson, Stevanović and Ilić; and James and Kalisperis take a more ethnographic approach, focusing on various aspects of the house/family interface in Sicily, Portugal, Serbia, and Greece. Part III pursues the more deeply symbolic and cognitive dimensions of houses in Ireland (Taylor) and for immigrants to France (Bahloul). Crosscutting this organizational scheme are some common themes regarding the hegemony of generation, gender, and class. Most of the chapters also highlight aspects of change as modern house forms replace premodern ones, with additional themes emerging about the hegemony of market and government and the counter-hegemonic agency of individuals.

Premodern Foundations of House and Family

Why is it so tempting to dichotomize the history of European house and family life into sequential periods labelled "traditional" and "modern"? Certainly for Europe, where the very labels themselves received their cultural genesis and definition, such a division would be appropriate. However, it is precisely because these terms are so deeply embedded in European culture history and so problematic in anthropology that they must not go unexamined here. Although Europeans themselves generally identify "tradition" with the past and with informal transmission and continuity, anthropologists have learned that tradition is dynamic and ever current. Hobsbawm and Ranger's (1983) lessons about the continuing invention of tradition in human societies are well known by now. Bourdier has even noted that, although we often position tradition in contrast to modernity, in fact "tradition defined as the past is a modernist idea" (1989: 38). Modernity, furthermore, has deep roots within "traditional" Europe, where the modern nuclear family became predominant by at least the sixteenth century in England (Laslett and Wall 1972) and where the so-called modern model of the house (with its rational allocations of space to specific functions and systematic separation of genders and generations) also originated.

This being said, it is still the case that there are certain configurations of houses and families that are more characteristic of past times and quite other configurations that are now, by tradition, recognized as "modern." Since the modern model of the house and family are easier to document and have clear salience, we choose here to use the contrast set "modern" and "premodern," although in the clear recognition that there is no abrupt break between the two in many parts of Europe and that "modern" is not, after all, a monolithic formal construct. In general, we assume that people's interaction with their built environment in Europe or anywhere else exhibits more continuity than discontinuity. If we had complete histories of all phases of housing change in all the societies documented here, the apparent contrast between premodern and modern would undoubtedly be less stark. Lawrence Taylor gives us a taste of this in his treatment of the "traditional" Irish west room (Chapter 9), as well as what came before and what comes after. In most cases, however, our historical purview is more limited.[8]

Built to Last: Investing in House and Family

Premodern European houses were generally built to last, often housing, sequentially, many generations of the same family. Such houses represented a considerable familial investment in biological, social and economic reproduction. The physical facts of houses – their durability, permanence, fixed location and degree of malleability – conditioned the ways in which they influenced and were influenced by family strategies. The durability of the house depended on the choice of materials and methods of construction, which was influenced by the intended use of the house as well as the type and amount of resources available. House longevity entered into family strategies as a consideration of life expectancy or "anticipated uselife" of the house in relation to householders' use of it (McGuire and Schiffer 1983).

Adapting a dwelling to householders' ongoing needs often required assembling further resources to make renovations; general upkeep also required continuing outlays of material and labor resources. Investments in houses were often substantial; but because houses are durable, they can bestow benefits over many generations. Brettell's study (Chapter 2) lucidly demonstrates the role that a house can play in the integrity of a family line across generations. Her detailed analysis of a northern Portuguese case reveals the complexities of how strategic expansion and contraction of family are linked to property through time. Sutton (Chapter 3) and James and Kalisperis (Chapter 8) describe the inheritance roles houses are expected to play and how such expectations affect house construction in Greece.

The symbolic associations arising from housing investments, especially over the long-term, have powerful implications for the attachment family members feel with home and locale. Material investment in houses is not unrelated to symbolic and emotional investment. Households often seize the potential of durable, permanent dwellings to generate associations with site and context through long-term territorial occupations, which in turn entail long-term implications for the resident families. The association of family with the land facilitated by the materiality of home is detailed in a historical manner by Birdwell-Pheasant (Chapter 4), who takes us back to ancient Ireland and the genesis of the Irish notion of "place." This type of family identity often imputes a more enduring presence in a particular locale than can be established in fact. Nonetheless, where dwellings are built beside the ruins of previous family occupations, they add a powerful legitimacy to ties of place. For Greece, Sutton (Chapter 3) details the way in which Irakliote household strategies historically included the construction of houses to legitimate claims to actual space, but also to construct a history of connection and identity within the Nemea Valley. Sutton argues that in spite of the historical mobility and flexibility of population and settlement in many parts of Greece, "the concept of the stable village community has . . . been part of the national invention of tradition in Greek life" (Chapter 3, p. 91). Thus, the durability of European houses may at times be more of a symbolic declaration than a historical reality. Sutton's Greek case demonstrates that the importance of the house as a symbol of familial unity, status, and continuity may in fact obscure the realities of "a shifting housing base" and the strategems implemented by family agents.

House form, with its implications of stability, enables household recruitment, but equally establishes limits to co-residence. Brettell's northern Portuguese family (Chapter 2) used the allocation of spaces in the main house for designating and accommodating core members while peripheralizing or excluding others; these spatial patterns were later finalized in inheritance distributions. Sutton (Chapter 3) relates how Greek families recruit members using the house as well as new house construction as an instrument of family control over migration and consolidation. Although the house may symbolically communicate family continuity, deep family history may similarly lend importance to the house. In Formentera, Bestard-Camps noted that prestige is associated with the house that has a successful, deep lineage, whereas "indigence" is associated with the "new" house (1991: 56).[9]

Houses, as vehicles of strategic recruitment to and exclusion from family lines, participated in the hegemony of the older generations. Generational hegemony was often strongly implemented through the regulation of access to means of livelihood via houses. Blanton shows how the predominant use of gender-specific interior spaces could act to remind younger household members that their control over family resources and choice of marriage partners were limited by an older generation (1994: 108). In Europe, where both family and its means of livelihood (whether retail establishment, workshop, or agricultural enterprise) were housed within a single structure or on common premises, the form and function of structures were affected and access to housing was tied up with access to livelihood. Such formal linkages also effectively reinforced the identification of the family or household as the unit of economic production. Houses described in this book often included spaces for agricultural equipment and storage, and even for the sheltering of farm animals. Brettell (northern Portugal), Sutton (Greece) and James and Kalisperis (also Greece) indicate that houses in their studies were often constructed on two levels, with humans occupying the upper floor. Control over houses not only regulated the next generation's access to means of livelihood, but also determined their ability to dispense hospitality, which in turn regulated their integration into larger communities (Segalen 1983).

As the size and composition of the household changed during its developmental cycle, the inventory of activities a household needed to accommodate could also change, requiring investment in alterations of house form (McGuire and Schiffer 1983: 285), such as the rearrangement of space or construction of new rooms and divisions. Changes in family size and composition could also be accommodated by building or acquiring more houses. The Portuguese (Chapter 2) house compound – the *lugar de vivenda* – could contain several houses and be associated with an extended set of family connections that transcended even national boundaries. Brettell also notes the continued interaction among family segments who lived in houses outside the primary *lugar*, introducing the concept of neighborhood. Greek families (Sutton, Chapter 3), in deference to the value of nuclear family autonomy, constructed new houses in clusters, creating virilocal neighborhoods. The settlement of new couples in physically separate structures falls short of true neolocality where the new house is in fact provided and controlled by the senior generation (see also Birdwell-Pheasant, Chapter 4; Collier 1997: 116–18).

Although European, as well as other highly differentiated societies, are characterized by relatively permanent settlements and substantial, often elaborate houses, there is considerable variability in the types and longevity of houses intentionally used for dwelling purposes. Under conditions of social inequality, dwellings have differential capacities to shelter multiple successive generations of a family and thereby enter into household strategies of resource deployment and inheritance. Birdwell-Pheasant's discussion (Chapter 4) of Ballyduff family and house systems identifies "long-" and "short-cycle" houses, which vary in durability and are allocated within a single family: the substantial house is inherited by the principal heir, while less substantial houses are built for siblings. Important families thus not only control recruitment to or exclusion from their own main premises, but often control sets of peripheral houses as well. In early nineteenth-century Ireland, successive generations of lesser heirs and their descendants became peripheralized from their core families and accumulated on the land in unprecedented numbers in the decades leading up to the Great Famine.

The seasonality of European rural activity also often required investment in the construction of more than one kind of house. David Gaunt has described a Carelian household in nineteenth-century Finland composed of forty-two members who lived together in two heated three-room houses during the winter, but in summer lived more outdoors and slept in seventeen sleeping sheds (1987: 127). Rasson *et al.* (Chapter 7) report changes in cooking and sleeping facilities in Serbia from winter to summer. Transhumant peoples often had different kinds of houses to meet seasonal needs required by the movement of livestock. Birdwell-Pheasant (Chapter 4) notes that the traditional Irish had their small "booley houses" near the places of summer pasturage, while maintaining primary houses on their farms. Such a pattern was once widespread among pastoral Europeans.

The furnishings and collected contents of a house represent yet another avenue of investment. Taylor (Chapter 9) refers to this as the "assembled environment," as seen in the Irish west room, where "all the objects of sentimental value" were kept (Arensberg and Kimball 1940: 129). Likewise, the traditional parlor in the French village of Minot was "a place in which to display family possessions," each of which had its remembered history and meaning (Zonabend 1984: 16). In Spain, Collier describes how the mothers of the bride and groom would "construct," through furnishings and décor, the requisite "wedding house" for their offspring, which sought to replicate, in so far as possible, an ideal house (1997: 116–18). Rasson *et al.* (Chapter 7) describe the assemblage of furnishings and smaller details necessary for the ideal or "complete" house in Serbia.

The studies in this volume show that investing in houses – both materially and emotionally – is an investment in the family and in its continuity. Upper classes, who control more wealth, understandably make more lavish investments in houses. This, in turn, can strengthen not only the hegemony of the upper class within the society, but also the hegemony of generation and gender within the upper class.

Structuring Space and Social Life

The mutually constituting relations between houses and families depend as much on reproductive strategies as they do on the physical facts of house form, but are actualized in the relationship between household members' daily activities and the specific form of their house. Family investments in house construction and renovation take advantage of the design of a house and its modifiability to meet the changing needs of the residents. This may be accomplished in a number of ways – through rapid or gradual construction and reconstruction; superficial treatments or structural additions, deletions and subdivisions; and modifications through changes in designated usages (functions) and names, or organization of relationships of usages (adjacencies) of particular domestic spaces.

Premodern European houses were designed and built by local craftsmen who employed local construction materials, methods and concepts of appropriate physically bounded, named spaces, or rooms, intended for use by people engaged in one or more activities, or to accommodate storage or animals. Presumably, houses were constructed with the input of household members for the purpose of accommodating to their size, composition and expected activities, a concept typically identified as "fit" or congruence (D. Lawrence and Low 1990: 460). Europe's premodern houses often afforded sufficient space and flexibility to accommodate gracefully the predictable or typical transformations of the family through its patterned developmental cycle. Nonetheless, as successive births, marriages and deaths, as well as migrations and returns, introduced new members to, or deleted them from, the domestic setting, tensions arose between the social group, its activities, and the existing house spaces, requiring solutions such as new construction or else renaming and reassigning spaces (or, on occasion, doubling-up).

Matthew Johnson's work on English houses from the fourteenth century onward establishes the roots of the modern house, but simultaneously highlights an important premodern feature, that of central multifunctional spaces. Premodern European houses were in general characterized by more open and multifunctional spaces and by ownership and control by the elder generation. The kitchen – the woman's domain – with its conceptually central hearth was generally the most multifunctional space in the house, accommodating cooking, eating and everyday social interaction among the family. Edelman describes the Russian *izba* as "one large, heated room" where "peasants ate, slept, worked, socialized, learned, pro-created, perhaps bathed, sometimes defecated, entered the world, and often left it" (1993: 8). Construction of additional hearths could catalyze formation of new nuclear segments within a larger family unit, as detailed in Brettell's Portuguese case (Chapter 2).[10]

Although activities within these multifunctional rooms were not bounded by physical walls and barriers, they were far from chaotic. Areas could be segregated by the use of props or conceptually designated by customary location of certain activities within the larger space (Johnson 1993; Kent 1984). James and Kalisperis (Chapter 8) describe the kitchens of many older houses on Chios as being divided conceptually by an "unmarked threshold" separating hospitality areas from regions used for food processing and other daily activities. On the other hand, Chios food preparation is not confined to specific spaces such as the kitchen, but may occur as well on the front steps of homes. Thus, although activities may tend to recur in specific spaces, they are not exclusive to these spaces, nor do these spaces remain dedicated to specific uses over time.

A classic description of a multifunctional space is found in Zonabend's study of the house in Minot, in the French province of Burgundy. The traditional *salle*[11] in Minot was a single room and the center of family life, in which there was "no separation between the living and the dead, between the healthy and the sick; and the generations were not isolated" (1984: 15). Within the room, however, certain furnishings and equipment marked male and female areas, and social rules were strictly enforced, including "the imposition of a strict discipline between generations" in which "the children kept silent, the old people stayed in the background" (1984: 15). Zonabend concludes that "what was lost in space was recovered in time, i.e. in the hierarchy of generations" (1984: 15). Some of these same observations about family life are echoed by Bestard-Camps in his study of the older houses on the island of Formentera, in the Balearics, in which the *porxo* served multiple functions for daily life and for managing the family farm (1991: 121–7).

In European cultures, although houses were most often built by men they were "made" and "kept" by "homemakers" and "housekeepers" – women, whose touch was required to make a house a home. In fact, houses (and kitchens in particular) are often considered to be the principal domain of women, such that domestic forms not only express gender relations but reproduce them. Bahloul (Chapter 10) finds the house, the locus of transplanted Algerian Jewish memory in France, essentially symbolic of women's position within a largely patriarchal family structure. Although motherhood was the venerated ideal for women, expressed in the central courtyard symbolizing the womb, the economic necessity and desire of women to work brought tensions. Bahloul clearly indicates how relations of gender and generation reverberate in house form and in the memory of house form.

In Greece and Sicily, home, and especially the kitchen, has been the center of women's activities, in contradistinction to the public arena, associated with men. James and Kalisperis (Chapter 8) describe the control over the kitchen a Greek woman could exercise (especially when she was an older grandmother), not only by cooking all the meals but by sleeping there as well. The working-class Sicilian women described by Booth (Chapter 5) favored a house in which kitchens opened onto a shared, semi-public courtyard and exterior balconies permitted women to "overview" and communicate from one house to another.

The communication of private household spaces with public streets and plaza is often expressed through the architectural form of thresholds, whether visible or conceptual. Permeable elements such as doors and windows identify transitions in space, use and social meaning. James and Kalisperis (Chapter 8) describe a wide range of thresholds on Chios, from balconies and open courtyards to abrupt stone walls linking houses to the street. While the relative openness of movable elements like shutters and gates can signal to passers-by the possibility of approach, the presence of residents in their open courtyard, the *avli*, is an active invitation to social interaction. In the Mastichochoria village residents temporarily appropriate the street with chairs, as they do in many Mediterranean settlements, to create a conceptual *avli* where there is no formal transitional space. Thresholds connecting interior and exterior, private and public, seem especially significant in Mediterranean cultures, where much work is done out-of-doors.

Householders regulate visitors' access into their private household space in a variety of ways. James and Kalisperis (Chapter 8) explain that, although close friends and family may be entertained in the kitchen, formal guests should be hosted in the salon; if no separate space is available, a portion of the kitchen bounded by furniture may serve that purpose. Among the Gorale of Poland there were two "parlors": the "white room" represented "formality, ritual and time-out-of-time" and stood in symbolic opposition to the "black room," where "the inhabitants' day-to-day life is played out" (Pine 1996: 447). In Ireland, the kitchen was the locus of daily life, while the west room came to be "reserved as a sort of parlor into which none but distinguished visitors are admitted" (Arensberg and Kimball: 1940: 129). In an extreme example – the French village of Minot – the public was generally kept at bay altogether. In fact, the house was so closed to public scrutiny that even house-cleaning, which required "opening up" the house, was minimized (Zonabend 1984: 16).

Social life is also constituted and reconstituted by the often selective remembrance of houses. Bahloul (Chapter 10) examines the North African Jewish home through memory – as a mnemonic for a way of life that has irrevocably changed for members of the community who emigrated to France. For the migrants, house form is a remembered narrative that strengthens family cohesion. The remembered central courtyard not only acts as a symbol of the womb, but is historically associated with the deceased mother around whom the family is organized. Bahloul argues that these reminiscences "transform the physicality of past experiences into intangible and irreversibly symbolic ones in the present. It is a discursive strategy whereby displaced ethnicity aims to restore its shattered geography" (Chapter 10, p. 247).

In a more practical vein, we can see that Europeans' remembrance of premodern houses may be a factor affecting their experiences with the modern house, not only precipitating resistance to change but also motivating nostalgic acquisition of older structures. (See further discussion below and in Booth, Chapter 5, and Lawrence-Zúñiga, Chapter 6.) Whole communities may even be structured by the memory of houses: Sutton (Chapter 3) explains the ideological importance of belief in the historic depth of family connections. Through memory, this belief lingers through generations of emigrants from these rural places.

Taylor (Chapter 9) stresses the symbolic and emotional – indeed, transformative – power of rooms within the house in his contribution, contrasting Arensberg and Kimball's classic description of the Irish west room with an Irish kitchen and parlor portrayed by novelist Frank O'Connor. Taylor describes the west room's transformation from a space reserved for the farm family's retired old couple into an English-style parlor to accommodate more bourgeois lifestyles. After exploring the origins of the west room itself, Taylor goes on to explore the development of Western cultural views of the material environment, especially those of the Victorian middle class, which viewed the built environment, especially the domestic one, as a civilizing force capable of reforming society and especially the working classes. Under the influence of Protestant landlord and government, and the Catholic Church, domesticating and civilizing forces were set in motion in order to bring concepts of family morality and individual privacy to the poor.

The issue of the parlor as a room set apart from daily life in which to represent the family and receive visitors is one of the most important developments in European rural house design before the start of the "modern" period after the Second World War. As a continuation of processes set in place by the landed elite late in the Middle Ages in England (Johnson 1993) and at other times elsewhere in Europe, the incorporation of a special room for hosting visitors to the house reflects concern for family reputation as well as the influence of increasing affluence on class consciousness. Lawrence-Zúñiga (Chapter 6) traces the changing hierarchies of domestic spaces in a rural southern Portuguese town to the first half of the twentieth century, when remodeling activities favored creation of an entry and a *sala* for guests, shifting the kitchen from its prominent position at the front of the house to the rear. The creation of new spaces acted to buffer and protect the private life of the family from public view and even from the view of welcomed visitors, but it also moved family activity, which often spilled into the rear and interior of the house, out of view altogether. But because the *sala* was already a part of older rural bourgeois homes, its appropriation by less affluent residents had a more powerful symbolic meaning related to family image; it was intended to signify readiness to engage in bourgeois civility and to signal a more dignified and respectable lifestyle. Further implications of this trend are discussed below in the context of the development of the modern model of the house.

The Modern Model of the House

The ascendancy of the modern model of the house in the twentieth century has had a far-reaching impact on European families. As noted earlier, the production of housing in Europe had long been managed by specialists, as is the case in most socially differentiated societies; but until recently the manufacture of the materials and the methods of construction used in housing were predominantly local. During the nineteenth century, the gradual growth of industrialization and the mass production of material goods began to alter significantly local control over the construction and form of housing; national and international urban industrial centers became the sources for products and ideas. Just as important in this regard was the increasing influence of bourgeois reformers and urban professionals whose design ideas began to shape private housing production and government housing policies and to change expectations regarding living standards. By the twentieth century, bourgeois reform ideas linked up with the progress and promise of science and technology to promote a single concept of family housing. This concept has since come to dominate the design and construction of urban and most rural houses, and government policies seeking to regulate them, in most European nations. The intention of this "modern model" of the house is to rationalize living patterns by providing the most economical and efficient spaces for everyday life (Tosi 1995) and by meeting the assumed needs of an idealized, relatively autonomous nuclear family.

The twentieth-century modern model of European housing was intended by its urban bourgeois and professional creators to provide spaces for domestic activities that would maximize efficiency and promote the well-being of the family. Ideally, it was to include *minimum* spaces for eating, cooking, resting, sleeping, bathing, socializing and leisure pursuits, while providing basic amenities for hygiene and health. Implicitly, formally undifferentiated space was seen as chaotic and somehow wasteful. The organization of spaces was conceived to provide for the privacy of the ideal nuclear family from its neighbors and of individuals from one another within the home. The proposed ideal minimum usually consisted of a room for a family's collective activities (a combined living/dining room), a small efficient kitchen equipped with "labor-saving" modern appliances, three bedrooms (one for parents and one for the children of each sex), and a bathroom. Many European governments eventually developed programs to build or subsidize new housing for working-class families whose houses did not meet these standards. Especially during reconstruction after the Second World War, such programs did equalize some housing conditions across classes in urban areas. As Rasson *et al.* (Chapter 7) describe, state-supplied apartments in the former Yugoslavia fell short of the ideal while also failing to meet expectations of residents. Although this was the case in most European countries at one time or another, it was chronic throughout Eastern Europe in the twentieth century.

Publicly financed housing projects stimulated the development of a housing industry centered on mass production of standardized building components and specialized labor, resulting in displacement of rural builders working in the local vernacular. International style-setting design trends and the mass production of consumer items such as furniture and appliances to fill new houses have further weakened local control over ideas about the proper way to live. Market forces increasingly enter into the construction and economics of housing and remove the immediate control of design, the organization of space and expression of domestic values from traditional key actors (Pavlides and Hesser 1989). The home ceases to be a center of production and becomes instead a locus of consumption; the domestic environment is commodified.

The ability of families to modify their homes, whether by simple renovation in the local vernacular or by appropriating and incorporating modern, commodified domestic designs sold in the marketplace, depends on a different aspect of their control – home ownership, or at least long-term tenancy, the rights to which can be passed on to descendants. Home ownership rates generally run higher in rural areas than in cities, allowing families to make the kind of substantial modifications to their housing that urban dwellers, especially those in rented apartments, find difficult or impossible. Occupant-initiated or self-managed changes to house form probably occur in both owned and rented properties alike, but to different degrees (Tosi 1995). Existing house and apartment forms can constrain outcomes. Brettell (Chapter 2) shows how inherited rights to a rural farm house and surrounding land permitted descendants of a Portuguese farmer to add on to the main house and build additional separate houses. In contrast, Rasson *et al.* (Chapter 7) describe the limitations faced by dissatisfied tenants of Belgrade apartments who can only alter a few interior walls or enclose balconies to create more usable spaces for daily living.

As the modern house becomes more widely available, the agency of individuals within European families and households generally is expressed in one of two ways, either (a) through vigorous adoption of modern amenities, often to counter the hegemony of generation and/or enhance status or (b) through distortion and transformation of the modern model itself, sometimes as a form of resistance to the hegemony of class and market that the modern model represents. Whereas the modern model of housing promises to improve material standards of living, the specialized skills and knowledge required in its construction effectively limit the control of local craftsmen and residents in determining the form of their housing and represent the penetration of hegemonic influences of the state and market into the intimate lives of European families. In some cases (e.g. Rasson *et al.*, Chapter 7, and Booth, Chapter 5) the hegemony of the state is resisted by families who pursue the reproductive strategies that keep faith with older patterns, in particular those that sustain gender relations that are consonant with shared memories of "traditional" house forms. In other cases, (Lawrence-Zúñiga, Chapter 6; Brettell, Chapter 2; and Sutton, Chapter 3), modern house forms are eagerly, if selectively, appropriated, partly for the comfort and convenience they promise, but also as local expressions of status distinction and even class consciousness.

Rural residents often selectively incorporate elements of the modern house that they value most, including indoor plumbing, electrical systems designed to accommodate modern domestic appliances, and discrete areas for cooking, dining, and watching television, as well as separate sleeping quarters for adult couples and their offspring of each sex. Sometimes the consequences of these new elements are unanticipated. Lawrence-Zúñiga (Chapter 6) describes the acquisition of the modern bathroom by residents living in older houses in a southern Portuguese town. With limited space, none offering easy installation of a bathroom, residents most often appropriated the kitchen's large fireplace, partly because of its location near water and sewer lines at the front of the house, but also because the fireplace was already considered polluting within the house interior. Then, in the space formerly taken up by the kitchen, a parlor was created for entertaining and leisure activities such as viewing television, while a new traditional kitchen, with its polluting fireplace, was built in the garden. This traditional kitchen becomes an important center for the daily domestic activities of cooking, eating and socializing. In the construction of new suburban-style houses, the traditional kitchen is often built as a temporary residence first while the modern house is being completed. Thus, the appropriation of new domestic forms may only awkwardly accommodate old behaviors, expectations and needs, but may also prod those aspiring to become more modern to acquire the desired habits.

The constraints imposed by the modern apartment in Belgrade (Chapter 7) result in family strategies that reassign and remodel spaces to accommodate domestic needs and changes in household composition. Serb residents encountered limited space for the storage of traditional preserved foods essential to a woman's reputation as a good homemaker, but also moved walls, enclosed balconies and reassigned rooms to create more bounded spaces for a grandparent or children. Rasson *et al.* make it clear that separating siblings at puberty (unless an adult sleeps with them) is an important principle in the organization and use of domestic space. But it is also apparent that, contrary to the modern architects' intentions in these apartment designs, housing a husband's widowed mother with the nuclear family is also an important obligation. Although urban Serbs are able to make some modifications to the state-provided apartments, they are clearly constrained by the fixed amount of space available to them. In rural areas where apartments and government programs are less prevalent and where home ownership is more common, residents may have more control over what aspects and what degree of modern designs and amenities are embraced.

Although changes in rural housing are more likely to be generated through the actions of local residents than through government programs and policies, there are exceptions. Birdwell-Pheasant (Chapter 4) describes Irish housing programs of the late nineteenth and early twentieth centuries that resulted in the construction of thousands of new cottages in rural Munster. These programs were implemented by the combined efforts of governments and landlords. Booth (Chapter 5) details how, in the aftermath of a devastating 1968 earthquake in Sicily's Belice Valley, the Italian government rebuilt the area with modern housing better suited to an urban middle class and largely unappreciated by the rural working-class population.

If there are any domestic spaces introduced from exogenous sources to which people seem particularly sensitive in their reception or rejection, these are the parlor (or *sala*) and the modern kitchen. Set apart from the rhythm and action of daily life, the parlor appeared commonly in both rural and urban houses and among both families of means and those with considerably less. While the parlor was often promoted as a key element of the bourgeois model of home by reformers who hoped it would have a "civilizing" effect on the working class and make them more bourgeois (see Taylor, Chapter 9), it was eagerly appropriated by families who had no particular desire for embourgeoisement (Lofgren 1984: 57). As Lawrence-Zúñiga (Chapter 6) points out, possessing the bourgeois parlor became a fairly straightforward remodeling job and brought significant improvements in the residents' sense of their importance and social standing.

By contrast, the efficiently organized and technologically equipped modern kitchen has been more roundly resisted. In Sicily, new forms of the kitchen were perceived almost as an assault on women's dominance within the domestic sector as well as on sociality among women. Booth (Chapter 5) suggests that designers of the modern kitchens in the new town housing assumed that women would work outside the home and depend on commodified food products rather than on processing foodstuffs themselves at home. Women objected to the modernist housing designs that relegated the kitchen to a back corner and positioned exterior balconies so as to prevent "overviewing" from one house to another, ostensibly to protect family privacy. This practice broke with traditional house forms and inhibited women's customary socializing across balconies. Booth notes that in defiance of housing regulations, the working-class women adapted their garages as kitchens that could be opened to restore the familiar flow of neighborhood social interaction that once occupied collective courtyards.

Lawrence-Zúñiga (Chapter 6) also describes how residents of modern houses who have a fully appointed modern kitchen build, in addition, a traditional kitchen as an alternative and spend much of their time there. As in the Sicilian case, women find little or no incentive to acquire or use the modern kitchen for status reasons, since their reputations are still judged by traditional cooking and homemaking skills. While the acquisition of the parlor by the Portuguese householders simply added a new space with a specialized function to the house, and residents lost nothing, the acquisition of the modern kitchen was intended to supplant the traditional one, a hegemonic imposition women have largely countered with creative and sometimes subversive alternatives.

Resistance to the commodification of housing may take many forms. Tosi discusses the "informal practices" of accessing housing through family network relations; this is not, he says, merely persistence of tradition, but "reinterpretive" practice in which non-modern elements are "refunctionalized." He notes: "self-help has turned to a metaphor of reappropriation of housing" (1995: 285). Home improvement is also important in Hungary, where the focus is more on self-built items in preference to purchased ones. Fahervary observes, "The activity of making something oneself contributes to a sense of autonomy and individuality – the made product is not only one-of-a-kind, but it enhances the sense of the object as an inalienable possession" (1996: 6). In Norway, Gullestad found that "values and identities are created and objectified in home decoration" (1993: 158) and especially in the continual renovation, rearrangement and redecoration of the home as a joint focus of the couple's domestic creative energies and shared values (1993: 145). Although most of these Norwegian home-improvement projects entail extensive use of commodified products, it is the process that seems to be important.

Despite repeated instances of rejection of various features of the modern house, its appropriation, whether via new construction or remodeling, has become the symbol *par excellence* of a family's becoming "modern" and achieving success. By contrast, older housing begins to look backward, obsolete, and distinctly unprosperous. The northern Portuguese family, whose members Brettell (Chapter 2) describes as expressing new affluence in modern house construction, finally turned their backs on the large antiquated house that for decades had been the locus of family power. In their quest to keep married offspring from migrating, the Greek families Sutton describes (Chapter 3) built modern houses to signal and to compete for equal status with urban domestic amenities. Some residents of Iraklio viewed old houses as representations of a backwardness and "rural decay" best relegated to the remoter corners of memory, while other residents saw the same houses as benchmarks of progress as well as validations of community membership (see also Bestard-Camps 1991: 121–2).

In Sicily, on the other hand, Booth (Chapter 5) reports that middle-class and professional families (and women in particular) have increasingly rejected town living in favor of the countryside, renovating abandoned farm houses or building villas imitating a rustic style, initially for vacations devoted to selective appreciation of "the peasant heritage." Lifestyles of professional women occupying these homes also imitate domestic tasks undertaken out of economic necessity by lower-class women in order to "savor the authentic experience of home production" (Booth, Chapter 5, p. 151). While dispersed rural houses bring greatly desired privacy, they also shift the use of such forms from loci of production to loci for the consumption of rural lifestyles. In many areas of Europe, the traditional houses, rejected by rural citizens desiring to be modern, are purchased by urban dwellers seeking a summer retreat into a romantic past and the evocation of lost – but often creatively remembered – lifeways (Bestard-Camps 1991: 136; Ward 1993: 81).

Other modernizing trends external to both house and family have also had profound effects. Transportation was increasingly affected by technological changes; the introduction of the railway and later the automobile meant that people no longer had to depend on slow transport on foot or on animal transport. Increased mobility certainly introduced people to new ideas about housing, but other results occurred as well. In her study of French peasant life, Zonabend describes how the advent of rapid motor transport facilitated day visits among relatives, resulting in the reallocation of traditional guest rooms for the use of household members, contributing to the segregation of sleeping functions formerly associated with the *salle* (1984). Booth (Chapter 5) observes that Sicilian towns, once planned around the activities of pedestrians and animal-drawn carts, have given way to planning schemes for new towns based on providing access and storage for automobiles. In Ireland (Birdwell-Pheasant, Chapter 4) farm houses, which used to mark the center of the home place, moved to the main roads with the advent of the automobile and tractor. All over Europe, large-scale factories have brought together increasingly large agglomerations of workers whose transport and communication have also transformed the pattern of activities in households; irregular residents often provide regular income and return frequently to participate in family rituals.

In the last half of the twentieth century, housing in most of Europe has increasingly become a commodity – an item to be purchased from inventory in the great economic marketplace. All the authors in this volume make some note of such changes in the production and form of housing in rural and urban European communities and their tremendous impact on family life. None of the local communities described here was isolated prior to the twentieth century; nonetheless, changes during the twentieth century have been dramatic. The social and economic forces set in motion during the late Middle Ages, which culminated in industrialization and the penetration of urban, national and international influences during the nineteenth century, have gradually altered the degree and type of local control residents exercise over the shape and appearance of their houses. New materials and methods of construction, increased government intervention, and altogether new housing design ideas developed by professionals of various types have meant that the production of house forms is centered outside local areas. Remodeling of older houses and construction of new houses converts them to commodities and changes their meaning in profound ways.

It is not just that the commodification of housing alters the relationship and meanings houses hold for their residents; it also signals a change in the signification of the home within its context. As Birdwell-Pheasant's Irish case indicates (Chapter 4), the bungalow that is intended to signal a family's modernity concomitantly loses its ability to symbolize the union with place that was once accomplished by more traditional structures. As she notes, these "generically modern" houses symbolize peripherality in a global community rather than centrality in a local one. But the apparent homogenization of housing and lifestyles across rural and urban settings as families increasingly reject older homes for modern ones, and as premodern alternatives disappear, will continue to be moderated by particular and highly local adaptations enriching house forms, as contributions in this volume vividly testify.

Conclusions

It is a goal of this volume to further "the critique and deconstruction of the central categories of European experience" (Verdery 1997: 715), specifically of constructions of the house and family that have originated within European folk discourse and blossomed into anthropological categories of analysis. In addition to concepts of house and family, we also have addressed the problem of modernity as a concept that arose in Europe and that has had – and is having – a profound impact on the redefinition of families and houses around the world.

Some of our anthropological dilemmas about the relationship between houses and domestic life – in particular our *impasse* over the priority of family versus household – may be informed by a return to the European roots of our discipline. It seems likely that while we anthropologists have been busily breaking things out into categories and typologies and neat oppositions, we have lost sight of why it was so hard for us to unravel the separate strands in the first place. Family and household, morphology and function, gender, generation and class are tightly knit together in the real world. We need to see the separate strands, but we also need to see the patterns the strands weave in various times, places, and cultural contexts.

European patterns are distinctively different from those originating in other cultures. Houses of the Zafimaniry of Madagascar have "bones" that must be "hardened" through various rituals of the family life cycle (Bloch 1995: 78–9). Among the Ara of Indonesia, the house has its own *balapati* or spirit, which enters the house at the precise moment "when the beam that runs through the male and female posts from front to back goes through the central hole in the male post. The erection of a house is thus closely analogous to the birth of a child" (Gibson 1995: 140). Japanese houses are characterized by *oku*, defined as "innermost core," which "does not really refer to the concept of core in the sense of a *substantial* center, as the Western metaphysics of Presence formulates it" (Bourdier and AlSayyad 1989b: 18). Rather, *oku* "is a convenience devised by a spirit and climate which deny absolute objects or symbols such as a notion of center" (1989b: 18). Khambatta explains that the traditional Hindu residence "invites us to follow an open metaphysical and architectural itinerary from *residence* to *residue*, interlinking the three houses: man, building and cosmos" (1989: 265). Clearly, many cultures introduce their own distinctive strands into the tapestry woven by houses and families.

Time is also a significant variable; the same strands weave different patterns in different periods. In Europe, for example, premodern houses – especially those of the poor – were more open in plan, with little physical demarcation of spaces. Over the past two centuries, there has been an increasing trend of subdivision and specialization of spaces. This European project is now being exported to the world. The potential global impact of Western housing must not be underestimated.

Because it is avowedly rational and even "scientific," the modern model of the house is inextricably associated with the global hegemony of Western civilization.

In this introduction, we have sought to tease out some basic and universal strands of house/family patterns, arguing that the house is vital in forming and reproducing the family in its biological, social, economic, and moral dimensions. We have emphasized that several material dimensions of houses are critical in this regard: family reproductive strategies are both constrained and facilitated by house durability and fixity to site. As a conservative element of material culture, houses not only shelter co-residing family members and their material possessions, but often outlast the lives of their current occupants and provide them with a sense of enduring security for future generations. Thus, houses constitute objects of considerable familial investment and provide different classes, through the differential deployment of resources, opportunities to secure space for future generations to occupy, and to advertise their status. As inheritance, and by housing several successive generations, the materiality of home typically aids in constituting the family group economically and symbolically over time. Belief in the durability and fixity of housing, however, may be mobilized to suggest a permanent association with place even where one does not actually exist; in this sense, the material aspects of the house add legitimacy to claims of a more perduring territorial occupation. The memory of home associated with sentiments of family life may also be stronger and more lasting than the physical durability, fixity, or occupation of any house. Thus, the conservative nature of home consists of its ability to endure and remain as a fixed piece of material culture that successive social groups appropriate and remember each in their time.

Recurring or cyclical changes, such as those involved in the developmental cycle of the family, are a near-universal feature and express themselves in the regular expansion, contraction, and reconfiguration of domestic spaces. Historical changes such as those associated with industrialization and the spread of bourgeois and modern house forms introduce new concepts of spatial organization. In the European case, spatial changes that promote family and individual privacy express as well as influence the organization of activities and values related to class and gender in the domestic sphere. The transformation of rural landscapes and urban settings not only reflects but proclaims new family lifestyles and values. Increasingly, these forms are communicated and marketed through contemporary media. Newspapers, magazines, catalogs, television, and even the internet are part of the global marketplace where people now shop for the latest houses, furnishings, and ideas and values regarding home and family life.

Familial control over the forms houses take is diminished by increasing government intervention as well as by commodification. Both introduce standardization and uniformity in house form, which tend to homogenize rural and urban domestic settings, despite attempts by residents to adapt forms to their specific needs. If, as we argue in this work, the physical form of houses can influence domestic behaviors and values as well as express them, then the homogenization of houses should also tend to homogenize families. In this sense, the material dimensions of home play a critical role in the global transformations of family life and local cultures.

We would argue that the house is potentially one of the most invasive agents of Western hegemony, outflanking even the ubiquitous television. This assessment is based on the realization that the restructuring of the most intimate lives of people within their domestic family settings cannot help but have profound consequences. On the other hand, as chapters in this volume clearly demonstrate, residents often resist such hegemonic intrusions in surprising and creative ways. Surely there are nascent postmodern trends in house and family life that have yet to be identified. The ongoing investigation of the mutually constitutive nature of house and family ought to be high on anthropology's global research agenda. It is our hope that this exploration of houses and families in Europe can in some way help to catalyze such research.

Notes

1. Rapoport's contribution of the concept of activity systems to the study of interactions between humans and their environments focuses on systems of settings rather than on built forms *per se*; one cannot assume that dwellings will contain exactly the same inventory of activities organized in the same ways from one cultural setting to the next (1990: 15). In a similar fashion, archaeologist Susan Kent argues that activity areas or the uses of space generate architectural form, in particular in the partitioning of spaces, which is related more to sociopolitical organization than to environment and technology (1990: 5).
2. The words were spoken by the wife of the employer of the "hired man" in Frost's poem, "The Death of the Hired Man."
3. Fustel de Coulanges observed over a century ago that in both ancient Greece and Rome the socioeconomic organization of the domestic unit was initially centered on ancestor worship of agnatic kin, the locus of which was identified with the sacred fire and the hearth of the house in which the members resided (original English version 1873: 31).
4. Gudeman found a similar set of meanings for *la casa* in Panama (1976: 86).
5. The French text states: "Par rapport au clan ou au lignage, la maison possède donc des caractères distinctifs qu'on peut énumérer comme suit. La maison est 1) une personne morale, 2) détentrice d'un domaine 3) composé à la fois de biens matériels et immatériels, et qui 4) se perpétue par la transmission de son nom, de sa fortune et de ses titres en ligne réelle ou fictive, 5) tenue pour légitime

à la condition que cette continuité puisse se traduire dans le langage de la parenté ou de l'alliance, ou 6) le plus souvent les deux ensemble" (Lévi-Strauss 1991: 435).

6. We must be wary not to overextend the distinction between "lineage society" and "house society." Grinker reports that Evans-Pritchard "could find no Nuer concept for lineage or clan, the closest word being *thok mac* (the hearth) or *thok dwiel* (the entrance to the hut)" (1996: 858).

7. Less durable types of house are built by women in much of Africa, including among the Ju/'hoansi, Mbuti, and Gabra (Prussin 1995).

8. Several of the authors in this volume use the contrast set "traditional/modern" rather than "premodern/modern," and we have seen no reason to impose uniformity.

9. Headley states that in Java it is possible to distinguish between "weak" and "strong" corporate houses, and that weak and strong houses "may well exist side by side" (1987: 213). Coexistence often merges into essential complementarity, in which continuity of the system itself entails differentiation. Carsten and Hugh-Jones attribute to Lévi-Strauss the idea that "as core institutions, the houses of high-ranking groups are linked to those of commoners" (1995: 11).

10. Birdwell-Pheasant (1986) has also detailed how the construction of kitchens and other domestic structures implemented household fissioning and family development among villagers in northern Belize, Central America.

11. *Salle* is rendered as "parlor" in the English edition of Zonabend's work. The English-style parlor, however, is called *salon* in French, and is translated as "drawing-room" (Zonabend 1984: 19).

References

Agnew, John. 1989. "The Devaluation of Place in Social Science." In *The Power of Place: Bringing Together Geographical and Sociological Imaginations*, ed. John Agnew and James Duncan, pp. 9–29. Boston, MA: Unwin Hyman.

Arensberg, Conrad M., and Solon T. Kimball. 1940. *Family and Community in Ireland*. Cambridge, MA: Harvard University Press.

Barnard, Henry. 1990. "Bourdieu and Ethnography: Reflexivity, Politics and Praxis." In *An Introduction to the Work of Pierre Bourdieu: The Practice of Theory*, ed. Richard Harker, Cheleen Mahar, and Chris Wilkes. New York: St Martin's.

Bestard-Camps, Joan. 1991 [1986 in Spanish]. *What's in a Relative? Household and Family in Formentera*. Oxford: Berg.

Binford, Lewis. 1981. *Bones, Ancient Men, and Modern Myths*. New York: Academic Press.

Birdwell-Pheasant, Donna. 1986. "Domestic Process in the Transition from Labor-flow to Cash-flow Enterprise in Belize." *Urban Anthropology and Studies of Cultural Systems and World Economic Development* 14(3): 367–90.

Blanton, Richard E. 1994. *Houses and Households: A Comparative Study*. New York: Plenum.

Bloch, Maurice. 1995. "The Resurrection of the House Amongst the Zafimaniry of Madagascar." In *About the House: Lévi-Strauss and Beyond*, ed. Janet Carsten and Stephen Hugh-Jones, pp. 69–83. Cambridge, UK: Cambridge University Press.

Bouquet, Mary. 1996. "Family Trees and Their Affinities: The Visual Imperative of the Genealogical Diagram." *Journal of the Royal Anthropological Institute (Incorporating Man)* 2(1): 43–66.

Bourdier, Jean-Paul. 1989. "Reading Tradition." In *Dwellings, Settlements and Tradition: Cross-cultural Perspectives*, ed. Jean-Paul Bourdier and Nezar AlSayyad, pp. 35–52. Berkeley, CA: International Association for the Study of Traditional Environments; New York: University Press of America.

Bourdier, Jean-Paul, and Nezar AlSayyad (eds). 1989a. *Dwellings, Settlements and Tradition: Cross-cultural Perspectives*. Berkeley, CA: International Association for the Study of Traditional Environments; New York: University Press of America.

——. 1989b. "Prologue." In *Dwellings, Settlements and Tradition: Cross-cultural Perspectives*, ed. Jean-Paul Bourdier and Nezar AlSayyad, pp. 5–26. Berkeley, CA: International Association for the Study of Traditional Environments; New York: University Press of America.

Bourdieu, Pierre. 1976. "Marriage Strategies as Strategies of Social Reproduction." In *Family and Society (Selections from the Annales, Economies, Sociétés, Civilisations)*, ed. R. Forster and O. Ranum, pp. 117–44. Baltimore, MD: Johns Hopkins University Press.

Brettell, Caroline B. 1986. *Men Who Migrate, Women Who Wait: Population and History in a Portuguese Parish*. Princeton, NJ: Princeton University Press.

——. 1988. "Emigration and Household Structure in a Portuguese Parish, 1850–1920." *Journal of Family History* 13: 33–58.

Brown, Donald E. 1991. *Human Universals*. New York: McGraw-Hill.

Carsten, Janet, and Stephen Hugh-Jones (eds). 1995. *About the House: Lévi-Strauss and Beyond*. Cambridge, UK: Cambridge University Press.

Clark, J. Desmond, and J. W. K. Harris. 1985. "Fire and Its Roles in Early Hominid Lifeways." *African Archaeological Review* 3: 3–28.

Collier, Jane Fishburne. 1997. *From Duty to Desire: Remaking Families in a Spanish Village*. Princeton, NJ: Princeton University Press.

Collier, Jane Fishburne, Michelle Z. Rosaldo, and Sylvia Yanagisako. 1987. "Is There a Family? New Anthropological Views." In *Gender: Essays Toward a*

Unified Analysis, ed. Jane F. Collier and Sylvia Yanagisako. Stanford, CA: Stanford University Press.

Danto, Arthur C. 1982. "Abide/ Abode." In *Housing: Symbol, Structure, Site*, ed. Lisa Taylor, pp. 8–9. New York: Rizzoli.

d'Argemir, Dolors Comas. 1988. "Household, Family, and Social Stratification: Inheritance and Labor Strategies in a Catalan Village (Nineteenth and Twentieth Centuries)." *Journal of Family History* 13(1): 143–63.

Eco, Umberto. 1972. "A Componential Analysis of the Architectural Sign /column." *Semiotica* 5(2): 97–117.

Edelman, Robert. 1993. "Everybody's Got to Be Someplace: Organizing Space in the Russian Peasant House, 1880 to 1930." In *Russian Housing in the Modern Age: Design and Social History*, ed. William Craft Brumfield and Blair A. Ruble, pp. 7–24. Cambridge, UK: Cambridge University Press.

Fahervary, K. 1996. "From the Private Sphere to Real Estate: Securing and Storing Value in Hungarian Family Homes." Paper Presented at the American Anthropological Association Annual Meeting. San Francisco, CA.

Fisher, Helen. 1983. *The Sex Contract: The Evolution of Human Behavior*. New York: Quill.

Fortes, Meyer. 1971 [1958]. "Introduction." In *The Developmental Cycle in Domestic Groups*, ed. Jack Goody, pp. 1–14. Cambridge, UK: Cambridge University Press.

Fustel de Coulanges, Numa Denis. 1873 [1864 in French]. *The Ancient City: A Study on the Religion, Laws, and Institutions of Greece and Rome*, transl. Willard Small. Garden City, NY: Doubleday Anchor Books.

Gaffin, Dennis. 1996. *In Place: Spatial and Social Order in a Faeroe Islands Community*. Prospect Heights, IL: Waveland.

Gaunt, David. 1987. "Rural Household Organization and Inheritance in Northern Europe." *Journal of Family History* 12(1–3): 121–41.

Gell, Alfred. 1998. *Art and Agency: An Anthropological Theory*. Oxford: Clarendon Press.

Gibson, Thomas. 1995. "Having Your House and Eating It: Houses and Siblings in Ara, South Sulawesi." In *About the House: Lévi-Strauss and Beyond*, ed. Janet Carsten and Stephen Hugh-Jones, pp. 129–48. Cambridge, UK: Cambridge University Press.

Giddens, A. 1984. *The Constitution of Society: Outline of the Theory of Structuration*. Berkeley, CA: University of California Press.

Goody, Jack. 1971 [1958]. "The Fission of Domestic Groups Among the LoDagaba." In *The Developmental Cycle in Domestic Groups*, ed. Jack Goody, pp. 53–91. Cambridge, UK: Cambridge University Press.

Grinker, Roy Richard. 1996. "Reconstructing the House in Anthropology." (Book Review.) *American Anthropologist* 98(4): 856–8.

Gudeman, Stephen. 1976. *Relationships, Residence and the Individual: A Rural Panamanian Community*. Minneapolis, MN: University of Minnesota Press.

Gullestad, Marianne. 1993. "Home Decoration as Popular Culture: Constructing Homes, Genders and Classes in Norway." In *Gendered Anthropology*, ed. Teresa del Valle, pp. 128–61. London: Routledge.

Hammel, Eugene. 1984. "On the *** of Investigating Household Form and Function." In *Households: Comparative and Historical Studies of the Domestic Group*, ed. Robert McC. Netting, Richard R. Wilk, and Eric J. Arnould, pp. 29–43. Berkeley, CA: University of California Press.

Hayward, D. Geoffrey. 1975. "Home as an Environmental and Psychological Concept." *Landscape* 20(1): 2–9.

Headley, Stephen C. 1987. "The Idiom of Siblingship: One Definition of House in Southeast Asia." In *De la Hutte Au Palais: Sociétés 'à Maison' en Asie Du Sud-Est Insulaire*, ed. C. Macdonald. Paris: Presses Universitaires de France.

Herlihy, David. 1985. *Medieval Households*. Cambridge, MA: Harvard University Press.

Hobsbawm, Eric. 1991. "Introduction (Exile: A Keynote Address)." *Social Research* 58(1): 65–8.

Hobsbawm, Eric, and Terence Ranger (eds). 1983. *The Invention of Tradition*. Cambridge, UK: Cambridge University Press.

Hollander, John. 1991. "It All Depends." *Social Research* 58 (Spring): 31–50.

Illich, Ivan. 1982. *Gender*. New York: Pantheon.

Jameson, Michael H. 1990. "Domestic Space in the Greek City-state." In *Domestic Architecture and the Use of Space: An Interdisciplinary Cross-cultural Study*, ed. Susan Kent, pp. 92–113. Cambridge, UK: Cambridge University Press.

Johnson, Matthew. 1993. *Housing Culture: Traditional Architecture in an English Landscape*. Washington, DC: Smithsonian Institution.

Kent, Susan. 1984. *Analyzing Activity Areas: An Ethnoarchaeological Study of the Use of Space*. Albuquerque, NM: University of New Mexico Press.

——. 1990a. "Activity Areas and Architecture: An Interdisciplinary View of the Relationship Between Use of Space and Domestic Built Environments." In *Domestic Architecture and the Use of Space: An Interdisciplinary Cross-cultural Study*, ed. Susan Kent, pp. 1–8. Cambridge, UK: Cambridge University Press.

—— (ed). 1990b. *Domestic Architecture and the Use of Space: An Interdisciplinary Cross-cultural Study*. Cambridge, UK: Cambridge University Press.

Khambatta, Ismet. 1989. "The Meaning of Residence in Traditional Hindu Society." In *Dwellings, Settlements and Tradition: Cross-Cultural Perspectives*, ed. Jean-Paul Bourdier and Nezar AlSayyad, pp. 257–73. New York: University Press of America.

Laslett, Peter. 1983. "Family and Household as Work Group and Kin Group: Areas of Traditional Europe Compared." In *Family Forms in Historic Europe*, ed. R. Wall, J. Robin, and P. Laslett, pp. 513–63. Cambridge, UK: Cambridge University Press.

——. 1984. "The Family as a Knot of Individual Interests." In *Households: Comparative and Historical Studies of the Domestic Group*, ed. Robert McC. Netting, Richard R. Wilk, and Eric J. Arnould, pp. 353–79. Berkeley, CA: University of California Press.

Laslett, Peter, and Richard Wall (eds). 1972. *Household and Family in Past Time*. Cambridge, UK: Cambridge University Press.

Lawrence, Denise L., and Setha M. Low. 1990. "The Built Environment and Spatial Form." *Annual Review of Anthropology* 19: 453–505.

Lawrence, Roderick J. 1987. "What Makes a House a Home?" *Environment and Behavior* 19 (March): 154–68.

Lévi-Strauss, Claude. 1982 [1975 Pt.I, 1979 Pt.II]. *The Way of the Masks*, transl. Sylvia Modelski. Vancouver, BC: Douglas & McIntyre.

——. 1987. *Anthropology and Myth: Lectures 1951–1982*. Oxford: Blackwell.

——. 1991. "*Maison.*" In *Dictionnaire de l'éthnologie et de l'anthropologie*, ed. P. Bonte and M. Izard, pp. 344–6. Paris: Presses Universitaires de France.

Lofgren, Orvar. 1984. "The Sweetness of Home: Class Culture and Family Life in Sweden." *Ethnologia Europea* 14: 44–64.

Lumley, Henry de. 1969. "A Paleolithic Camp Near Nice." *Scientific American* 87: 23–32.

Macdonald, C. (ed.). 1987. *De la hutte au palais: sociétés 'à maison' en Asie du Sud-Est insulaire*. Paris: Presses Universitaires de France.

McGuire, R. H., and M. B. Schiffer. 1983. "A Theory of Architectural Design." *Journal of Anthropological Archaeology* 2: 227–303.

Morgan, Lewis Henry. 1981 [1881]. *Houses and House-life of the American Aborigines*. Chicago, IL: University of Chicago Press.

Netting, Robert McC., Richard R. Wilk, and Eric J. Arnould. 1984. "Introduction." In *Households: Comparative and Historical Studies of the Domestic Group*, ed. Robert McC. Netting, Richard R. Wilk, and Eric J. Arnould, pp. xiii–xxxviii. Berkeley, CA: University of California Press.

Oliver, Paul. 1987. *Dwellings: The House Across the World*. Oxford, UK: Phaidon.

—— (ed). 1997. *Encyclopedia of Vernacular Architecture of the World*. Cambridge, UK: Cambridge University Press.

Parkin, Robert. 1997. *Kinship: An Introduction to the Basic Concepts*. Oxford: Blackwell.

Pavlides, Eleftherios, and Jana E. Hesser. 1989. "Vernacular Architecture as an Expression of Its Social Context in Eressos, Greece." In *Housing, Culture and Design: A Comparative Perspective*, ed. Setha M. Low and Erve Chambers, pp. 357–74. Philadelphia, PA: University of Pennsylvania Press.

Pina-Cabral, João de. 1986. *Sons of Adam, Daughters of Eve*. Oxford: Clarendon Press.

Pine, Frances. 1996. "Naming the House and Naming the Land: Kinship and Social Groups in Highland Poland." *The Journal of the Royal Anthropological Institute (Incorporating Man)* 2(5): 443–60.

Pitkin, Donald S. 1985. *The House That Giacomo Built: History of an Italian Family, 1898–1978*. Cambridge, UK: Cambridge University Press.

Potts, Richard. 1984. "Home Bases and Early Hominids." *American Scientist* 72: 338–47.

———. 1988. *Early Hominid Activities at Olduvai*. New York: Aldine de Gruyter.

Prussin, Labelle. 1995. *African Nomadic Architecture: Space, Place and Gender*, with Amina Adan, Peter A. Andrews, Arlene Fullerton, Anders Grum, and Uta Holter. Washington, DC: Smithsonian Institution Press and the National Museum of African Art.

Rapoport, Amos. 1969. *House Form and Culture*. Englewood Cliffs, NJ: Prentice-Hall.

———. 1982. *The Meaning of the Built Environment: A Nonverbal Communication Approach*. Beverly Hills, CA: Sage.

———. 1990. "Systems of Activities and Systems of Settings." In *Domestic Architecture and the Use of Space: An Interdisciplinary Cross-cultural Study*, ed. Susan Kent, pp. 9–20. Cambridge, UK: Cambridge University Press.

Richardson, Miles. 1989. "Place and Culture: Two Disciplines, Two Concepts, Two Images of Christ and a Single Goal." In *The Power of Place: Bringing Together Geographical and Sociological Imaginations*, ed. John Agnew and James Duncan. Boston, MA: Unwin Hyman.

Rykwert, Joseph. 1991. "House and Home." *Social Research* 58 (Spring): 51–62.

Segalen, Martine. 1983. *Love and Power in the Peasant Family: Rural France in the Nineteenth Century*. Chicago: University of Chicago Press.

Soja, Edward. 1989. *Postmodern Geographies: The Reassertion of Space in Critical Social Theory*. London: Verso.

Stringer, Christopher, and Clive Gamble. 1993. *The Search for the Neanderthals*. London: Thames and Hudson.

Tosi, Antonio. 1995. "Shifting Paradigms: The Sociology of Housing, the Sociology of the Family, and the Crisis of Modernity." In *Housing and Family Wealth: Comparative International Perspectives*, ed. Ray Forrest and Alan Murie, pp. 260–88. New York: Routledge.

Verdery, Katherine. 1997. "The 'New' Eastern Europe in an Anthropology of Europe." In "Provocations of European Ethnology," with Talal Asad, James W. Fernandez, Michael Herzfeld, Andrew Lass, Susan Carol Rogers, and Jane Schneider. *American Anthropologist* 99(4): 715–17.

Wallerstein, Immanuel, and Joan Smith. 1992. "Introduction: Households as an

Institution of the World-economy." In *Creating and Transforming Households: The Constraints of the World-economy*, ed. Immanuel Wallerstein and Joan Smith, pp. 3–23. Cambridge, UK: Cambridge University Press.

Ward, Martha C. 1993. *The Hidden Life of Tirol*. Prospect Heights, IL: Waveland.

Wilk, Richard R. 1984. "Households in Process: Agricultural Change and Domestic Transformation Among the Kekchi Maya of Belize." In *Households: Comparative and Historical Studies of the Domestic Group*, ed. Robert McC. Netting, Richard R. Wilk, and Eric J. Arnould, pp. 217–44. Berkeley, CA: University of California Press.

———. 1990. "The Built Environment and Consumer Decisions." In *Domestic Architecture and the Use of Space: An Interdisciplinary Cross-cultural Study*, ed. Susan Kent, pp. 34–42. Cambridge, UK: Cambridge University Press.

Wilson, Peter J. 1988. *The Domestication of the Human Species*. New Haven, CT: Yale University Press.

Wissler, Clark. 1923. *Man and Culture*. New York: Crowell Company.

Zonabend, Françoise. 1984. *The Enduring Memory: Time and History in a French Village*. Manchester: Manchester University Press.

Part I:
House, Family and the
Construction of History

–2–

The *Casa* of José dos Santos Caldas:
Family and Household in a Northwestern
Portuguese Village, 1850–1993

Caroline B. Brettell

Introduction

In April of 1991 I received a letter from Virginia dos Santos Caldas, a Portuguese woman who has been a friend ever since I first met her early in 1975 when I was in Paris working on a dissertation about Portuguese immigrant women (Brettell 1995 [1982]). She apologized for not responding sooner to my Christmas card, blaming her delay, as always, on her embarrassment about her written Portuguese. But she wanted to let me know that she was now living full-time in her little apartment in the town of Viana do Castelo in northern Portugal rather than in her natal village of Lanheses, where I had last visited her during the summer of 1990. She had had a falling out with her cousin Mia, who still lives in the paternal home in which they both grew up. "I will go to Lanheses to visit because it is my home village (*a minha terra*)," she told me, "but I will no longer live and work there. I was very offended by my cousin. I was a slave to her and her family because in that house, since my mother's death, there is only her family. I cooked and also worked in the fields and in the end was criticized and I can take no more." Virginia closed her letter by telling me that she had spent Easter with her maternal uncles in her mother's natal village of São Miguel de Fontoura, a place she recalled us visiting together fifteen years earlier.

Virginia's letter records the latest episode in a family history that revolves around a particular house, its appended properties, and their transmission across genera-tions. This history dates back to the middle of the nineteenth century. It is a history characterized by processes of augmentation and consolidation, as well as by the periodic exclusion of some members from the household so that others remain in control and so that the unity of the house is maintained not only as the focus of economic activity but also as a symbol of the social status of the family. This exclusion has been achieved by particular strategies of marriage and heirship as well as by the construction or acquisition of other domestic spaces nearby or elsewhere in the village. And yet in some cases exclusion from the natal house does not mean exclusion from the family. Over several generations not only has a family compound of domestic units that are linked through ties of kinship been created, but also, and as Virginia's letter suggests, one village in northern Portugal has been intimately tied to another that is at some distance from it.

It is this history, reconstructed through both ethnographic and archival sources,[1] that I present in this chapter. In doing so, I will explore how a house shapes the lives of its inhabitants as they shape it (Lawrence and Low 1990), as well as how both the form and function of houses are influenced by the institutions of kinship and inheritance. Finally, this chapter also addresses the question of how house forms affirm social status within communities. A house that was the symbol of a prosperous peasant family until the 1970s may soon be abandoned as a relic of the past in a present where homes with modern amenities are highly desired and where the agricultural land that sustained peasant households has diminished in value.

The Founding Generation: José dos Santos Caldas

Sometime between 1855 and 1857, José dos Santos Caldas (Figure 2.1), a resident of the town of Caminha in northwestern Portugal, arrived in the parish of Lanheses, in the district of Viana do Castelo, with his wife and children. José was born in 1827 in the village of São Miguel de Fontoura south of the provincial town of Valença. Valença is situated on the Minho river, the river that forms the northern border of Portugal (Map 2.1).

In August of 1848, José married Ana Rita Sousa Pinto, a native of Caminha, a town to the west of Valença at the mouth of the Minho river. Ana Rita's sister Maria had married José's older brother António five years earlier. This exchange of siblings was one variant of a strategy of consolidation characteristic of the Caldas family across the generations. Ana Rita's brothers António and José married two sisters, Leonor and Maria, both of whom were cousins of José dos Santos Caldas. In the succeeding generation marriages between close kin rather than sibling exchange were the practice.

José and Ana lived in Caminha for the first seven to nine years of their married life and had three children baptized in the town. In all the historical records, José dos Santos Caldas is listed as a *marchante*, an individual who negotiates in livestock for butcher shops. This was a profession that "ran" in the family. José's father, his paternal grandfather, his brother, and later his own son were also *marchantes*. Although we might speculate that the semi-monthly *feira* (market) in Lanheses, a *feira* where livestock was and is routinely bought and sold, drew José dos Santos Caldas to the village, a full explanation for his arrival in this region is locked in history.

– 40 –

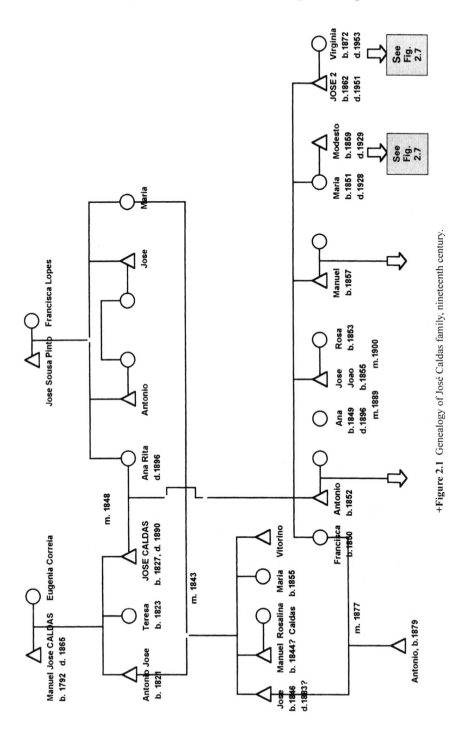

+**Figure 2.1** Genealogy of José Caldas family, nineteenth century.

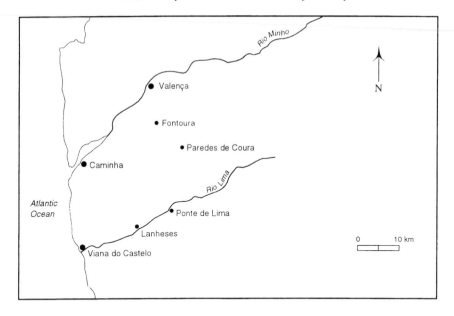

Map 2.1 Map of Minho – Northwestern Portugal.

His presence there can be dated by the birth of a son, baptized Manuel, in September of 1857. At that time the couple lived in a house on the village square, and they remained there at least through August of 1859, when another child, Maria da Conceição, was born. By 1862 the family had moved to the nearby *lugar* of Seara, where their last child, a son named José (#2) after his father, was born in May of that year.[2]

The eight members of the José dos Santos Caldas family set up residence in a house that is still standing today (Figure 2.2). It is a two-story stone and tiled-roof structure with a kitchen, a pantry (*dispensa*), five bedrooms, a parlor (*sala*), a water closet (like an internal outhouse), and a covered wooden veranda on the top floor. On the ground floor there are animal sheds and a wine cellar (*adega*). Located in the vine-covered courtyard at the front of the house is a well. At the back of the house there is a threshing floor (*eira*) and beyond that a kitchen garden and a field of maize. At some point, two covered stalls to house pigs, two sheds for the storage of farm equipment, and another shed to house an oven for the baking of *broa*, the traditional regional bread made from maize meal, were added to the original structure (Figure 2.3). All of these items constitute the northwestern Portuguese *casa* (the residential space as well as the domestic group of people who occupy it and eat together; translated as "house" or "household") and *lugar de vivenda* (literally the dwelling place; it includes the courtyard, sheds, outdoor working spaces, and adjacent fields).[3] Domestic space in rural northwestern Portugal

Figure 2.2 The Caldas House (Photo credit Caroline Brettell).

comprises both the *casa* and the *lugar de vivenda*, and together they form the focal unit of economic and social life for the peasants of the region.

The house of José dos Santos Caldas (Figure 2.4) was large and substantial by nineteenth-century rural standards, and therefore stood as a symbol of a prosperous peasant (*lavrador*) family. José's social status is confirmed by his listing on extant electoral rolls for the early 1870s. His assets were valued at 360 *milreis* (360$000). This placed him at the upper end of the range for voting males of the parish at the time. Sixty-four men were assessed lower, and only seventeen were assessed higher.

The Marriages of the Children of José dos Santos Caldas

In 1877 Francisca Rosa, the eldest daughter of José dos Santos Caldas and Ana Rita de Sousa, married her thirty-year-old double first cousin (their fathers were brothers and their mothers were sisters), José António dos Santos Caldas, a *marchante* who lived in the natal parish of Fontoura (Figure 2.1). The interconnections between closely related kin groups were thereby reinforced yet again.[4]

Francisca Rosa went to live with her husband in Fontoura and in December of 1879 gave birth to a son. By 1883 she was a widow, and there is no further information about her.[5] Evidently José dos Santos Caldas kept in touch with his kin in Fontoura despite his residence in Lanheses. This is substantiated by the

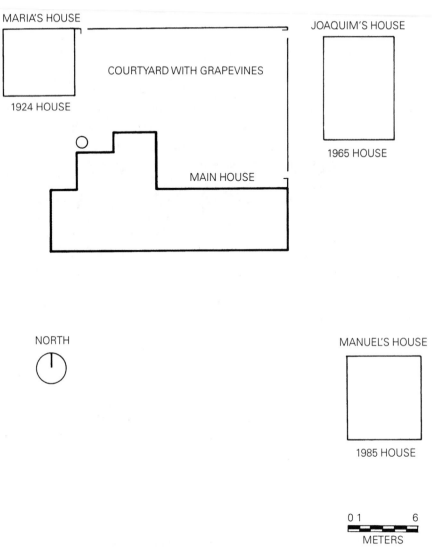

Figure 2.3 Site Plan of Caldas Lugar de Vivenda (Drawn by Silke Metzler).

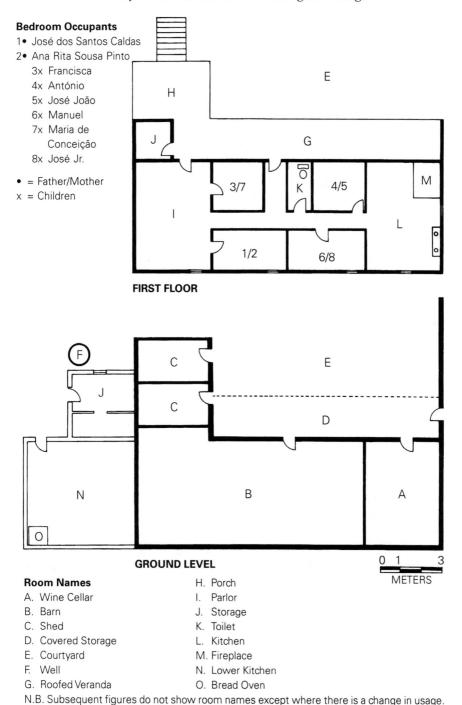

Bedroom Occupants
1• José dos Santos Caldas
2• Ana Rita Sousa Pinto
  3x Francisca
  4x António
  5x José João
  6x Manuel
  7x Maria de
     Conceição
  8x José Jr.

• = Father/Mother
x = Children

FIRST FLOOR

GROUND LEVEL

0 1 3
METERS

Room Names
A. Wine Cellar
B. Barn
C. Shed
D. Covered Storage
E. Courtyard
F. Well
G. Roofed Veranda
H. Porch
I. Parlor
J. Storage
K. Toilet
L. Kitchen
M. Fireplace
N. Lower Kitchen
O. Bread Oven
N.B. Subsequent figures do not show room names except where there is a change in usage.

Figure 2.4 1870 Plan (Drawn by Silke Metzler).

fact that the next marriage to occur, in January of 1881, was that of the youngest daughter Maria da Conceição to a young man of twenty-four named Modesto de Castro, who was originally from Galicia in Spain but a resident of Fontoura at the time he was wed. Maria was also a resident of Fontoura just prior to her marriage, perhaps sent there to live with kinfolk. By December of 1881 the couple had moved back to Lanheses, because on the nineteenth of that month Maria gave birth to a daughter, Ana, who died fourteen months later.

Rather than residing in the big house, Maria and her husband occupied two ground-level rooms that were appended to the main house on the western side (Figure 2.5). The family slept in these rooms and used the room with the bread oven as a kitchen. This was the first new-built structure added to the *lugar de vivenda*, and the first step in the creation of a family compound of interconnected domestic spaces. The needs of the family were expressed in this modification. New and independent living quarters were required, but preferably nearby, so that members of the family could continue to work together on agricultural land that remained undivided.

On the 1881 Rol da Desobriga (the annual list of communicants kept by the parish priest), the two eldest sons of José dos Santos Caldas and Ana Rita de Sousa, José João and António, were marked as absent, possibly in Spain or Brazil. This was the period of extensive emigration of men, both single and married, and the Caldas family was no different from any other in this region of Portugal in sending family members off, whether temporarily or more permanently (Brettell 1986).

Both these sons returned, António to Fontoura to marry a cousin and settle there and José João to Lanheses, where he married a woman six years his senior in 1889.[6] José João and his bride, Ana Margarida de Sousa, moved into a house in the neighboring *lugar* of Romão. It is almost as if José João, who did not reside in the main house or the *lugar de vivenda*, who had not married a kinswoman, and who had no heirs, has been dropped from genealogical memory. No one in the family living today remembers anything about him.

It was the youngest son, José, who remained with his parents in the structure into which the family had moved in the early 1860s. In this region of Portugal the goal for propertied peasant families was to have one child marry into the *casa*; but there were no hard and fast rules for which child it would be in terms of sex or birth order (Brettell 1991). Indeed, very often daughters were favored over sons. Why young José was chosen over his other siblings is unclear, and may have had as much to do with personal qualities as anything else.

By 1887, Maria da Conceição had moved back temporarily into the big house with her parents and her as yet unmarried brother José. This was a common practice when husbands were absent as emigrants (Brettell 1988). Modesto was not present in the parish, although we do not know precisely where he was. His absence

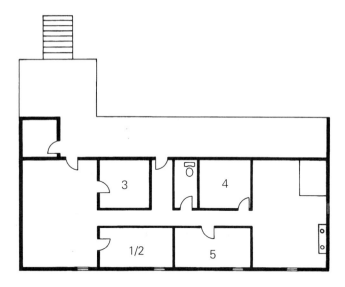

Bedroom Occupants

1• José dos Santos Caldas
2• Ana Rita Sousa Pinto
   3x José Jr.
   4x José João
   5x Manuel
   6x Maria de Conceição and Modesto de Castro

  • = Father/Mother
  x = Children

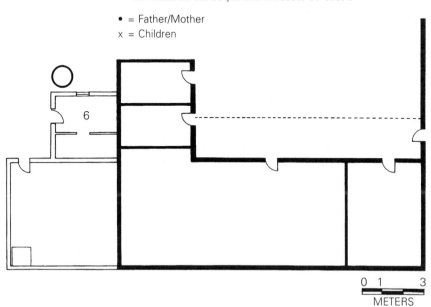

Figure 2.5 1881 Plan (Drawn by Silke Metzler).

certainly explains the ten-year interval between the birth of his daughter Francisca in 1883 and the next child and first son João, born in 1893. In 1892, Modesto de Castro had returned and was living with his family in a household headed by his now widowed mother-in-law (Figure 2.6). Two more children followed João, a son Manuel and a daughter Maria who died three days after her birth. In 1904 Modesto left again, having applied for a passport for Brazil in April of that year. He had returned by 1907.

To summarize, the *casa*, as a physical structure, set certain limitations on its inhabitants. Faced with these limitations, and through a process of strategic dispersal, José dos Santos Caldas could maintain his *casa* as a viable economic and social unit. Four of José's children were excluded (from the house but not, as will be shown, from their rights of patrimony), three of them returning to their father's place of birth, São Miguel de Fontoura, to marry and make their living, and the other moving to another *lugar* in Lanheses. The fifth, the daughter Maria da Conceição, remained in the *lugar de vivenda*, where there was room for expansion. After her marriage she moved into a small two-room structure affixed to the western wall of the main house. José, the youngest son, became the child who married into the *casa*.

The Second Generation: José dos Santos Caldas Junior

In 1895, five years after his father's death, José dos Santos Caldas Jr. (#2) married Virginia da Conceição Pereira of Lanheses[7] (Figure 2.7). In that year eight individuals, five adults and three children who spanned three generations, lived in the big house – the widow Ana Rita, her son José and his wife, her daughter Maria da Conceição and her husband, and their three children Francisca, João, and Manuel. A year later Ana Rita de Sousa died, and the younger couples created two independent households, José and his wife occupying the main *casa* and Maria da Conceição and her family living again in the adjacent and smaller two-room structure. This residential configuration endured for several decades (Figure 2.8).

Despite the separation shortly after the death of the widow Ana Rita, it was only in 1909 that the *partilhas* (the legal division of property) took place.[8] Present at the *partilhas* were José João dos Santos Caldas and his wife Rosa de Brito, Maria da Conceição Santos Caldas and her husband Modesto de Castro, and José dos Santos Caldas Jr. and his wife Virginia. José was also acting as the agent or proxy for his brothers and in-laws António José dos Santos Caldas and his wife Maria da Conceição, Francisca Rosa dos Santos Caldas, widow, and Manuel dos Santos Caldas and his wife Margarida, all of whom were residents in the parish of São Miguel de Fontoura.

José dos Santos Caldas (#1) and Ana Rita de Sousa had died without wills, a common occurrence among the populations of rural Portugal. Their assets

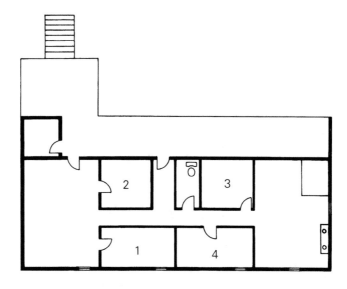

Bedroom Occupants

1• Ana Rita Sousa Pinto
2x José Jr.
3x Francisca
4x Maria de Conceição and Modesto de Castro

• = Mother
x = Children

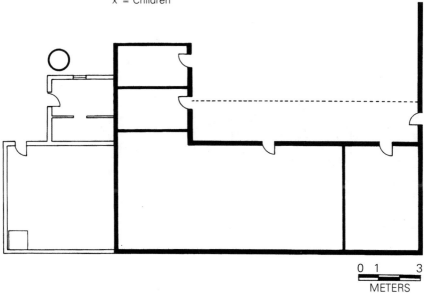

0 1   3
METERS

Figure 2.6 1892 Plan (Drawn by Silke Metzler).

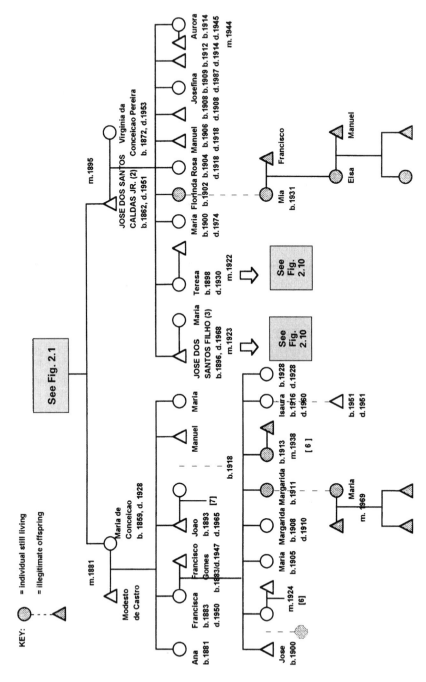

Figure 2.7 Genealogy, early twentieth century, José dos Santos Caldas Jr.

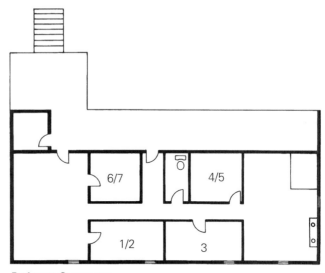

Bedroom Occupants

1• José dos Santos Caldas Jr.
2• Virgínia da Conceição Pereira
  3x José Filho
  4x Teresa
  5x Maria
  6x Florinda
  7x Rosa
8• Maria da Conceição and Modesto de Castro
  9x João Manuel and x Maria

• = Father/Mother
x = Children

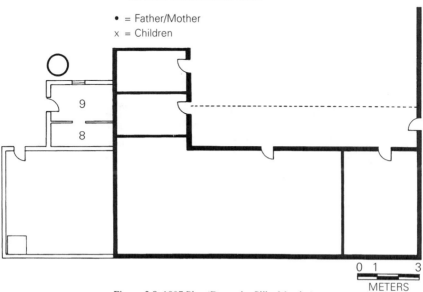

Figure 2.8 1907 Plan (Drawn by Silke Metzler).

(including jewelry and money) were valued at 840 *milreis* (840$000) which, according to law, had to be divided into six equal parts. The division occurred in the following manner:

- José João and his wife received, in money and other movable goods, the value of 140$000.
- Francisca Rosa, António, and Manuel (the children living in Fontoura) received, in movable property, money, and jewelry the value of 140$000 each.
- Maria da Conceição and Modesto received the low houses on the western side of the *lugar de vivenda* and the western half of the kitchen garden and land with vines adjacent to the property in the *lugar* of Seara. A well located in their half was to be shared with José. They also received half of a field with vines and fruit trees in the *lugar* of Agra.
- José inherited the big house, half of the field, vines and kitchen garden in the *lugar* of Seara and half of the arable field with vines and fruit trees in the *lugar* of Agra.

With this *partilha* those siblings no longer resident in the parish of Lanheses were bought out and could lay no further claims to the *casa* and *lugar de vivenda* of José dos Santos Caldas. They were permanently excluded. While Maria da Conceição and her brother José (#2) clearly partitioned the residential property – a partition that was to have implications in the future – the division of the field in the *lugar* of Agra was not to last long. According to a notarial note of November 1909, Maria da Conceição sold her half to her brother José for 60 *milreis* (60$000).[9]

This transaction marked the beginning of José Jr.'s socioeconomic ascent within the parish of Lanheses and the concurrent descent of his sister and brother-in-law. To some extent, this ascent was symbolically represented by the built structure he continued to occupy, the structure of a *lavrador abastado* – a prosperous peasant-farmer. Exclusion of some family members from the primary domestic space, reconsolidation of agricultural land that had been divided by the regulations of inheritance, and, later, augmentation that resulted from access to the property of his wife's family were the processes that contributed to and sustained this social status. It is in this sense that yet again the house and what it stood for shaped the lives of those who occupied it as they shaped it.

The Children of Maria da Conceição and José Junior

Only two of the children of Maria da Conceição and Modesto married in Lanheses, Francisca in 1900 at the age of seventeen, and João in 1921 at the age of twenty-eight. Francisca married Francisco Gomes, the nineteen-year-old son of a share-cropping couple from the parish of Santa Marta to the west, who came to work the lands of the wealthy and ennobled Pimenta Gama family – hence his nickname, "Chico da Pimenta." Francisco was a boatman (*barqueiro*), not a particularly lucrative profession.

Francisca's brother João, who also worked as a *barqueiro*, married a *jornaleira* (day laborer) from the *lugar* of Outeiro who had given birth to an illegitimate child three years earlier. Both these marriages, to people who were not property-owners in the parish, represented a further step down the socioeconomic ladder for the branch of the dos Santos Caldas family that had been denied access to the symbol of social status represented by the *casa* of José dos Santos Caldas.

Francisco and Francisca lived in a rented house on the village square for almost two decades, but by 1924 they had moved with their four daughters Maria, Margarida, Albertina, and Isaura into a new one-story, two-room structure built on the northwest corner of the *lugar de vivenda* on land inherited by Francisca's mother (Figure 2.9). Francisca's parents, Modesto and Maria da Conceição, remained in the space built for them at the time of their marriage. Although their son Manuel was still officially listed as a resident of their household, he was absent from the village in the mid-1920s. By the end of the decade, both Modesto and Maria da Conceição were dead. Francisco and Francisca had moved into the two-room structure appended to the main house and their daughters continued to sleep in the free-standing structure. The kitchen remained where it had always been.

Three of the daughters of Francisco and Francisca had illegitimate children. Only one of them, Virginia, eventually married the father of her illegitimate child.[10] The father of Margarida's child was married and there was, therefore, no possibility of legitimization. Margarida Gomes, described by some villagers as "*muito popular*" (familiar, outgoing), worked as a *jornaleira* for various families throughout the village. She raised her daughter in the free-standing house in the northwestern corner of the *lugar de vivenda* in Seara. José dos Santos Caldas Jr. (#2) had purchased the other two structures (the attached two rooms and the bread oven building) from his niece Francisca before her death, although she retained usufruct rights.

In the late 1970s Margarida's daughter and son-in-law, both of whom were emigrants in France, expanded and remodeled the free-standing house after buying out all the other heirs. They added another floor, a modern kitchen, and two bathrooms. The exterior gives it the appearance of a chalet more familiar to the countryside of France or Switzerland. Today Margarida, who spent several years in Paris helping her daughter raise her children, lives in this house by herself. Her cousin Mia sleeps there each night to keep her company. Each summer she is joined by her daughter, son-in-law, and grandsons.

By contrast with his sister Maria da Conceição and her family, José dos Santos Caldas Jr. (#2) and his wife Virginia da Conceição Pereira were one of the most respected couples in Lanheses during the early part of the twentieth century. They

1924 House Residents

1• Francisco Gomes and
   Francisca Caldas
2x Maria
3x Margarida
4x Albertina
5x Isaura

• = Father/Mother
x = Children

Bedroom Occupants

1• José dos Santos Caldas Jr.
2• Virgínia da Conceição Pereira
   3x José Filho and Maria de Conceição Fernandes
   4x Maria
   5x Florinda
   6x Josefina
   7x Aurora
8• Maria da Conceição and Modesto de Castro
   9x João Manuel

• = Father/Mother
x = Children

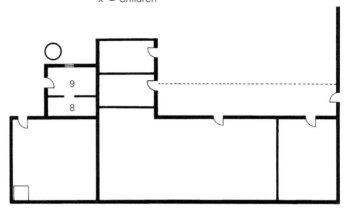

Figure 2.9 1924 Plan (Drawn by Silke Metzler).

were regular churchgoers and have been described by villagers who knew them as friends of one another as well as husband and wife. José is remembered by both his children and grandchildren as having been a true patriarch, a trait manifested particularly in the control which he seems to have had over his daughters' lives. His daughter Florinda recalled how her father used to greet their suitors with a knife in his hand. They quickly ran off. He allowed neither his children nor his grandchildren to go out to the cafes in the village square, preferring to keep them around the house. When there was work to do in the fields his children were kept out of school, and as a result only his son José and his daughter Florinda ever learned to read and write. Children, in his view, were workers. "That was the custom then," commented Florinda. "Today all children do is high jinks and merry-making (*a pandega*)."

Those who worked for José Jr. remember him as a man with a sense of humor who treated them well. He was also admired as a shrewd businessman. He earned extra capital by making and trading leather goods used in farm work, and was therefore known throughout the region. Although by no means the richest in the village, the household was never wanting. It was "*uma casa farta* (a household of abundance)," according to several local residents.

Pursuing a strategy of augmentation, José converted the cash earned from his business endeavors into additional property-holdings in the parish. In September of 1919, for example, after obtaining the consent of his wife's siblings, he purchased from his widowed father-in-law a two-story house in the *lugar* of Corredoura as well as the land, vines and trees nearby. He paid 305 *escudos*.[11] This was a clear effort at land consolidation, since he already owned property to the west of this house. Furthermore, it is quite likely that José was already thinking about a home to which he could send one of his daughters after marriage. This is indeed what happened; the eldest daughter Teresa married in 1922 and set up her household in the Corredoura house. With so many unmarried siblings still occupying the main house it was virtually impossible to include a new married couple there.[12]

In 1925, two years after his father-in-law's death, the property of José Jr.'s in-laws (valued at 1: 998$00) was divided equally between two sisters, one brother (living in Lisbon and represented at the *partilhas* by proxy) and three grandchildren, one the daughter of a dead brother named António (also living in Lisbon) and the other two the daughters of a dead brother named Manuel. As a result of this inheritance, José Jr. and Virginia received four-fifths of two-thirds of an arable field with vines, brush and pines in the *lugar* of Outeiro valued at 1598$40. (The other one-fifth was acquired by Virginia's sister.) Since this was greater than their due share they paid the excess in equal parts to the four other heirs – the living brother and the three children of the two dead brothers. Again, José and Virginia's strategy was to increase their holdings of fixed assets by buying out those kin who were no longer resident in the parish. The settlement worked to everyone's advantage.[13]

José dos Santos Caldas Jr. (#2) and Virginia da Conceição Pereira had ten children (Figure 2.7). Of the five daughters who survived to adulthood, only two married, one (Teresa) bearing four children of her own and the other (Aurora) dying in childbirth. The eldest and only surviving son, also named José (#3), was born in December of 1896, and in 1923 he married a first cousin once removed (Maria Fernandes), who was from the natal parish of Fontoura.

The Third Generation: José dos Santos Caldas, Filho

José *filho* (#3) had been courting a young women, a *jornaleira* (day laborer) of modest means, who lived in the *lugar* of Lamas. However, in November of 1922 this woman gave birth to an illegitimate child fathered by her employer, a *lavrador* with entrepreneurial interests. Although the child died, the disgrace propelled José's father to send him off to fulfill his military service in the town of Valença. José *filho* spent his free weekends with his kin in Fontoura, and there became interested in his cousin Maria da Conceição Fernandes, a woman "in whom one could have confidence (*confiança*)."

Like his father, José *filho* (#3) brought his bride to live with his parents in the *casa* established by his grandfather. This laid the foundation for the recreation of a three-generation household such as had existed for a brief period in the latter decade of the nineteenth century.

José dos Santos Caldas *filho* and his wife Maria had four children: a son Joaquim born in 1925, a son Manuel born in 1928, and two daughters, Virginia and Rosa, born in 1931 and 1935 respectively (Figure 2.10).[14] To accommodate this growing family, two new rooms were added to the main structure on the east end with a door opening onto the kitchen, the focus of family life in every northern Portuguese peasant household (Figure 2.11). This was a different form of augmentation and inclusion from that two generations earlier when Maria and Modesto moved into a domestic space that was within the *lugar de vivenda* but separate, independent, and with its own kitchen. José *filho* and Maria were fully a part of the *casa*, and they remained there throughout their lives.

This domestic situation was never easy for Maria. Her daughter Virginia described the problem in the following way: "My mother never had a house of her own. My father simply built two extra rooms for us and we all shared the kitchen. Although my grandparents were very friendly with my mother, some of my aunts made her life difficult."

Virginia's mother, throughout her childbearing years, continued to work along-side her husband in the fields, leaving her children in the household with her mother-in-law or a sister-in-law. One daughter-in-law observed that these children never developed the attachment to their mother that other children might, because they were being cared for by their aunts and their grandmother as well. Virginia

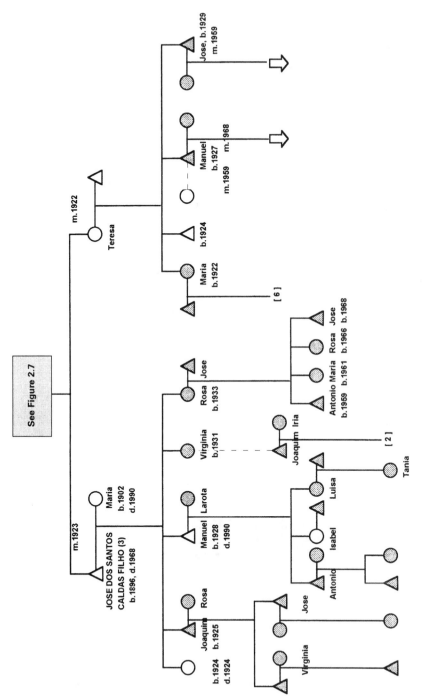

Figure 2.10 Genealogy, later twentieth century, José dos Santos Caldas Filho.

1924 House Residents

1x Maria
2x Margarida
3x Albertina
4x Isaura

• = Father/Mother
x = Children

Bedroom Occupants

1• José dos Santos Caldas Jr.
2• Virgínia da Conceição Pereira
  3x Maria
  4x Josefina
  5x Aurora
  6x Florinda
   7* Mia
  8x José Filho and Maria de
    Conceição

  9* Manuel
10* Joaquim
11* Virgínia
12* Rosa
13• Francisco Gomes and
    Francisca Caldas

• = Father/Mother
x = Children
* = Grandchildren

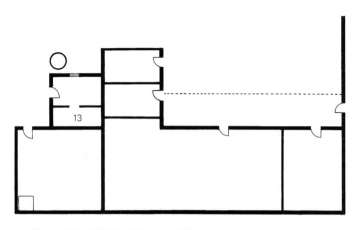

Figure 2.11 1935 Plan (Drawn by Silke Metzler).

added: "My father never had that special affection for my mother because she was not the only one looking after his needs. He had his three unmarried sisters to dote on him as well."

Maria's life, in short, was fundamentally shaped by the Caldas *casa*: by a domestic arrangement where everybody lived, worked, and ate together and where everything was held in common. When Maria's mother-in-law Virginia da Conceição married into this *casa*, José Jr.'s father was already dead, and three years later her mother-in-law passed away. In a short amount of time a three-generation household became a two-generation nuclear family household, and Virginia da Conceição was able to claim the role of *dona* (mistress) of the household. Maria, by contrast, had been married for almost thirty years before her father-in-law died. Furthermore, Virginia da Conceição had no sisters-in-law to contend with. Maria had to share a house with spinster sisters-in-law throughout her married life.

There is yet another way in which Maria differed from her mother-in-law. She was a stranger to the community of Lanheses at the time of her marriage, a person with no pre-established social position. Furthermore, one parish old-timer described José *filho* as "not half the man his father was." He did not garner the same respect, and this too contributed to Maria's vulnerable position in both the household and the parish at large.

Clearly the present difficulties of Maria's daughter Virginia (referred to at the beginning of this chapter) stem from the fact that her final tie to the paternal home was through an aged mother who lived in the house but had no legal right to it. In the eyes of the law Virginia does have a legal right to a share through her father; but as long as the house remains undivided this right does not always translate into being made to feel welcome.

To this three-generation household composed of grandparents, a son and his wife and children, and several unmarried daughters, another individual was added when one of these daughters, Florinda, gave birth in 1931 to an illegitimate child, baptized Maria do Carmo (called Mia). Mia married in 1952, but her husband went to Brazil a month later. She joined him there in 1957, staying just long enough to conceive a child. She returned to Lanheses and there gave birth to a daughter, Elsa, who is now herself grown up and married. It is this particular branch that now occupies the main house and is the source of tension for Virginia.

In March of 1951, almost thirty years after the marriage of José dos Santos Caldas *filho*, José dos Santos Caldas Jr. (#2), the patriarch, died. However, it was not until December of that year that the family came before a notary to divide the property. José had left no will, and his marriage to Virginia da Conceição, like most peasant marriages, was one of community property (*comunhão de bens*). His widow was therefore entitled to half the assets and her children to the other half in equal shares. The children of Virginia da Conceição's daughter Teresa, who had died in 1930, instigated the *partilhas*. The integrity of the *casa* and *lugar de vivenda* was at stake, and the *partilhas* had to be executed in such a way as to sustain this integrity. In the early 1950s a peasant way of life that had endured for centuries still predominated, and the *casa* was still fundamental to that way of life.

The assets of the Caldas family were valued at what was a rather substantial sum at the time – 41,789$30. The division proceeded as follows: [15] The widow Virginia received half of the big house and its sheds; a quarter went to José *filho* (#3) and another quarter to his eldest surviving sister Maria das Dores. Two other sisters, Florinda and Josefina, received in common and equal parts the house in the *lugar* of Corredoura that José Jr. (#2) had purchased from his father-in-law, as well as a field of underbrush in the same *lugar* and a portion (13/29 *avos*) of a cultivated field in the same *lugar*.[16] The cultivated field with vines and olive trees adjacent to the big house in the *lugar* of Seara was divided (on paper) between the widow Virginia (17/61 *avos*), her son (22/61 *avos*), and her daughter Maria das Dores (22/61 *avos*). The widow retained title to four other plots of land in different areas of the village, while a field near the river was divided between her (32/41 *avos*) and her daughters Florinda and Josefina (9/41 *avos*). The three children of Teresa (Maria, Manuel, José) received in common and equal parts a field of underbrush (*mato*) in the *lugar* of Bacelo and the other portion (16/29 *avos*) of the field in the *lugar* of Corredoura.

To settle everything, sums of money were owed. It is likely that the children of Teresa paid what they owed to their uncle José and aunt Maria das Dores in order to achieve full independence; it is unlikely that any money owed by Florinda and Josefina to their mother and brother was actually paid. Certainly, the land continued to be cultivated in common.

On January 16, 1952, a few weeks after this *partilha*, Virginia returned to a notary in the town of Viana do Castelo in the company of her son José and daughter Maria das Dores to declare her last will and testament.[17] In this will she left the legally disposable share of her assets to her son and her three daughters in equal and common parts. These included the half of the big house as well as the various fields, cultivated and uncultivated, that had been left to her by her husband and her parents. By including her daughters Josefina and Florinda, Virginia ensured that the big house and the supporting land would remain undivided and that her married son and spinster daughters would continue to live and work together for the duration of their lives. The disposition of the *casa*, in short, would continue to shape family relations.

One snag in this legacy was settled on January 22, 1954, three months after the death of Virginia on October 18, 1953. The children of Teresa, all of whom were adults, married, and living in the parish of Lanheses, appeared before a notary to cede to their cousin José dos Santos Caldas (#3) all their rights and action with regard to the undivided inheritance of immovable property to which they were entitled as a result of the death of their grandmother. In return, they were paid eleven thousand *escudos* by José, who raised the cash by selling a piece of his wife's inherited property in Fontoura. The sum was high because another *lavrador* with property adjacent to a prime field that Teresa's children had inherited offered them that much for it. José wanted to keep it within the family.

Each participant to this agreement placed his or her thumbprint on the document (none of them could write). By this act and the two preceding it, yet another branch of the family (the descendants of Teresa) was excluded from any future claim on the *casa* and supporting agricultural fields of the José dos Santos Caldas family. Land that had been divided in name or in reality was reconsolidated. Each of the surviving children of José Jr. (#2) (José *filho*, Maria das Dores, Florinda, and Josefina) owned a share of the *casa* and therefore a rightful place in it. As in the previous generation, the *casa* remained as a single and sacred unit representing the continuity of the Caldas family within the sphere of village life. Despite or maybe because of the economic hard times of the 1930s and 1940s, little had changed in northern rural Portugal during the first half of the twentieth century. A peasant way of life predominated, agricultural land was a valuable asset, and any family that drew on its own labor to cultivate this land could survive. In the next generation, everything changed.

The Present Generation

Both sons and one of the daughters of the younger José *filho* and Maria da Conceição married, while the other daughter, named Virginia after her grandmother, bore an illegitimate son in 1954. The eldest son, Joaquim, trained himself as an electrician and worked for many years in Lisbon and in Trás os Montes. In the early 1950s he was courting a distant cousin (a girl from Caminha), who was very interested in marriage. Then one day his father saw this girl in Viana with another man and warned his son. Joaquim decided to stop seeing her, feeling that he wanted to make a little money before marrying. In 1961, when he was thirty-six, he wed Rosa da Silva, a woman from the suburbs of Porto who was working as a cook in a mining camp near Vila Real, where Joaquim was employed as an electrician. The couple returned to Lanheses, and there Rosa gave birth to a daughter, Virginia, in 1962 and a son, José, in 1963.

During the first few years of their marriage, Joaquim and Rosa lived in a rented house on the village square and Joaquim worked in the town of Viana. Later he was able to secure employment at the gas pump which was built at the entrance to the village. They decided to build their own house and sold some land that his wife owned in Trás os Montes to help cover the cost. With the permission of Joaquim's father they built this house on a corner of agricultural land adjacent to the old house. After many years, another new structure appeared within the *lugar de vivenda* (Figure 2.12).

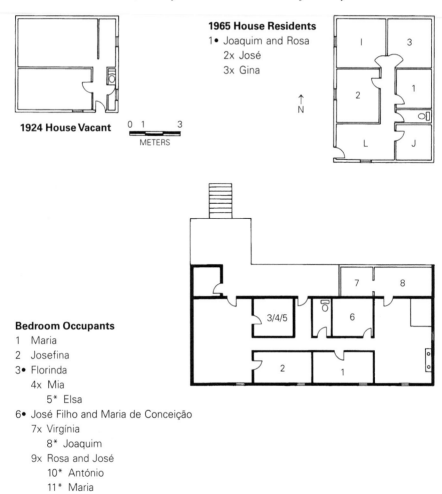

1965 House Residents
1• Joaquim and Rosa
2x José
3x Gina

↑
N

1924 House Vacant

0 1 3
METERS

Bedroom Occupants
1 Maria
2 Josefina
3• Florinda
  4x Mia
    5* Elsa
6• José Filho and Maria de Conceição
  7x Virgínia
    8* Joaquim
    9x Rosa and José
      10* António
      11* Maria

• = Father/Mother
x = Children
* = Grandchildren

Figure 2.12 1965 Plan (Drawn by Silke Metzler).

When Joaquim's father (José #3) died in 1968, he left the major portion (the third share) of his share of the Caldas family property to his second son Manuel (feeling he had already provided for his son Joaquim by permitting him to build a house within the *lugar de vivenda*, and not fully considering his daughters) with the stipulation that the spinster aunts retain rights of usufruct until their deaths. Before the eldest aunt, Maria das Dores, died (in 1974) she also signed over her share to Manuel. The house in Corredoura, which had been left to Josefina and Florinda, has fallen into the hands of Florinda's daughter Maria, her aunt Josefina having signed over her share in it. They rented it out, everyone preferring to remain in the *casa* in Seara. In 1974, a niece of Josefina and Florinda moved into the small house in the northwest corner with her new husband and remained there until she and her husband were able to build a new house elsewhere in the parish.

The favoring of Manuel became a source of some bitterness among the current generation, especially since he made no move to register any further divisions (the other two-thirds legally had to be shared equally among all heirs) with the Finance Office in Viana do Castelo. Although his siblings argued that he did not want to pay the taxes on these transactions, the fact that his two remaining spinster aunts and his mother were still living in the big house and working the land together with him and his cousin Mia made it, in Manuel's view, inadvisable to act.

Manuel's sister Rosa, the youngest daughter of José dos Santos Caldas *filho* (#3) and his wife Maria da Conceição Fernandes, was married in 1958 at age twenty-three to José Franco. The couple moved into the two rooms adjacent to the old house, which José Jr. had purchased from his widowed niece Francisca prior to her death (Figure 2.12). Rosa had two children rather quickly, a son António in 1959 and a daughter Maria da Conceição in 1961. José Franco then departed for France, where he remained for nine years before calling his wife and family to join him. He was able, however, to make visits back to Portugal after a few years, and thus two more children were conceived, a daughter Rosa born in August of 1966 and a son José born in August of 1968. When Rosa left for France, she took her sister Virginia with her. The two youngest children remained in Portugal until they were settled. Today, this family remains in France, essentially for good, returning to the village every other year during the summer. They have built a new house in the *lugar* of Cutarelos. Joaquim and Rosa's son José, his wife, and their children lived there for a few years, but recently moved back in with José's parents, who remain in their home in the *lugar de vivenda*. José's mother Rosa is ill and her daughter-in-law has been helping out with the housework. One of the daughters of José Franco and Rosa Caldas is now living in their house in Cutarelos. She decided to return from France.

Also within the *lugar de vivenda* is the new home of José *filho*'s son Manuel, who died in March of 1990. It is a one-story structure with three bedrooms, a modern bathroom and kitchen, and a parlor. It is occupied by Manuel's widow,

Larota, his daughter Luisa, and her husband and baby daughter Tania. Larota speaks of this house as her daughter's – she helped to pay for it with the salary she earns as a teacher. However, Larota also has a legal interest in the old house that comes to her through her husband. She readily laments the fact that people own things because "it creates family problems. My son is angry with me because I am living with my daughter, but daughters are different from daughters-in-law." During the spring of 1993 when I talked with her she admitted that she had not seen her son's children in many months, even though they live in the village.

José *filho* (#3) told his daughter Virginia that she could have the two rooms adjacent to the big house (the ones built for Maria and Modesto at the time of their marriage in 1881) for herself, but any suggestion on her part about renovation was blocked by her brother Manuel, who did not want any obstruction to the passage around the house on the west side. Virginia, as indicated at the beginning of this chapter, lives in an apartment (with a parlor, a dining room, two bedrooms, a full bath and a half bath, and a kitchen) in the town of Viana do Castelo, a place provided to her by the father of her illegitimate son Joaquim.[18] Her son is married and living with his wife and mother-in-law in another parish in the region.

In 1993, a complex family spanning four generations occupied the old *casa* (Figure 2.13). From José Jr.'s (#2) generation only his sister Florinda survives. Josefina died in 1987 and José *filho*'s widow, Maria da Conceição Fernandes, in December of 1989. Florinda's daughter Mia represents the next generation, and her granddaughter Elsa the third. Elsa was married in 1979, and she and her husband moved into the old house after a short sojourn working in Venezuela. They have two children.

During the fall of 1992 Elsa and her husband began to work with an architect to develop plans for the renovation of the old house in Corredoura, which has been rented for many years. This renovation may take time. Although Elsa has recently inherited money as a result of the *partilhas* of her father's family, the resources are as yet limited. But when it is finished they will abandon the old house and move in there. They, like everyone else in the family and in the village in general, want a more modern place to live in. Virginia explained their desires as follows. "In the past we lived okay. We had sardines and animals and pork. But our houses were poor. Today everyone wants a better place, each with his or her own room, and apart from the animals." With fewer and fewer people depending on agriculture to make a living, a *lavrador* house of the kind represented by the Caldas house has become an anachronism.

The main house remains unchanged and unrenovated largely because it has no single owner. Although there has been electric light since the 1930s, when electricity came to this region of Portugal,[19] there is still no piped water and therefore no modern bathroom or kitchen. The only signs of modernity are several items of twentieth-century technology: a refrigerator, a television, a gas stove. There is no

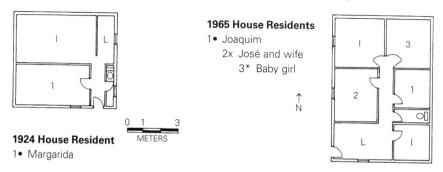

1965 House Residents
1• Joaquim
  2x José and wife
    3* Baby girl

0 1   3
METERS

1924 House Resident
1• Margarida

Bedroom Occupants
1• Florinda
  2x Mia
    3* Elsa and Manuel
    4+ Marisa
    5+ Luis

• = Father/Mother
x = Children
* = Grandchildren
+ = Great Grandchildren

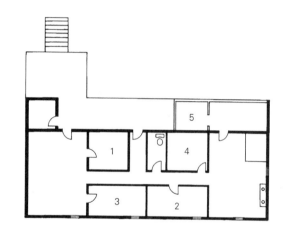

1985 House Residents
1• Larota
  2x Luisa and Manuel
    3* Tania

Figure 2.13 1993 Plan (Drawn by Silke Metzler).

telephone in the main house, but the three other houses are equipped. Within the family compound, there are three cars, one owned by Elsa's husband, one by Luisa and her husband, and the third by Joaquim's son José.

The acquisition of all these items reflects the changes that have come to Lanheses in general during the past twenty to twenty-five years as a result of money flowing back from France as well as the prosperity brought by Portugal's membership in the European Economic Community. No family is poor anymore; new houses are being built throughout the village; the village square has been revived as new stores, cafes, and other businesses have been opened. In 1978 a new health clinic and recreation center was built at the western entrance to the village, and in 1991 a new high school was opened. Although a bus service between Lanheses and the towns of Viana do Castelo and Ponte de Lima has existed since the 1930s, a new bridge built across the Lima River at Lanheses was opened in 1980 and has facilitated access to the city of Porto and points south. All these changes have affected the present generation in a manner unlike the experience of the previous generations of the Caldas family. It is in this context that the final fate of the *casa* has to be understood.

Conclusion

In this chapter I have engaged in a close analysis of a single case by combining data drawn from historical records with that furnished through ethnographic fieldwork and oral history. The approach I adopt is analogous to what Lila Abu-Lughod (1991: 153) proposes as one method by which to recapture anthropology – telling a story about particular individuals in time and place and exploring how these individuals experience and live the institutions of their society.

Here, I have paid particular attention to the institution of family. For several generations, life for the Caldas family has revolved around a particular domestic structure, its various built appendages, and the agricultural property that supported the house and household. The way that these items were transmitted across generations ensured not only the continuity of a space and place that was closely identified with a particular family, but also that certain family members would live and work together during their lifetimes while others were expelled. Laws calling for the equal division of property were circumvented by specific patterns of marriage as well as through transactions of sale or equivalent compensation.

Through processes of consolidation and exclusion the *casa* of the Caldas family remained intact as a symbol of a well-to-do and respected peasant family. Through a process of augmentation the physical structure of the *casa* was occasionally modified, for example by the addition of rooms, to suit the needs of an expanding and contracting family across several generations. This augmentation also occurred within the *lugar de vivenda* by means of the construction of additional domestic spaces to house related family members. However, until the most recent generation it was those who occupied the main two-story structure who were of higher social and economic status than the kin who resided in the smaller one-story structures built on other parts of the *lugar de vivenda*.

The house as a symbol of social status is a phenomenon documented in a wide range of social contexts (Duncan 1981), and in Portugal it is further manifested in the new houses covered in ceramic tiles, girded by wrought-iron balconies, and surrounded by well-kept gardens that are homes to those who have emigrated to France, Germany, or the United States and have returned to display their success abroad (Brettell 1979).[20]

Today, it is the chalet-like home of "Maria da Gida," the illegitimate daughter of Margarida Gomes, that is the best-appointed of all the structures in the Caldas *lugar de vivenda*. Originally a member of the "poor" branch of the family, Maria da Gida has had the most success abroad, and this success is manifested, if not stated, in her home. Rosa Caldas and her husband José Franco have also built a house with monies earned in France, but it is a modest structure located near the soccer field in another hamlet of the village.

If I have argued here that the house cannot be separated from those who live in it, it has equally been suggested that in this region of Portugal the concepts of house, household, and family are themselves difficult to distinguish. Pina-Cabral (1986: 37) has suggested that among the peasants of rural Minho the term *casa* is most commonly used to refer to household, while among the bourgeoisie *familia* is favored to mean the same thing. For the bourgeoisie, he argues,

> the nuclear family is the household, and other persons living with the *familia* are seen largely as extrinsic to it even when they are related by ties of kinship to the head couple. For the peasants . . . these co-residents are full members of the household. The choice of the word casa (house) reflects this conception, as it stresses the spatial unity of the members rather than the kinship relations among them. The casa is a compound of land, buildings, animals, people, absent relatives, and even the dead of the household (Pina-Cabral 1986: 37–8).

For the Caldas family this spatial unity exists both within the *casa* and within the *lugar de vivenda*. Across the generations, some of those who were expelled from the main house remained associated with the family by means of the creation of a family compound of households connected by close relations of kinship. Even if individuals live in a separate house in the physical sense, they are adjacent to and hence interact with other kin who live in close proximity. They share domesticated space in a larger sense. Pina-Cabral (1984; 1991) proposes a concept of sibling vicinality to describe this phenomenon, and Oppo's (1990) work in Sardinia suggests that it is certainly not unique to Portugal. In nineteenth-century

Sardinia marital residential units were "grouped together in a closely packed *vicinati* (neighborhood) of brothers and sisters, around the home of the parents, or sometimes of a widowed mother or an unmarried sister who continued to live in the parental home" (Oppo 1990: 492) In Sardinia, these *vicinati* were mainly structured on an uxorilocal basis. Uxorilocality is also quite common in northwestern Portugal (Pina-Cabral 1984; Brettell 1988), although the Caldas family example demonstrates that there is both variation and flexibility.

It has by now become commonplace to accept the fact that "an overemphasis on the bounded household leads to a misleading conceptualization of households as autonomous units where marriage is the defining relationship between the genders and conjugal relations are privileged over other types of relations and strategies" (Moore 1988: 50). In the case of the Caldas family, sibling relations, as well as relations between sisters and wives, are clearly as important to consider. As a modification to Karen Sacks' (1979) argument, the Caldas family illustrates that in a class-based society such as Portugal the sister relationship is not necessarily obliterated by an in-marrying wife. Virginia's mother's problem was that none of her children married into the old house, and therefore the control of this particular family line was lost.

In a period where bourgeois values have infiltrated the countryside, the younger generation of the Caldas family may be more eager to establish separate *casas* and independent nuclear family households. Yet, if this motivated the present-day descendants of José dos Santos Caldas at first, they have nevertheless reproduced the complex multi-generation households that were characteristic of the *lavrador* families of the past, albeit accommodated to non-agricultural employment, and, in two cases, in house forms that are very different from those of the past. Luisa is a teacher and her husband is a carpenter; Elsa's husband works in a factory and she is employed in a social service office in Viana do Castelo; José, Joaquim's son, runs a restaurant that he built on an adjacent piece of property. In an economy where wages are still low (in 1990, for example, Elsa's husband Manuel was earning 30 *contos* per month)[21] but costs are rising, the pooling of resources in a collective living arrangement is an excellent strategy to make ends meet.

What will happen to the *casa* of José dos Santos Caldas during the next generation? Increasingly, families in this region are reducing the amount of land they cultivate and the number of animals they keep. As Manuel's widow said to me, "we can longer maintain our rented properties because to hire *jornaleiros* these days is too expensive; and today seeds come from elsewhere and you need chemical fertilizer. The land no longer responds to natural fertilizer. All this costs money, so we have given up several fields." A farmhouse with all its sheds and equipment becomes obsolete when agricultural work itself declines. And a house without modern amenities cannot satisfy the needs and values of the late twentieth century. The house to which José dos Santos Caldas moved with his family sometime around 1860 is most likely to become a relic of a peasant way of life that is progressively vanishing.

Acknowledgements

The author would like to thank the American Philosophical Society for supporting the archival research for this paper during the summer of 1990. She is also grateful to Donna Birdwell-Pheasant and Denise Lawrence-Zúñiga for their editorial suggestions.

Notes

1. This history has been reconstructed by supplementing material gathered from family members during formal interviews and informal conversation with data drawn from notarial records, parish registers, books of testaments, and communicant lists kept by parish priests.
2. A *lugar* is a locality within a village. In the 1860s, Lanheses had 25 *lugares*. Today three new ones have been added. The godparents of all these children were António José Caldas and Maria de Sousa Lopes, José's brother and sister-in-law, who lived with António José's parents in São Miguel de Fontoura. Choosing kin as godparents is quite common in northern Portugal, and is yet another example of a strategy of familial consolidation.
3. For further discussion see Pina-Cabral 1984 and 1991. The Portuguese *lugar de vivenda* is roughly equivalent to the Irish "home place" described by Birdwell-Pheasant in Chapter 4 of this book.
4. Another example of consanguineal marriages in this family occurred in December of 1885 when Manuel José Caldas, a forty-one-year-old landowner (*proprietário*) married Rosalina Conceição Caldas, aged thirty. Manuel was the son of António José Caldas and Maria de Sousa and Rosalina was the daughter of João António Caldas and Ana Rosa Caldas. The marriage required dispensations of the second and third degree of consanguinity – they were first cousins on one side and second cousins on the other.
5. In May of 1858, as a young boy of eleven, José António applied in the town of Viana do Castelo for a passport to go to Brazil. He left with his older brother Manuel, aged thirteen. How long he remained in Brazil is unknown, but at his marriage he was required to "justify his time there," presumably to prove that he had no other wife. It is possible that he returned to Brazil after marriage and, like so many emigrants of this period, died while abroad.
6. José dos Santos Caldas' son Manuel, who was also a *marchante*, moved to Fontoura with his wife Margarida (a woman from the parish of Darque across the river from the provincial town of Viana do Castelo), whom he had married

sometime in the early 1880s. The parish registers of Fontoura provide us with evidence of the marriage and the move. In February of 1883 Margarida gave birth to a daughter, baptized Francisca, who was herself married in 1902 and widowed in 1934. Francisca died in 1968.

7. Numerous studies have explored the relationship between father's age at death and mean age at marriage for sons and/or daughters. While there appears to have been some relationship between these two variables in Lanheses, it is not clear-cut. Only about one-quarter of those sons and daughters whose fathers died at over the age of sixty waited until after the death of their fathers to marry (Brettell 1986: 110). Nor do I think there is any clear relationship between father's death and marriage when we take co-residence into account. Three-generation stem-family households with two co-residing conjugal couples were quite common.

8. Tabelião João Felipe de Castro, volume 228, p. 17, 13-8-1909. (A *tabelião* is a notary; notarial records are organized by name of notary and volume.) Despite a law in 1867 calling for *partilhas*, many peasant families delayed property division for as long as they could. Agricultural families today complain that new laws in the 1980s are more rigorously enforced, and *partilhas* must now be carried out more expeditiously.

9. Tabelião António José Alves, volume 230, p. 1.

10. Illegitimacy was common in northern Portugal, especially during the later nineteenth and early twentieth centuries. Between 1860 and 1919, 13 percent of all baptisms in Lanheses were those of illegitimate children. Illegitimacy ran in families, and was particularly prevalent among *jornaleiras*. It was, in short, partly a function of social class, but also associated with extensive male emigration. See Brettell (1986), Pina-Cabral (1986) and O'Neill (1987) for further discussion of this topic.

11. Tabelião Francisco José de Aquiar, volume 135, p. 48. By this time the denomination of Portuguese currency was the *escudo*. One *escudo* was equivalent to one *milréis*. From henceforth, the notation in this text is as follows: 100$00=100 *escudos*; 1: 000$00=1,000 *escudos* or 1 *conto*.

12. Teresa died prematurely in 1930. Her widowed husband moved back in with his parents in a house in the *lugar* of Romão. His mother helped to raise the three young children. Teresa's daughter Maria, after her marriage in 1954, moved into a small room built on to her paternal grandparents' house.

13. This accumulation of land continued into the 1930s. In February of 1935 José bought a field in the *lugar* of Corredoura that was to the south and west of property he already owned from a widow named Maria Franco da Rua for 780$00. This widow, together with her children, sons-in-law, and daughters-in-law, was selling a lot of property at this time, perhaps as a result of the

eventual *partilhas* following her husband's death in 1922. (Tabelião António Gonçalves de Amorím, volume 257, p. 22.)

14. In fact Virginia was one of twins, but the second infant died soon after birth.

15. Tabelião Abílio Menezes Lopes de Carvalho, Partilhas, volume 34A, page 6.

16. An *avo* is a fraction of a unity when divided into more than ten parts.

17. Tabelião Alberto Teixeira Botelho, Testamentos, volume 15, page 11.

18. Virginia's life story is detailed in Brettell (1995 [1982]). However, since the writing of that story there have been changes in her life. She married and later divorced the father of her son. He in turn married another woman, and lives in the parish to the west of Lanheses. He never sees Virginia, but does pay the rent on her apartment. To make ends meet, Virginia takes care of an old woman in the town of Viana for five afternoons a week.

19. Electricity was brought to some regions of interior Portugal only after the 1974 revolution.

20. The predecessors of these modern emigrant houses are to be found in the *casas dos brasileiros*, the houses built by those who emigrated to and returned from Brazil during the late nineteenth and early twentieth centuries (Brettell 1979, 1986; Rocha-Trindade 1990).

21. One *conto*=1,000 *escudos*. At the 1990 exchange rate of roughly 140 escudos/ dollar, this sum is equivalent to $214/month.

References

Abu-Lughod, Lila. 1991. "Writing Against Culture." In *Recapturing Anthropology: Working in the Present*, ed. Richard G. Fox, pp. 137–62. Santa Fe, NM: School of American Research.

Brettell, Caroline B. 1979. "Emigrar Para Voltar: A Portuguese Ideology of Return Migration." *Papers in Anthropology* 20: 1–20.

——. 1986. *Men Who Migrate, Women Who Wait: Population and History in a Portuguese Parish*. Princeton, NJ: Princeton University Press.

——. 1988. "Emigration and Household Structure in a Portuguese Parish, 1850–1920." *Journal of Family History* 13: 33–58.

——. 1991. "Kinship and Contract: Property Transmission and Family Relations in Northwestern Portugal." *Comparative Studies in Society and History* 33(4): 443–65.

——. 1995 [1982]. *We Have Already Cried Many Tears: The Stories of Three Portuguese Migrant Women*. Prospect Heights, IL: Waveland [Original publisher Schenkman.]

Duncan, James S. 1981. *Housing and Identity: Cross-cultural Perspectives*. London: Croom Helm.

Lawrence, Denise L., and Setha M. Low. 1990. "The Built Environment and Spatial Form." *Annual Review of Anthropology* 19: 453–505.

Moore, Henrietta. 1988. *Feminism and Anthropology*. Ann Arbor, MI: University of Michigan Press.

O'Neill, Brian. 1987. *Social Inequality in a Portuguese Hamlet*. Cambridge, UK: Cambridge University Press.

Oppo, Anna. 1990. "'Where There's No Woman There's No Home': Profile of the Agro-pastoral Family in Nineteenth-century Sardinia." *Journal of Family History* 15: 438–502.

Pina-Cabral, João de. 1984. "Comentários Críticos Sobre a Casa e a Família No Alto Minho Rural." *Análise Social* 20: 263–84.

——. 1986. *Sons of Adam, Daughters of Eve*. Oxford: Clarendon Press.

——. 1991. *Os Contextos Da Antropologia*. Lisbon: Difusão Editorial, Lda.

Rocha-Trindade, Maria Beatriz. 1990. "Portuguese Migration to Brazil in the Nineteenth and Twentieth Centuries: An Example of International Cultural Exchanges." In *Portuguese Migration in Global Perspective*, ed. David Higgs, pp. 29–42. Toronto: The Multicultural History Society of Ontario.

Sacks, Karen. 1979. *Sisters and Wives: The Past and Future of Sexual Equality*. Westport, CN: Greenwood Press.

–3–

Fleeting Villages, Moving Households: Greek Housing Strategies in Historical Perspective

Susan Buck Sutton

Housing is the premier symbol of Greek familial autonomy and status, yet actual houses have been repeatedly abandoned or altered during the many migrations of Greek history. Architectural homage to the classic peasant house notwithstanding, this chapter argues that for at least the last five centuries, control over a shifting housing base, rather than maintenance of any one particular house, has been the driving force making these seemingly contradictory statements possible. Greek life has long favored mobile, household-based systems of production that encouraged frequent migration in response to the shifting fortunes of different geographical regions. Greek villages have thus appeared and disappeared with some regularity over the millennia. By examining the shifting housing base surrounding the historical foundation and growth of one particular village, this chapter explores how the ability to leave or transform houses operated as a key familial strategy, and how this strategy created a social landscape in which spaces acquired meaning and houses became markers for varying interpretations of the past.

Examining such formative processes also illuminates how rural Greeks attained some sense of agency and refuge as they meshed their domestic world with larger systems of political economy, an issue of great interest in the study of households (Maclachlan 1987; Netting, Wilk and Arnould 1984; Turner and Brush 1987; Smith, Wallerstein and Evers 1984; Yanagisako 1979). Houses encircle families with walls of defense, but also establish points of contact with the outside. Changes in housing reveal much about the ways families reproduce or transform their articulation with wider systems.

In another sense, I am also discussing how I learned to look at Greek villages differently. As an urban anthropologist, I originally saw Greek villages as a respite from Athenian smog, and an unplumbed foundation for recent change. When in them, my gaze quickly moved to older, well-maintained houses that spoke of rural strength and stability. Collapsing buildings evoked the sadness of disruption, and newly built structures seemed like grafted impositions. Much scholarly, nationalistic, and touristic literature implicitly verified my impressions by presenting the

"Greek house" and the "Greek village" as eternal types (e.g. Megas 1951). When local leaders spoke of village unity and longevity, I did not consider this as selective history. Only as village after village presented evidence of growth as well as decline, did I return these villages to a fuller place in history. Their mixed housing of various ages and states of repair then emerged as road maps to the familial strategies operating in that history and provoked a reconsideration of why such dynamic processes were often conceived in more static terms.

Iraklio, a village founded shortly after 1876 in the northeastern Peloponnesos, provides a good case for pursuing these issues.[1] It is located in the Nemea Valley, the second in a series of upland basins that rise steadily westward from the National Highway to the interior mountains of Corinthia. The valley and its surrounding hillsides circumscribe a ten square kilometer area, ranging from 370 meters to 730 meters in altitude, and containing three standing columns from a classical temple to Zeus at its center. The nearest market town, Ayios Yeorgos (also now known as Nemea), stands some two kilometers over the western ridge. The larger cities of Corinth and Argos are thirty kilometers northeast and twenty kilometers southeast, respectively.

Working with the interdisciplinary Nemea Valley Archaeological Project (Wright, Cherry, Davis, Mantzourani and Sutton 1990), I pursued issues of economics, settlement and land use in Iraklio for seven summers between 1985 and 1994.[2] Upon learning that Iraklio was a relatively recent village, we assembled a variety of ethnohistorical data, including interviews on familial, house and local history. We also conducted a full-coverage archaeological survey of surface remains of past settlements and examined the village population register, existing structures in the valley, historical aerial and hilltop photographs, nineteenth-century travelers' accounts and descriptions, annual records of agricultural production, field ownership maps, and such archival documents as annual British consular reports, Venetian cadastral records, regional newspapers, and notebooks from a 1920s archaeological excavation.[3]

After brief discussion of certain issues from modern Greek history and anthropology, I will present the housing history which has emerged from this effort. Significant demographic transitions divide this account into three phases: first, the assembling of families between 1800 and 1890 that resulted in Iraklio's foundation; second, its continued growth and consolidation from 1890 to 1940; and, third, the steadying and subsequent diminution of its population from 1940 to the present (see Table 3.1).

Households, Migration, and Modern Greek History

The great importance of the house for Greek families is an enduring maxim, well elaborated in the classic ethnographies of Friedl (1962), Campbell (1964), and

Table 3.1 Population Growth (*de facto* population)

Year	Iraklio	Nemea Valley	Ayios Yeorgos
PHASE THREE			
1991	487	704	3991
1981	512	748	4182
1971	534	804	4356
1961	549	871	4720
1951	452	776	3872
PHASE TWO			
1940	534	834	4247
1928	499	671	3485
1920	397	618	2630
1907		490	2331
1896		387	2189
PHASE ONE			
1889		315	1974
1879	90*	216	1517
1851		140	960
1821		125*	575
1700		200	211

* Estimate, based on number of households and average household size at
that time.

Source: Based on correlation of Greek census reports with Houliarakis 1973;
Kousoulos 1971; Mansolas 1872; Miliarakis 1886; Nouhakis 1901; Panayiotopoulos 1985; Pouqueville 1820; Ragkavis 1853.

DuBoulay (1974). Indeed the common word for family, *oikoyenia*, quite literally
means "relatives of the house," showing how inextricably the two concepts are
intertwined.[4] Such terms are used, however, with a flexibility revealing the fluid
nature of what actually constitutes a house, household, or family. *Oikoyenia* can
variously encompass a nuclear family, all the kin actually sharing a house, or an
entire bilateral kindred, depending on context. The common word for house, *spiti*,
can describe the building itself or the inhabitants thereof, related or not. Such
linguistic ambiguity is reflected in the varying composition of Greek households,
which as Friedl (1962), Bennett (1988) and I (Sutton 1983) have shown, may be
composed of a single person or several unrelated individuals, although nuclear
family households are the most common.

Direct control of houses has long been an important part of the tenacity, mobility
and flexibility of Greek families. The house wall establishes a boundary between
public and private domains (Dimen 1986; Dubisch 1986; Seremetakis 1991). Even
under imperial and feudal circumstances, house ownership established some

measure of independence, and successful management of housing remains central to familial power and status (Sant Cassia 1992: 150). Houses are key components of dowry and patrimony, two-thirds of migrant remittances go to housing, and real estate remains the most common investment in Greece (Shinn 1986: 106,172).

This chapter explores how such pursuit of housing autonomy created different social landscapes at different points in Greek history. Recent work on the malleability of both kin and house systems bodes well for this investigation. Sant Cassia (1992) has chronicled the initial production in the nineteenth century of certain kinship practices now taken for granted. Just (1991), Kenna (1976) and Loizos and Papataxiarchis (1991), among others, have probed the present-day manipulation of kinship within a wider set of social relations. Friedl (1976) and Allen (1979) have shown how contemporary rural families dower their daughters with urban apartments to facilitate their migration to Athens, and Hirschon (1989) has documented the creative use of minimal housing resources by urban refugees. Pavlides (Pavlides and Hesser 1989; Pavlides 1995) and Saccopoulos (1995) have revealed the dynamic nature of "traditional" architecture, while Clark (1995) has recorded successive changes in the housing stock of one village. Finally, Moore (1995) and Herzfeld (1991) have examined local response to the constraints of historic preservation and tourism on housing. Such studies make all the more plausible the idea that housing, household, and village structures have shuffled and reshuffled themselves at different points in Greek history.

This task is also supported by recent work on the history and nature of Greek society, particularly during the last two centuries of Ottoman domination and first century of the modern Greek state. Turkish rule of Greek lands changed significantly in the 200 years leading to the outbreak of the Greek Revolution in 1821. As Mouzelis (1978), Vacalopoulos (1976), McNeill (1977), Kremmydas (1972) and others have established, the expanding commercial economies of western Europe evoked much internal change in the Empire at this time. While some Greek peasants came under heightened demands for production on Turkish estates, others lived in greater autonomy from weakening Ottoman administrative structures. In this atmosphere, some produced specialized crops and handicrafts for European markets, while others became shippers traveling between the Empire and parts of Europe. Many Greeks thus had direct contact with international economic networks well before independence, a circumstance that only intensified after creation of the Greek nation (Mouzelis 1978; Vergopoulos 1975; Hadjimichalis 1987; Evangelinides 1979).

In this atmosphere, most rural Greeks operated as small-scale entrepreneurs even before national independence, responding to international markets while using household structures for labor and support. The great divide between domestic and wider economic systems attributed to some peasants does not apply well to

Greece.[5] Familial organization and entrepreneurship remain central features of the Greek economy, both rural and urban, to this day (McNeill 1977; Hadjimichalis 1987).[6] Ethnohistorical studies of rural political economy by Costa (1988), Gavrielides (1976), Bialor (1976), Aschenbrenner (1986), Vermeulen (1976), Karakasidou (1992), and Gallant (1988) further support this point. Greek peasants emerge as the sort described by Sheridan (1988), for whom the household equals or surpasses the village as a basic unit of resource control. While most Greeks have lived in villages of a few hundred people for centuries (Zakynthos 1976: 56–70), most villages were not particularly stable, long-lived, or compelling in their hold on Greek households. They provided collaboration and refuge, but were put together, disassembled, and reassembled with some regularity, a process that continued well after independence.

Indeed, the instability of villages on the Greek landscape has now been established in multiple ways. Archaeological surveys, such as those by van Andel and Runnels (1987), Cherry, Davis and Mantzourani (1991) and Renfrew and Wagstaff (1982) show small settlements appearing and disappearing throughout Greek history. Historical data affirm this pattern for Byzantine and early Turkish times (Laiou-Thomadakis 1977; Antoniadi-Bibicou 1965),[7] and increasing evidence shows the late Ottoman Empire and the succeeding Greek nation as periods of even greater migratory flux.[8] The move to freer regions toward the end of the Empire, the availability of lands vacated by Turks after independence, and increasing integration into global systems of political economy all generated great mobility. The creation of new settlement allegiances has thus been part of Greek life for some time. The case of Iraklio, to which I now turn, demonstrates how some families managed their housing resources in this situation.

Iraklio: Development and Foundation, 1800–1890

Toward the end of Ottoman control, the Nemea Valley was a sparsely inhabited buffer between the strong Turkish presence at Corinth and less dominated areas to the west. By the time of the Greek Revolution, the nearby town of Ayios Yeorgos was solidly under Greek control and a center of anti-Turkish sentiment.[9] In the Nemea Valley itself, only one of the three small settlements recorded for the early eighteenth century was still going strong (Panayiotopoulos 1985: 193–5). Koutsomadi, a free village of some 20 to 34 families (Pouqueville 1820: 182; Bory de Saint-Vincent 1834: 68) lay midway up the western hillside, close to the town of Ayios Yeorgos and its monastery, which owned some of the valley's land.[10] The formerly Turkish-controlled communities of Lekosi and Bekiri Bei were in rapid demographic decline, soon to disappear.[11]

Koutsomadi, with its roughly 120 inhabitants, was home to some five to eight patrilines.[12] The now elderly sons of those who eventually left recall it as a poor place, full of shepherds, with marginal farming of grains and vines. The valley floor was considered open grazing land, home to a few shepherds in scattered, seasonal huts (*kalivia*).[13] This combination of herding and viticulture is confirmed by several travelers (Dodwell 1819: 209; Curtius 1851; Pouqueville 1820: 186). The vineyards did not extend far onto the valley floor, for these travelers also comment on the uncultivated, uninhabited nature of the area. Some of the vintage was pressed into *mousto* (must) in vats just at the bottom of the hill. The small, mostly mud-brick houses of Koutsomadi, a few with cut stone foundations, clustered around its small church.

With Greek independence, the entire Peloponnesos became part of the new nation of Greece, and the Nemea Valley was placed into the administrative township (*demos*) of Ayios Yeorgos established in 1834 (Kousoulos 1971: 407). Removal of the Ottomans spurred new waves of migration by the rural Greek population. Much land formerly controlled by Turks, as well as vacant areas and some monastic property, became part of the National Lands, gradually made available to Greek peasants during the nineteenth century (McGrew 1985). A surge of migration down from the interior mountains to the lowland coasts and plains resulted (Anagnosto-poulos and Aivaliotakis 1939: 17–18; Aschenbrenner 1986; Beuermann 1954; Bialor 1976; Burgel 1965; Cvijić 1918; McGrew 1985: 225; Mansolas 1867: 9; Sivignon 1981; Philippson 1892; Wagstaff 1982: 19–21). Other families entered the Peloponnesos from Greek lands not yet free of Turkish rule (Anagnostopoulos and Gagalis 1938: 40). The Peloponnesian population thus grew throughout the nineteenth century (Alexopoulos 1971; Baxevanis 1972), and many new settlements, referred to by one nineteenth-century observer as both *choria* (villages) and *komidia* (hamlets), appeared on the landscape (Miliarakis 1886).[14]

The Nemea Valley was no exception to this pattern. Its uninhabited sections fell under the National Lands, and peasants who used them hoped eventually to obtain legal title.[15] Many families moved into the valley to stake claims, and residents of Koutsomadi attempted to solidify their hold on parts of the valley floor. All were encouraged by the valley's potential for several important commercial crops of the period. Miliarakis (1886: 161) described the Nemea and the nearby Ayios Yeorgos Valleys as the two best inland farming areas of Corinthia. By the 1880s, they exported dried currants abroad and sold must to wine merchants in Argos.[16] Currants were the main Greek export of the nineteenth century, rising to great favor in British cooking, and, from 1877 to 1890, forming a key element in French wine-making (Beaujour 1800; Burlumi 1899; Lambrinidos 1905; Mansolas 1867). Vineyards thus spread across the Nemea Valley, although many families also continued herding and other agricultural activities as well.

Family histories reveal the number of patrilines living in the valley had increased to over a dozen by the mid-nineteenth century.[17] These new families came from both free and unredeemed Greece: Euboea, Central Greece, the Aegean Islands, the Argolid, and the interior mountains of the Peloponnesos. Approximately half attached themselves to Koutsomadi, while several brothers took over the former Turkish hamlet of Lekosi. The remaining new families built isolated farmsteads scattered around the area, sheltering from one to six patrilineally related households. As elsewhere in the Peloponnesos, these new hamlets often had names that combined "-*aika*," "-*eika*," or "-*ika*" endings with the familial patronym (Beuermann 1954; Sivignon 1981: 34; Vayiakakos 1974: 75–6; Wagstaff 1982). Transhumant shepherds added to their winter sites in the area and initiated some farming.Land use and settlement in the valley thus became denser during this period. Most new houses were one-story with one or two rooms. A few were rough stone held together by mortar, while most were mud-brick. Low mud-brick or stone walls generally surrounded these houses and their accompanying ovens, storage sheds, and courtyards. Household composition was quite variable, most likely a fluid mix of nuclear and extended families.[18]

A major earthquake in 1876 precipitated further settlement change.[19] Koutsomadi suffered much damage, and its residents chose to abandon it rather than rebuild. Its isolated hillside location did not suit the expanding commercial economy. About half the Koutsomadi residents left the valley altogether, settling in Ayios Yeorgos and more distant villages and towns. The remainder created two new hamlets on the valley floor (Miliarakis 1886; Nouhakis 1901: 488; Kousoulos 1971: 411).[20] The smaller hamlet, Linos, arose near the Koutsomadi wine vats at the bottom of the hillside.[21] The larger one, Iraklio, emerged as a set of widely spaced homesteads centrally located along the dirt road running east–west through the valley.[22] This road was important for transporting produce from Ayios Yeorgos and the valley to the Argos–Corinth highway, something enhanced in the 1880s by the upgrading of the latter to a carriage road, and construction of a railroad along its length (Papayiannakis 1982: 99; Vardouniotis 1913: 225). Family histories indicate around eight patrilines from Koutsomadi settled in Iraklio, and 15 households were listed there soon after the earthquake (Miliarakis 1886).

Within ten years, these two hamlets moved to the status of *chorio*, or village, with larger populations, communal space, and churches. This was a conscious strategy by several families to create more viable settlements. Some even gave land to non-related families from outlying homesteads to encourage their inward movement. Such village formation allowed both coordination and control over the further development of the valley. There had been numerous land disputes during its initial settlement, preserved today in bitter tales of strong-arm tactics. Village consolidation and the fixing of most property lines by the national government by 1890 ended these disagreements.

As these two villages emerged, new families were thus incorporated. This sometimes occurred through intermarriage of various patrilines which had entered the valley since 1830. Between 1850 and 1900, local records indicate that the endogamy rate within the valley was 46 percent. Older residents remember this practice, and suggest it was used to consolidate land claims. An additional 16 patrilines joined Iraklio between 1876 and 1890, attached to the village either through marriage or the acquisition of property there. This increasing concentration in Iraklio and Linos also caused the abandonment of some scattered patrilineal hamlets, such as Lekosi.

Owning a house in Iraklio or Linos thus meant village membership and conveyed leverage in the valley's development. The households settling there acted quickly, initially constructing small, one-story, generally mud-brick structures with considerable open land or fields in between. In several cases, former stables or field huts were reused for houses, and in Linos, temporary huts were put up over wine vats.

Iraklio: Growth and Expansion, 1890–1940

For the next fifty years, Iraklio expanded its position within the valley, growing from roughly 100 inhabitants in 1889 to 534 by 1940. While there was some out-migration, particularly women marrying husbands from other areas and poorer families leaving altogether, these trends were more than offset by in-migration and natural increase. As a result, in 1912 the Nemea Valley became a separate *koinotis*, breaking away from Ayios Yeorgos, under the national reorganization that stressed these smaller administrative units rather than the former *demoi* (Kousoulos 1971: 409; Houliarakis 1973). Iraklio, Linos, and two hamlets outside the valley to the east (Dervenakia and Damatina) were designated *sinoikismoi* (settlements) of the *Koinotis* of Koutsomadi (renamed Archaia Nemea in 1958). As Linos and Iraklio thus grew and gained importance, more small hamlets in the area were abandoned.

Growth was spurred by the region's continued prosperity. While those Peloponnesian districts that had relied exclusively on currants suffered greatly when France imposed a boycott to protect its wine industry in the 1890s,[23] Iraklio emerged relatively unscathed from this event. Its high-quality produce still found markets both locally and abroad. The valley's production of must, and now also sultana raisins, olives and a local wine, also dampened the boycott's effects. Indeed, most shepherding ended in the 1920s, as families turned exclusively to commercial farming. A new road running through Iraklio to Ayios Yeorgos added to village stability, although it also exemplified the fragility of village cooperation as families vied to have it pass their houses.

The Irakliote population grew largely within established patrilines and families absorbed into these lines by marriage. Only twelve wholly new families entered the village after 1900. The exogamy rate, however, was around 80 percent, and among such couples who stayed in Iraklio, 85 percent contained brides from outside and 15 percent contained in-marrying grooms.[24] Most marriages were arranged by parents, and the ability to establish a suitable household for the new couple in Iraklio figured in these deliberations. Some shepherd men from the interior mountains are still described as having "come into land and house through marriage" at this time.[25] There was considerable play in these patterns, however, as adoption and other mechanisms were sometimes used to create households. Some selling and shifting of agricultural plots also occurred as families solidified their positions in the village.[26]

Postmarital residence tended to create virilocal neighborhoods in Iraklio, a pattern noted elsewhere in Greece (Seremetakis 1991: 22; Couroucli 1985; Piault 1985; Herzfeld 1985: 72).[27] New houses, or house additions were often built for married sons (and occasionally daughters) near the paternal house. Such practices increased the village housing stock in sponge-like fashion, with open areas increasingly filled in. These virilocal neighborhoods often became known by the name of the dominant family. Each household had distinct quarters and was listed separately on local records. On another level, however, closely related households often acted in compound fashion, sharing considerable labor and resources in common. Those few families entering Iraklio without marriage ties during this phase built on its outskirts. Most were poor shepherds who bought or were given peripheral land in exchange for creating clientage relations with established Irakliote families.[28]

This second phase of Irakliote history thus witnessed much building and rebuilding of houses (something also noted for other regions at this time: Wagstaff 1982; Clark 1995). New families constructed their initial houses, while many existing families replaced their original dwellings. Two main styles resulted.[29] Wealthier families built substantial two-story houses, many dating between 1890 and 1910 (Figures 3.1 and 3.2).[30] These larger houses contained storage for wine vats and farming equipment on the ground floor, and usually a balcony and three mixed-purpose rooms where the residents lived on the upper floor.[31] Most had cut stone foundations, constructed by itinerant masons from distant Arkadia or Macedonia, with either stone or mud-brick walls, depending on the household's wealth. Some families also used stones from the ruined houses of Koutsomadi for these foundations. In constructing these two-story houses, some families relegated their former one-story dwellings to workspace, and others incorporated them into the new house by raising the roof. Additional indications of status and wealth involved applying plaster both inside and out, and the occasional painting of romanticized scenes of antiquity on the interior walls.[32]

Poorer Irakliote families remained in or built houses of only one story, usually mud-brick, and typically eight meters by four meters with two rooms and a packed earth floor. One room contained the hearth, beds, cooking area, table, and sleeping mats. The other held additional tables, a mirror, clothes chests, and often a sewing

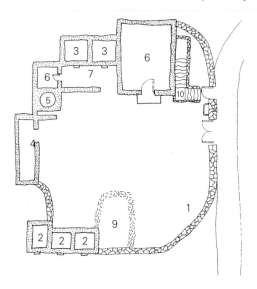

Figure 3.1a Plan of ground-level housing compound of a prosperous family, initially constructed in 1892 (Drawn by Lisa Teichgraeber, 1997).

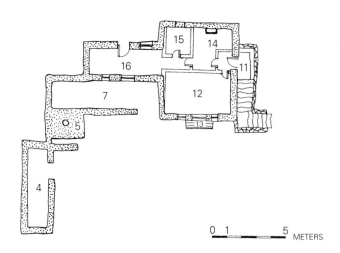

Figure 3.1b Plan of upper level of same housing compound.

1. Compound wall.
2. Wine vat (*linos*).
3. Wine vat now converted to pigeon roost (*peristeriona*).
4. Stable (*stavlos*).
5. Oven (*fournos*).
6. Storage room.
7. Open storage area; also flyway to pigeon roost.
8. Water trough.

9. Ruins of older structure for rabbits.
10. Stairs.
11. Entry porch (*hayiati*).
12. Summer parlor (*sala*).
13. Balcony.
14. Winter parlor (*sala*).
15. Bedroom.
16. Work room.

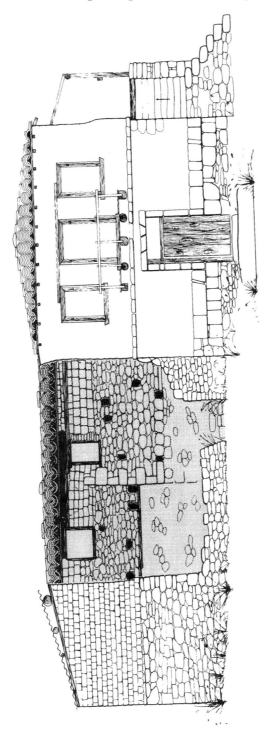

Figure 3.2 Elevation of the compound in Figure 3.1 (Drawn by Rosemary Robertson, 1987).

machine. Both large and small houses usually had walled courtyards within which were an oven, a stable, and space for agricultural activities. A second wave of renovations was sparked by another earthquake in 1928, after which the Greek government provided some financial assistance with repairs.

Several considerations bore upon Irakliote households as they built, rebuilt, or left the village during this period. To achieve housing autonomy and economic well-being, they weighed their ability to conduct commercial agriculture in the valley, their accessibility to land for houses in the village, their connections to established Irakliote families, the resources needed for either a one- or two-story house, the wealth to pay itinerant specialists, and the social networks they could mobilize for mud-brick construction. Mud-brick houses were built largely by the people who resided in them, calling upon friends and relatives for assistance. A group of fifteen people could make the 5,000 bricks needed for a house in about three days and then dry the bricks and assemble the house in the next few weeks (Figure 3.3).

Iraklio: Stabilization and Decline, 1940–Present

The Second World War and the ensuing Greek Civil War were watersheds in Greek life, ushering in another demographic shift in Irakliote history. Out-migration exceeded both in-migration and natural increase, resulting in little growth and, eventually, some decline in the village's *de facto* population.[33] Those households that remain are actually in moderate to good economic circumstances, producing wine, currants, olives, and recently such specialty crops as kiwi fruit. Increased education, expectations, and consumerism have, however, drawn many young people to nearby towns, to Athens, and to destinations abroad. While all but one of the original patrilines are still represented in Iraklio, all also now have branches outside the village. Exogamy rates continue high, and grooms are as likely as brides to leave Iraklio after marriage. Indeed, many marry spouses in the cities to which they hope to move. Only a few new families have entered Iraklio during the last fifty years, buying or receiving land, once again on its outskirts.

Housing strategies have changed correspondingly. On the one hand, those leaving Iraklio manipulate housing resources to claim a spot in Athens, Corinth, Argos, and other destinations. In patterns common throughout Greece, families sometimes purchase urban apartments for their children, while others arrange to live with relatives already established in these cities (Allen 1979; Friedl 1976; Moustaka 1964: 13–14; Sutton 1983). On the other hand, other Irakliote families use houses to keep their children in the village. Construction of new, modern-style houses for children in their teens is used as enticement for them and their eventual spouses to stay.

Figure 3.3 Irakliote man demonstrating how to make mud bricks (Photo credit Susan Sutton).

This last phase has thus led to further changes in Irakliote houses. A flurry of building and rebuilding contrasts with the village's demographic decline.[34] Even the poorest families have remodeled or added rooms or initiated new houses. Older houses have become quarters for elderly parents, uninhabited storehouses, or work areas. Some of this building, as already indicated, accommodates newly married couples. The rest, however, responds to changing patterns of consumption and display. While making houses accessible to even the poorest Irakliote families in the past, mud bricks ceased to be used around 1965. New houses are constructed from cinder blocks, bricks, poured cement, ceramic tiles and other commercial materials requiring specialist labor. Virtually all new houses are larger than previous ones, and the idealized dwelling is two-story, with separate dining, cooking, and living rooms as well as three bedrooms, all on the upper floor over storage space for agricultural machinery. A balcony often surrounds the upper story, making household activities visible all over the village.

Irakliote neighborhoods, which remain largely virilocal, are now dense with a combination of old and new housing. They also contain great variety in household composition, ranging from stem families living in old one-story houses to nuclear families inhabiting new two-story dwellings, to several houses within the same courtyard wall containing related but distinct households.[35] In altering their houses, families must consider how many individuals they must accommodate in the future, the lucky chance of receiving government funds for earthquake damage in the 1950s or 1970s, and their overall finances for rebuilding or starting a house. They also balance the availability of land and how soon they will need the house. Many houses are built progressively over a decade, with half-finished foundations or shells standing for years on end. Of course, these partially completed houses can still be used for shading flocks of sheep and storage, can be rented to visiting archaeologists, and may not be needed until now-young children are grown.[36] Families also weigh their desire for wooden floors and other such amenities against their finances. Some have shown skill in using regional social networks to garner lower prices or favors from various construction specialists. Others go into debt for their houses, a new development that nationally has increased bank loans for construction to unprecedented levels.[37]

Irakliote Houses: Negotiated Metaphors

The current array of Irakliote housing gives a visual history of the village, interpreted in significant but different ways by various residents. The housing strategies of this and previous periods have created a series of built environments structuring human action and acting as metaphors for social relations, in ways suggested by Pred (1990), Robben (1989), Glassie (1975), and Giddens (1984). This environment makes various statements about the present social structure and significant past of the village, and with each new building these are rephrased. Conceptions of the village are thus negotiated and reworked by its houses in ways that parallel the debate over village identity in the celebrations Caraveli (1985) has examined for another Greek village. In Iraklio, where houses are situated, how they look, and what public spaces and buildings surround them are part of this negotiation. Certain elements of this landscape provoke the most discourse.

Abandoned or decaying older dwellings, both in the village and nearby fields, are seen as markers of the Irakliote past (Lowenthal 1985: 187). In the absence of a written history, these architectural relics, together with old stories, build a sense of local history. For some Irakliotes, these disintegrating structures speak of rural decay and a backwardness they wish to leave. For others, they demonstrate sure progress from the past. In either case, however, these houses also establish the longevity of certain patrilines in the region and verify their legitimate membership in the village, in ways parallel to Birdwell-Pheasant's discussion (Chapter 4, this volume) of Irish home places.[38] Even the scant foundations of old, outlying patrilineal compounds mark claims to their descendants' long-term presence in the area (Figures 3.4 and 3.5). Correspondingly, those few households still living in unrenovated, older houses are pitied for their decrepit quarters, but also respected for the local longevity to which these houses attest. One of these houses, which has been elaborately renovated, is particularly interesting because it shows both familial longevity and the wealth to pay for expensive modern materials. Veneration for these markers of patrilineal legitimacy does not mean most families actually wish to live in them. Indeed in another interesting case, the old *patriko* house stands now occupied not by people but the family's pigeon roost.[39]

The village's varied housing also marks its class structure. By and large, poorer families live in one-story houses with three to four multipurpose rooms, and chicken wire fencing around their courtyards. These households frequently complain that their houses are "too low," specifying that they do not catch the healthful breezes of the valley, but implying low social status as well. Many strive to replace them with the two-story houses of the wealthier families, even at the expense of a considerable drain on household resources. Wealthier families, on the other hand, tend to have newer, larger houses, often grouped into clusters of closely related and cooperating households. The same wall may circumscribe an older house occupied by an elderly couple, a new two-story house for one of their married children, and several farm buildings, some of which may previously have been houses. These wealthier houses show the separation of work and family space that has marked the entry of farm families into urban-generated styles in northern Europe and North America (e.g. McMurray 1988; Pardailhe-Galabrun 1991; Lawrence-Zúñiga, Chapter 6 in this volume).[40]

The symbolic connotations of this new-style architecture bear scrutiny. In some ways, such houses convey a loss of familial control, for they are expensive and

Figure 3.4 Late nineteenth-century house, now elaborately renovated (Photo credit Susan Sutton).

Figure 3.5 Late nineteenth-century mud-brick house with recent manufactured brick additions (Photo credit Susan Sutton).

depend on labor outside the household. On another level, however, owning such houses demonstrates a new kind of control, one that many Irakliote families now strive to display. These houses show a family's knowledge of urban styles (or even international styles, as noted by Brettell for Portuguese housing) and its ability to operate in fully monetized economic systems. The complexity of commandeering and paying for specialists to come to Iraklio to build these houses, bit by bit over the years, demonstrates mastery in dealing with craftsmen and other representatives of the wider world on which Irakliotes fully depend (Figure 3.6). These houses thus display a new kind of household power and mastery. In making such statements, however, those who overspend their means or push the display value toward ostentation incur much criticism. The display must be viewed as legitimate to have full social value. And, of course, on another level, such modern-style architecture is the commoditization of one of the items peasant families value most, and what feels like control to families who incur debt to build these houses can also be seen as increasing dependence in a larger arena.

Irakliote housing thus establishes a visual framework and history for the relative standing of its inhabitants. In such a recently founded village, as Sheridan points out for a different part of the world, there is often tension between the goals of household autonomy and village cooperation. The tenuousness of village allegiances thus also appears in the Irakliote landscape. The legitimacy and primacy that some houses convey also stand as a reminder of class domination. The placement of a road recalls the machinations to have it built near one household rather than another. The sterile new *plateia* (square) is an emblem of Iraklio's difficulty in creating a viable center. An elderly man teases his *soghambros* (in-marrying) son-in-law that the house is not really his, and the son-in-law builds a larger one across the street. A young man bent on leaving sees the ruins of a former hamlet as simply where some old people used to live, while his mother displays them as proof of ancestry in the valley. In these, and many other ways, Irakliotes read their landscape differently. Village divisions – men and women, poor and rich, old and new, winners and losers – are mirrored and reworked through it.

Conclusions

In sum, Irakliote houses have been used to establish both continuity and change in family fortunes. Houses have served as basic shelter, a way of claiming space, a statement of household status, and an independent base for operating in larger systems. Housing control has been a major force in familial mobility, both past and present, and various strategies have been used to achieve this in situations of both migration and consolidation. Over time, these housing strategies have also turned an open valley into a nucleated village controlled by those families most long-lived in the area. This, in turn, has affected housing strategies in varied ways.

Figure 3.6 Construction specialist completing finishing touches on a new house (Photo credit Susan Sutton).

Social class, village longevity, changing construction techniques, and the varied symbolism of different styles and materials significantly influence the shape, status, and composition of both house and household. This is an ongoing process, shaped by both material constraints and normative ideals, control and contestation, opportunism and luck.

Certainly not all villages are like Iraklio, either in Greece or throughout Europe. The relationship between houses, households and village residence that this case illuminates, however, throws into relief forces that might be investigated elsewhere. Issues of land tenure and inheritance emerge as important for Iraklio, as they have in most studies. So do some less examined factors such as settlement formation, inward migration, changing marriage strategies, and village longevity. Repeated migrations and village turnover may have been more common in the European past than is generally thought.[41]

Even where such events have not occurred, however, there is something to be learned from the Irakliote case. The forces causing villages to be endogamous or exogamous, long-lived or short-lived, agonistic or communal bear scrutiny and affect housing strategies.[42] The contrast between villages with shrinking economic bases, and those with expanding ones, like Iraklio, is also significant. The advent of such forces as historical preservation and tourism and the transition of housing from transient to durable possession under such circumstances (Herzfeld 1991; Moore 1995) sets into motion yet another housing dynamic.[43]

All villages, of course, have a history worth investigating. As Wolf (1986) has elaborated, even closed corporate villages arose through their reaction to larger systems, and not as a mere survival of tradition. This, in turn, can contribute to the ongoing discussion of European household and family by scholars such as Hareven (1977), Laslett and Wall (1972), Berkner (1975), Goody (1983) and Plakans (1984). Studies such as those by Brettell (1991), Kertzer (1984), and Shaffer (1982) have detailed the complex interaction of land tenure and inheritance patterns with household form. Rogers (1991) has even shown how seemingly traditional household forms are produced by contemporary circumstances. This chapter suggests migration into villages and changing village composition as additional shaping forces. In so doing, it also affirms the growing understanding of peasant agency and resistance to the forces impinging on their lives (e.g. Rosenberg 1988).

Given this, the question remains why the Greek house and the European village have often been seen as more historically fixed than they actually have been. For many scholars, paradigmatic constraints classified villages as base factors, not variables.[44] They were the benchmark for measuring recent change, and a way of fixing a population in space. Certainly, modernization theorists viewed the village as primordial tradition. Even within dependency theory, however, discussions of peasant domination often treated the village as the stable bedrock being invaded. More broadly, the search for peasants rooted to both soil and community has been an important myth for measuring and interpreting change in Western society since the late nineteenth century (Lowenthal 1985: 122–3; Macfarlane 1977). Bell's (1979) otherwise very insightful study of *campanilismo* in Italian life thus assumes a stable, endogamous village base to validate its sense of the authentic.

Within Greece, this search for the primordial village or house is connected to nationalism. As Herzfeld (1982) has outlined, an unbroken peasant heritage established modern Greek claims to ancient Greek grandeur in the nineteenth century. More recently, Leontis (1991: 46–8) has shown how such nationalists found it important to connect actual villages with this past. The concept of the stable village community has thus been part of the national invention of tradition in Greek life (Hobsbawm and Ranger 1983; Friedman 1992). For those who leave these villages, such imagery is an artifact of memory, along lines suggested by Bahloul in this volume. This can even lead urban Greek scholars to constrict the data of rural life to fit their nostalgic image of what a village must have been (as Couroucli 1989 points out).

As was discussed earlier, statements by villagers themselves can also stress village and housing longevity to reinforce the legitimacy of certain families in an area. This is part of the creation of socially meaningful space and the negotiation of familial status.[45] If we take these statements as definitive, however, we miss those households that came later and those that have already left the village.

Ultimately, we miss the full dynamics of housing and village life. Housing control is an enduring goal of Greek life, but different historical moments have arranged and rearranged the ways families attempt to achieve it and the social landscapes that have resulted.

Notes

1. Names for this region and its settlements are problematic. For the purposes of this chapter, I have chosen a single variant for each. The village under examination is here called Iraklio, but also known as Archaia (or "Ancient") Nemea. The nearby village of Linos is now officially called Koutsomadi. Koutsomadi was also the name of the older village on the hillside destroyed by the earthquake in 1876. The site of that former village is now referred to as Palaiochori. The valley in which these sites is located is here called the Nemea Valley, but is also known as the Koutsomadi Valley. The next valley westward is also sometimes known as the Nemea Valley, although more accurately it is the Phleiasian or Ayios Yeorgos Valley. The market town in that valley is here called Ayios Yeorgos, but is also known as Nemea.

2. The Nemea Valley Archaeological Project was directed by James Wright, John Cherry, Jack L. Davis, and Eleni Mantzourani. It has been funded by major grants from the National Endowment for the Humanities, the National Geographic Society, and the Institute for Aegean Prehistory. I am indebted to all members of this collaborative endeavor, but particularly to William Alexander and Anastasia Karakasidou, who worked with me in interviewing villagers and documenting structures.

3. These various types of data were correlated with each other to reach more definitive conclusions. For example, I linked the population register, family histories, and other records to create genealogies extending back well into the nineteenth century.

4. While *oikos* is the ancient Greek word for house, it is only used that way in formalized speech today. The more common contemporary word for house is *spiti*, which probably derives from the late Latin *hospitium*, meaning inn or hospice.

5. Turner and Brush (1987) and Smith, Wallerstein, and Evers (1984) have especially good discussions on this point.

6. In the late 1980s, 90 percent of all Greek farms were family-run and under 20 hectares in size; 90 percent of all Greek manufacturing occurred in family-run workshops of fewer than 10 workers (Hadjimichalis 1987).

7. The terms *chorio* (village) and *koinotis* (community) have existed for such settlements in Greece since Antiquity. While the first is simply used for any small settlement that contains several family lines and some public facilities,

the second takes on more of an administrative or political meaning. As Laiou-Thomadakis points out, the *koinotis* was granted certain communal rights in Byzantine times, and carried some emphasis on shared pasturage and other resources. It is a major administrative division of the Greek state today (Houliarakis 1973), where it combines a number of closely related settlements for political functions.

8. The major demographic studies on this migration have been done by Wagstaff (1982), Kayser (1963), Frangakis and Wagstaff (1987), Spirinodakis (1977), Panayiotopoulos (1985), Sutton (1988), McGrew (1985), Kolodny (1974), Vacalopoulos (1976), Baxevanis (1972) and Beuermann (1954). Case studies such as those by Beopoulou (1981), Vermeulen (1976), Handman (1981) and Collard (1981) have shown how some villages and towns grew into commercial centers in the late Ottoman Empire. Several historians have stressed the increasing emphasis on small village life as a source of freedom at this time (Zakynthos 1976: 56–70; Vacalopoulos 1976). Many small settlements appeared and disappeared between 1700 and 1800 as rural Greeks rearranged themselves across the landscape (Panayiotopoulos 1985: 173). Continuing into the modern period, villages continued to appear, disappear and grow as government policies favored small farmers and villages (McGrew 1985) and rural Greek families sought their fortunes in settings, both rural and urban, deemed better vantage points in various new systems.

9. Ayios Yeorgos served as a Greek command post during the Revolution and was the scene of several skirmishes with Turks even before that (Zegkinis 1968: 235–48; Vardouniotis 1913: 221–4). Travelers described it as almost entirely Greek and much less closely governed by the Turks than Corinth (Pouqueville 1820: 187; Dodwell 1819: 211–12).

10. The monastery Panayias tou Vachou (also known as the Koimisis tou Theotokou) had some smallholdings scattered throughout the Ayios Yeorgos region (Belia 1975: 98; Kordosis 1981). It is also possible that the more distant monastery of Ayios Yeorgos Feneou had some lands in the area.

11. This corresponds with both oral history in the Nemea Valley and the disappearance of these two settlements from official records in the early nineteenth century.

12. Koutsomadi was representative of Peloponnesian villages at this time, which averaged between 34 and 140 inhabitants in the eighteenth century (Anoyatis-Pele 1987; Sauerwein 1969).

13. Clarke (1814: 714–15) mentions the hamlet of Colonna, consisting of three to four one-room shepherd huts near the ruins of the ancient temple. A corresponding cluster of late Turkish sherds was found at the modern-day place still called Colonitsa only a short distance north of the temple. A few other such small clusters of late Turkish sherds have been found at scattered

distances around the valley, one of them at a place locally thought to have been inhabited in Turkish times and called Aspra Spitia.

14. A British consular report from the late nineteenth century summed up these migrations in the following manner: "Among these classes the desire to obtain land and house is very strong, and owing to their careful and thrifty habits they are generally able to satisfy this craving, and there is scarcely a family which does not own a small cottage or a plot of land or vineyard . . ." (Great Britain 1891: 7).

15. McGrew (1985) gives a very full account of the distribution of the National Lands. The original Dotation Law of 1835 set up the principle that these lands could be transferred to the peasants. This law was cumbersome and confusing, and little was officially done until after the Distribution Laws of 1871, by which time there were some 50,000 squatters occupying lands without title in the Peloponnesos.

16. Currants, a variety of *Vitis vinifera*, are small, sweet grapes, known in Greece as either *Korinthiaki* or *mavri stafida*. Must is the initial pressing of grapes, which must then be further treated to produce wine. By the late nineteenth century, the must produced in the Nemea and Ayios Yeorgos valleys was important enough for the annual harvests to be reported in the Argos newspapers. Winemakers in Argos bought it to use as the basis of their wine. The wines thus originating in the Nemea/Ayios Yeorgos area were even graced with their own name, Ayioryitiko wine.

17. Indeed, only one of the old family names from the Venetian records of 1700 was still present in the valley by 1880.

18. The nearby town of Ayios Yeorgos had a ratio of 1.3 families per house according to the 1870 census.

19. The study by Galanopoulos (1955: 10) on nineteenth-century earthquakes in Greece confirms that a serious earthquake damaged the Nemea area in 1876. This event and date are also recalled by many elderly residents to this day.

20. These new hamlets remained part of the *Demos* of Ayios Yeorgos. Both Iraklio and Linos continued to be referred to collectively as Koutsomadi in Greek census reports, which gave no indication of their separate development until 1920.

21. *Linos* (also sometimes referred to in the plural, *Linoi*) is the Greek word for these particular wine vats. This hamlet eventually took the name of the old village, Koutsomadi, while the site where that village once stood became known as Palaiochori (literally Old Village).

22. Iraklio is a form of the name Hercules. The hamlet was named for the ancient myth of Hercules' killing of a ferocious and seemingly invincible lion in the Nemea Valley.

23. Baxevanis (1972) has shown that the collapse of the currant market in the 1890s led to the first widespread emigration from the Peloponnesos.

24. In virilocal areas of Greece, husbands who go to live in their bride's village are called *soghambroi*, and are often accorded lesser status than other men in the village because they are living on their wife's property.

25. Anagnostopoulos and Aivaliotakis (1939) note, for a nearby region, that some shepherds continued to move back and forth between winter and summer villages during this period, although most gradually settled down.

26. Some of this land was bought from those families moving out of the village. The rest was shifted among remaining families to produce better combinations in terms of location.

27. This pattern has also been noted for maturing Byzantine villages (Laiou-Thomadakis 1977: 101–3). It should also be mentioned that while most of Greece tends toward virilocality, the Aegean Islands are uxorilocal (Casselberry and Valvanes 1976: 222–3).

28. The attachment of such families on the outskirts of Iraklio is confirmed by a map drawn by local officials in 1960.

29. These two styles were very like those noted in the studies of nearby regions by Anagnostopoulos and Aivaliotakis (1939: 20–1) and Anagnostopoulos and Gagalis (1938: 42–52).

30. This period also corresponds with the dates for several of the isolated churches constructed throughout the valley, all built by families to mark their field areas.

31. These upper rooms tended to include: (1) a *sala* or sitting room with beds and table, (2) a clothes storage room, and (3) a second sitting/bedroom for winter.

32. This plaster was a mixture of lime with either cement, crushed tile or sand.

33. This parallels what has happened for much of the Peloponnesian population (Baxevanis 1972), although Iraklio in particular and the Corinthia in general have not lost as much population as most other areas (Alexopoulos 1971: 351).

34. See Aschenbrenner 1986; Clark 1988; Wagstaff 1982 for parallels elsewhere.

35. From an ethnoarchaeological standpoint, it is interesting to note that there is little correspondence between house size and the number of people living in the house.

36. The presence of a major archaeological project in the village over the last decade has also contributed its share to the rebuilding of the village landscape, as partially built houses were rented, wages paid, and food and goods purchased.

37. The credits owed the Mortgage Bank of Greece have gone from 466,700,000 drachmai at the end of 1955 to 251,597,000,000 drachmai at the end of 1984, an increase of over 500 times (Greece, National Statistical Service, *Statistical Yearbooks*, 1958, 1985).

38. Although it is not yet particularly true for Iraklio, such abandoned housing in other parts of Greece also leaves the door open for a return to an area by out-migrants.

39. Herzfeld (1991) gives a fascinating discussion of old houses in Rethemnnos, Crete, and how their history is sometimes "reread" to stress the patrilineal line.

40. Even within the houses with designated bedrooms, living room, dining room, and kitchen, however, Irakliote families still mix the use of these rooms. It is not unusual to find a bed placed in a dining room, for example.

41. Macfarlane (1977), for example, argues for the historical appearing and disappearing of many English villages. Knodel (1988), as another example, presents data showing considerable inward migration to several German villages.

42. Village marriage patterns in Greece have ranged between virtual exogamy and 80 to 90 percent endogamy (Kayser, Pechoux and Sivignon 1971).

43. Indeed Herzfeld's (1991) discussion of the frustration that Rethemniot houseowners feel at no longer being able to modify their houses freely is given even greater meaning when we consider the historical importance of housing control in Greek life.

44. As Chartier (1988: 5,102) says, historians often adopt certain categories by which they perceive the world, and once such a motif is established it takes on a life of its own. Thus Blum (1982) talks of the stable, closed peasant village even while he elsewhere acknowledges the historical formation of many new villages.

45. See Lagopoulos (1992) for a fascinating discussion of the social production of regional space in Greece.

References

Adams, Keith (forthcoming). "Mutable Boundaries: Subdivision and Consolidation in a Greek Village, 1936–1978." In *A Contingent Countryside: Settlement, Economy, and Land Use in the Southern Argolid Since 1700*, ed. Susan B. Sutton. Stanford, CA: Stanford University Press.

Alexopoulos, Anastasios A. 1971. "O Plithismos tis Korinthias." *Archeio Korinthiakon Meleton* 1: 346–86.

Allen, Peter. 1979. "Internal Migrations and the Changing Dowry in Modern Greece." *The Indiana Social Studies Quarterly* 32: 142–56.

Anagnostopoulos, N. H., and N. Aivaliotakis. 1939. *I Perifereia Xilokastro-Derveniou*. Athens: Agricultural Bank of Greece.

Anagnostopoulos, N. H., and G. Gagalis. 1938. *I Argoliki Pedias*. Athens: Agricultural Bank of Greece.

Anoyatis-Pele, Dimitris. 1987. *Connaissance de la Population et des productions de la Morée à travers un manuscrit anonyme de la fin du XVIIe siècle*. Athens: Manourtios.

Antoniadi-Bibicou, H. 1965. "Villages désertes en Grèce: un bilan provisoire." In

Villages désertes et histoire économique, pp. 343–417. Paris: École Pratique Des Hautes Études.

Aschenbrenner, Stanley. 1986. *Life in a Changing Greek Village*, Publications in Ancient Studies. Minneapolis, MN: University of Minnesota.

Baxevanis, John J. 1972. *Economy and Population Movements in the Peloponnesos of Greece*. Athens: National Centre of Social Research.

Beaujour, Félix. 1800. *A View of the Commerce of Greece*, transl. R. H. Horne. London: James Wallis.

Belia, Eleni. 1975. "Eidiseis peri tinon Korinthakon monastirion kata tin Kapodistriakin periodon." *Peloponnisiaka Parartima Praktika* 2: 92–102.

Bell, Rudolph M. 1979. *Fate and Honor, Family and Village: Demographic and Cultural Change in Rural Italy Since 1800*. Chicago, IL: University of Chicago Press.

Bennett, Diane. 1988. "'The Poor Have Much More Money': Changing Socioeconomic Relations in a Greek Village." *Journal of Modern Greek Studies* 6: 217–44.

Beopoulou, Ioanna. 1981. "Trikeri: mobilité et rapports d'appartenance." In *Aspects du changement social dans la campagne Grecque*, ed. Stathis Damianakos, pp. 191–9. Athens: National Centre for Social Research.

Berkner, Lutz. 1975. "The Use and Misuse of Census Data for the Historical Analysis of Family Structure." *Journal of Interdisciplinary History* 4: 721–38.

Beuermann, Arnold. 1954. "Kalyviendorfer Im Peloponnes." In *Ergebnisse und Probleme Moderner Geographischer Forschung*, pp. 229–38. Bremen: Walter Dorn.

Bialor, Perry. 1976. "The Northwestern Corner of the Peloponnesos: Mavrikion and Its Region." In *Regional Variation in Modern Greece and Cyprus*, ed. Muriel Dimen and Ernestine Friedl, pp. 222–35, Annals of the New York Academy of Sciences. New York: New York Academy of Sciences.

Blum, Jerome. 1982. "The Village and the Family." In *Our Forgotten Past: Seven Centuries of Life on the Land*, ed. Jerome Blum, pp. 10–24. London: Thames and Hudson.

Bory de Saint-Vincent, J. B. G. M. 1834. *Expédition scientifique de Morée*. Paris: Levrault.

Brettell, Caroline B. 1991. "Kinship and Contract: Property Transmission and Family Relations in Northwestern Portugal." *Comparative Studies in Society and History* 33(4): 443–65.

Burgel, Guy. 1965. *Pobia*. Athens: National Centre of Social Research.

Burlumi, Theodore A. 1899. "The Overproduction of Currants." *The Economic Journal* 9: 633–50.

Campbell, John. 1964. *Honour, Family and Patronage*. Oxford: Oxford University Press.

Caraveli, Anna. 1985. "The Symbolic Village: Community Born in Performance." *Journal of American Folklore* 98: 259–86.

Casselberry, Samuel, and Nancy Valvanes. 1976. "'Matrilocal' Greek Peasants and a Reconsideration of Residence Terminology." *American Ethnologist* 3: 215–26.

Chartier, Roger. 1988. *Cultural History: Between Practices and Representations*, transl. L. G. Cochrane. Ithaca, NY: Cornell University Press.

Cherry, John, Jack L. Davis, and Eleni Mantzourani (eds). 1991. *Landscape Archaeology as Long-term History: Northern Keos in the Cycladic Islands*. Institute of Archaeology. Los Angeles, CA: University of California at Los Angeles.

Clark, Mari. 1988. "The Transformation of Households on Methana, Greece 1931–1987." Ph.D. Thesis, University of North Carolina.

——. 1995. "From Shelters to Villas: Changing House and Settlement Form on Methana, 1880–1987." *Yearbook of Modern Greek Studies* 10/11: 511–36.

Clarke, Edward Daniel. 1814. *Travels in Various Countries of Europe, Asia and Africa*. London: T. Cadell and W. Davies.

Collard, A. 1981. "The Inequalities of Change in a Greek Mountain Village (Sterea Hellas: Evritania)." In *Aspects du changement social dans la campagne Grecque*, ed. Stathis Damianakos, pp. 208–20. Athens: National Centre of Social Research.

Costa, Janeen Arnold. 1988. "The History of Migration and Political Economy in Rural Greece: A Case Study." *Journal of Modern Greek Studies* 6: 159–86.

Couroucli, Maria. 1985. *Les oliviers du lignage: un Grèce de tradition Vénitienne*. Paris: Maisonneuve et Larose.

——. 1989. "Review of D. Psychoyios, *Proikes, Foroi, Stafida, Kai Psomi*." [Book Review.] *Journal of Modern Greek Studies* 7: 355–6.

Curtius, Ernst. 1851. *Peloponnesos*. Gotha: Justus Perthes.

Cvijić, J. 1918. "La Peninsule Balkanique." In *Geographie Humaine*.

Dimen, Muriel. 1986. "Servants and Sentries: Women, Power and Social Reproduction in Kriovrisi." *Journal of Modern Greek Studies* 1: 225–42.

Dodwell, Edward. 1819. *A Classical and Topographical Tour Through Greece During the Years 1801, 1805 and 1806*. London: Rodwell and Martin.

Dubisch, Jill. 1986. "Culture Enters Through the Kitchen: Women, Food, and Social Boundaries in Rural Greece." In *Gender and Power in Rural Greece*, ed. Jill Dubisch, pp. 195–214. Princeton, NJ: Princeton University Press.

du Boulay, Juliet. 1974. *Portrait of a Greek Mountain Village*. Oxford: Clarendon Press.

Evangelinides, Mary. 1979. "Core–Periphery Relations in the Greek Case." In *Underdeveloped Europe: Studies in Core-Periphery Relations*, ed. D. Seers, B. Schaffer, and M. Kiljunen, pp. 177–95. Atlantic Highlands, NJ: Humanities Press.

Frangakis, Elena, and Malcolm Wagstaff. 1987. "Settlement Pattern Change in the Morea (Peloponnisos) *c.* A.D. 1700–1830." *Byzantine and Modern Greek Studies* 11: 163–92.

Friedl, Ernestine. 1962. *Vasilika: A Village in Modern Greece*. New York: Holt, Rinehart and Winston.

———. 1976. *Women and Men: An Anthropologist's View*. New York: Holt, Rinehart and Winston.

Friedman, Jonathan. 1992. "The Past in the Future: History and the Politics of Identity." *American Anthropologist* 94(4): 837–59.

Galanopoulos, Angelos. 1955. "Seismiki geografia tis Ellados." *Geoloyikoi chronikoi ton Ellinikon choron* 6: 83–121.

Gallant, Thomas. 1988. "Greek Bandits: Lone Wolves or a Family Affair?" *Journal of Modern Greek Studies* 6: 269–90.

Gavrielides, Nicolas. 1976. "The Cultural Ecology of Olive Growing in the Fourni Valley." In *Regional Variation in Modern Greece and Cyprus: Toward a Perspective on the Ethnography of Greece*, Annals of the New York Academy of Sciences, Vol. 268, ed. Muriel Dimen and Ernestine Friedl, pp. 265–74. New York: New York Academy of Sciences.

Giddens, A. 1984. *The Constitution of Society: Outline of the Theory of Structuration*. Berkeley, CA: University of California Press.

Glassie, Henry. 1975. *Folk Housing in Middle Virginia: A Structural Analysis of Historic Artifacts*. Knoxville, TN: University of Tennessee Press.

Goody, Jack. 1983. *The Development of the Family and Marriage in Europe*. Cambridge, UK: Cambridge University Press.

Great Britain, Foreign Office. 1891. *Diplomatic and Consular Reports on Trade and Finance*. London: Foreign Office.

Hadjimichalis, Costis. 1987. *Uneven Development and Regionalism: State, Territory and Class in Southern Europe*. London: Croom Helm.

Handman, Marie-Elisabeth. 1981. "De la Soumission à la Dependance." In *Aspects du changement social dans la campagne Grecque*, ed. Stathis Damianakos, pp. 221–44. Athens: National Centre of Social Research.

Hareven, Tamara. 1977. "Family Time and Historical Time." In *The Family*, ed. A. Rossi, J. Kagan, and T. Hareven. New York: Norton.

Herzfeld, Michael. 1982. *Ours Once More: Folklore, Ideology, and the Making of Modern Greece*. Austin, TX: University of Texas Press.

———. 1985. *The Poetics of Manhood: Contest and Identity in a Cretan Mountain Village*. Princeton, NJ: Princeton University Press.

———. 1991. *A Place in History; Social and Monumental Time in a Cretan Town*. Princeton, NJ: Princeton University Press.

Hirschon, Renée. 1989. *Heirs of the Greek Catastrophe: The Social Life of Asia Minor Refugees in Piraeus*. Oxford: Clarendon Press.

Hobsbawm, Eric, and Terence Ranger (eds). 1983. *The Invention of Tradition.* Cambridge, UK: Cambridge University Press.

Houliarakis, Michail. 1973. *Geografiki dioikitiki kai plithismiaki exelixis tis Ellados, 1821–1973.* Athens: National Centre of Social Research.

Just, Roger. 1991. "The Limits of Kinship." In *Contested Identities: Gender and Kinship in Modern Greece,* ed. Peter Loizos and Evthymios Papataxiarchis, pp. 114–32. Princeton, NJ: Princeton University Press.

Karakasidou, Anastasia N. 1992. "Fields of Wheat, Hills of Shrub: Agrarian Development and the Dialectics of Ethnicity and Nationality in Northern Greece, 1870–1990." Ph.D. Thesis, Columbia University.

Kayser, Bernard. 1963. "Les migrations interieures en Grèce." In *Contributions to Mediterranean Sociology,* ed. J. G. Peristiany, pp. 192–200. The Hague: Mouton.

——, Pierre-Yves Pechoux, and Michel Sivignon. 1971. *Exode rural et attraction urbaine en Grèce.* Athens: National Centre for Social Research.

Kenna, Margaret. 1976. "The Idiom of Family." In *Mediterranean Family Structures,* ed. J. G. Peristiany, pp. 347–62. Cambridge, UK: Cambridge University Press.

Kertzer, David I. 1984. *Family Life in Central Italy, 1880–1910: Sharecropping, Wage Labor and Coresidence.* New Brunswick, NJ: Rutgers University Press.

Knodel, John. 1988. *Demographic Behavior in the Past: A Study of Fourteen German Village Populations in the Eighteenth and Nineteenth Centuries.* Cambridge, UK: Cambridge University Press.

Kolodny, Emile. 1974. *La population des îles de la Grèce.* Aix-en-Provence: EDISUD.

Kordosis, Michail. 1981. *Simvoli stin istoria kai topografia tis periochis Korinthou stous mesous chronous.* Athens: Vivliothiki Istorikon Meleton.

Kousoulos, Konstantinos. 1971. "Dioikitiki diarthrosis tis Korinthias apo to etos 1833 eos to 1964." *Archeio Korinthiakon Meleton* 1: 405–27.

Kremmydas, Vasilis. 1972. *To emporio tis Peloponnisou sto 18° aiona (1715–1792).* Athens: Emm. I. Moschonas.

Lagopoulos, Alexandros. 1992. *Meaning and Geography: The Social Conception of the Region in Northern Greece.* New York: Mouton de Gruyter.

Laiou-Thomadakis, Angeliki. 1977. *Peasant Society in the Late Byzantine Empire: A Social and Demographic Study.* Princeton, NJ: Princeton University Press.

Lambrinidos, Michail G. 1905. *Meletai kai arthra peri tis Korinthiakis stafidos (1844–1905).* Athens: Sakellarios.

Laslett, Peter, and Richard Wall (eds). 1972. *Household and Family in Past Time.* Cambridge, UK: Cambridge University Press.

Leontis, Artemis. 1991. "Cultural Politics and Populist Uses of the Ancients." *Journal of Modern Greek Studies* 9: 191–214.

Loizos, Peter, and Evthymios Papataxiarchis (eds). 1991. *Contested Identities:*

Gender and Kinship in Modern Greece. Princeton, NJ: Princeton University Press.

Lowenthal, David. 1985. *The Past is a Foreign Country*. Cambridge, UK: Cambridge University Press.

Macfarlane, Alan. 1977. *Reconstructing Historical Communities*. Cambridge, UK: Cambridge University Press.

McGrew, William. 1985. *Land and Revolution in Modern Greece, 1800–1991*. Kent, OH: Kent State University Press.

Maclachlan, Morgan (ed.). 1987. *Household Economies and Their Transformation*. Lanham, MD: University Press of America.

McMurry, Sally. 1988. *Families and Farmhouses in Nineteenth-century America: Vernacular Design and Social Change*. New York: Oxford University Press.

McNeill, William. 1977. *The Metamorphosis of Greece Since World War II*. Chicago, IL: University of Chicago Press.

Mansolas, Alexandros. 1867. *Politeiografikai pliroforiai peri Ellados*. Athens: Ethnikou Tipografeiou.

——. 1872. *Rapport sur l'etat de la statistique en Grèce*. Athens: Perris.

Megas, Georgios A. 1951. *The Greek House: Its Evolution and Its Relation to the House of Other Balkan Peoples*. Athens: Ministry of Reconstruction.

Miliarakis, Antonios. 1886. *Geografia politiki nea kai archaia tou Nomou Argolidos kai Korinthias*. Athens: Estias.

Moore, Roland. 1995. "Constructing Tradition: Architecture in a Boeotian Tourist Town." *Modern Greek Studies Yearbook* 10/11: 479–510.

Moustaka, Calliope. 1964. *The Internal Migrant*. Athens: National Centre for Social Research.

Mouzelis, Nicos. 1978. *Modern Greece: Facets of Underdevelopment*. New York: Holmes and Meier.

Netting, Robert, Richard Wilk, and Eric Arnould (eds). 1984. *Households: Comparative and Historical Studies of the Domestic Group*. Berkeley, CA: University of California Press.

Nouhakis, Ioannis Emm. 1901. *Elliniki Chorografia*. Athens: Kousoulinos.

Panayiotopoulos, Vasilis. 1985. *Plithismos kai oikismoi tis Peloponnisou 13os– 18os aionas*. Athens: Commercial Bank of Greece.

Papayiannakis, Lefteris. 1982. *Oi Ellinikoi sidirodromoi (1882–1910)*. Athens: National Bank of Greece.

Pardailhe-Galabrun, Annik. 1991. *The Birth of Intimacy: Privacy and Domestic Life in Early Paris*, transl. J. Phelps. Philadelphia: University of Pennsylvania Press.

Pavlides, Eleftherios. 1995. "The Expression of Institutional Meaning in Greek Domestic Architecture." In *Constructed Meaning: Form and Process in Greek Architecture*, Modern Greek Studies Yearbook, ed. Eleftherios Pavlides and Susan Buck Sutton. Minneapolis, MN: University of Minnesota.

——, and Jana E. Hesser. 1989. "Vernacular Architecture as an Expression of Its

Social Context in Eressos, Greece." In *Housing, Culture and Design: A Comparative Perspective*, ed. Setha M. Low and Erve Chambers, pp. 357–74. Philadelphia, PA: University of Pennsylvania Press.

Philippson, Alfred. 1892. *Der Peloponnes: Versuch einer Landeskunde auf Geologischer Grundlage*. Berlin: R. Friedlander.

Piault, Colette. 1985. *Familles et biens en Grèce et à Chypre*. Paris: Centre National de la Recherche Scientifique.

Plakans, Andrejs. 1984. *Kinship in the Past: An Anthropology of European Family Life, 1500–1900*. Oxford: Basil Blackwell.

Pouqueville, F. C. H. L. 1820. *Voyage dans la Grèce*. Paris: Firmin Didot.

Pred, Allan Richard. 1990. *Making Histories and Constructing Human Geographies: The Local Transformation of Practice, Power Relations, and Consciousness*. Boulder, CO: Westview Press.

Ragkavis, I. 1853. *Ta Ellinika*. Athens: K. Antoniadou.

Renfrew, Colin, and Malcolm Wagstaff (eds). 1982. *An Island Polity: The Archaeology of Exploitation in Melos*. Cambridge, UK: Cambridge University Press.

Robben, Antonius C. G. M. 1989. "Habits of the Home: Spatial Hegemony and the Structuration of House and Society in Brazil." *American Anthropologist* 91: 570–88.

Rogers, Susan Carol. 1991. *Shaping Modern Times in Rural France: The Transformation and Reproduction of an Aveyronnais Community*. Princeton, NJ: Princeton University Press.

Rosenberg, Harriet G. 1988. *A Negotiated World: Three Centuries of Change in a French Alpine Community*. Toronto: University of Toronto Press.

Saccopoulos, Christos. 1995. "The Codification of Tradition in Cycladic Architecture." *Yearbook of Modern Greek Studies* 10/11: 463–78.

Sant Cassia, Paul. 1992. *The Making of the Modern Greek Family: Marriage and Exchange in Nineteenth Century Athens*. Cambridge, UK: Cambridge University Press.

Sauerwein, Friedrich. 1969. "Das Siedlungsbild der Peloponnes Um das Jahr 1700." *Erdkunde* 23: 237–44.

Seremetakis, Nadia. 1991. *The Last Word: Women, Death, and Divination in Inner Mani*. Chicago: University of Chicago Press.

Shaffer, John W. 1982. *Family and Farm: Agrarian Change and Household Organization in the Loire Valley, 1500–1900*. Albany, NY: State University of New York Press.

Sheridan, Thomas E. 1988. *Where the Dove Calls: The Political Economy of a Peasant Corporate Community in Northwestern Mexico*. Tucson, AZ: University of Arizona Press.

Shinn, Rinn S. (ed.). 1986. *Greece: A Country Study*. Washington, DC: American University Press.

Sivignon, Michel. 1981. "Evolution de la société rurale dans l'ouest du Peloponnese – Metochi (Achaie)." In *Aspects du changement social dans la campagne Grecque*, ed. Stathis Damianakos, pp. 32–41. Athens: National Centre for Social Research.

Smith, Joan, Immanuel Wallerstein, and Hans-Dieter Evers (eds). 1984. *Households and the World Economy*. Beverly Hills, CA: Sage.

Spirinodakis, B. G. 1977. *Essays on the Historical Geography of the Greek World in the Balkans During the Turkokratia*. Thessaloniki: Institute for Balkan Studies.

Sutton, Susan Buck. 1983. "Rural–Urban Migration in Greece." In *Urban Life in Mediterranean Europe*. ed. M. Kenny and D. Kertzer. Urbana: University of Illinois Press.

——. 1988. "What is a 'Village' in a Nation of Migrants?" *Journal of Modern Greek Studies* 6: 187–215.

Turner, B. L., and Stephen Brush (eds). 1987. *Comparative Farming Systems*. New York: The Guilford Press.

Vacalopoulos, Apostolos. 1976. *The Greek Nation, 1453–1669*, transl. I. Moles and P. Moles. New Brunswick, NJ: Rutgers University Press.

van Andel, Tjeerd H., and Curtis Runnels. 1987. *Beyond the Acropolis: A Rural Greek Past*. Palo Alto, CA: Stanford University Press.

Vardouniotis, Dimitrios K. 1913. *I Katastrofi tou Dramali*. Tripolis: Efimeridos Moreas.

Vayiakakos, Dikaios. 1974. "Glossikai-laografikai-toponimikai erevnai peri Korinthias." *Peloponnisiaka Parartima Praktika* 2: 47–91.

Vergopoulos, Kostas. 1975. *To agrotiko zitima stin Ellada*. Athens: Exantas.

Vermeulen, Cornelius J. J. 1976. "Development and Migration in the Serres Basin." In *Regional Variation in Modern Greece and Cyprus*, Annals of the New York Academy of Sciences, ed. Muriel Dimen and Ernestine Friedl, pp. 59–70. New York: New York Academy of Sciences.

Wagstaff, Malcolm. 1982. *The Development of Rural Settlements*. Aldershot, UK: Avebury Publishing Company.

Wolf, Eric. 1986. "The Vicissitudes of the Closed Corporate Peasant Community." *American Ethnologist* 13: 325–29.

Wright, James, John F. Cherry, Jack L. Davis, Eleni Mantzourani, and Susan Buck Sutton. 1990. "The Nemea Valley Archaeological Project: A Preliminary Report." *Hesperia* 59: 579–645.

Yanagisako, S. J. 1979. "Family and Household: The Analysis of Domestic Groups." *Annual Review of Anthropology* 8: 161–205.

Zakynthos, D. A. 1976. *The Making of Modern Greece: From Byzantium to Independence*, transl. K. R. Johnstone. Totowa, NJ: Rowman and Littlefield.

Zegkinis, Ioannis E. 1968. *To Argos dia mesou ton aionon*. Athens: Pirgos.

–4–

The Home "Place": Center and Periphery in Irish House and Family Systems
Donna Birdwell-Pheasant

Directions within the home are set by motion around the fire. You are going 'down' when the hearth's open mouth is behind you, and 'up' when it is toward you . . . Beyond the home you go 'down' to the north and east and 'up' to the south and west. Like a swirling swastika, space spins, its four directions extend, then curve, spiraling down or up, merging to embrace half the world, returning, turning through the house to center precisely on the hearth.

— Henry Glassie, *Passing the Time in Ballymenone* (1982: 325)

Although land often emerges as the leitmotif in accounts of the last couple of centuries of Irish history, land was not the ruling symbol in Irish reality. Land was conceptually embedded in a vital nexus of rural life that was governed by two deeply consonant ideas – the idea of family and the idea of place. In this chapter, I describe the patterning of house systems and family systems[1] in rural Ireland from early times to the present. Both systems manifest a common deep structure, found also in Glassie's description above of spatial orientations around the house and hearth.

The dynamic linkage of center and periphery, so powerfully evoked by Glassie's image, emerges in both the systems discussed here. In the family, the center is constituted by the so-called "stem," from which the non-heirs spiral out in patterned waves. In houses, the complementary pattern is wrought by distinctions between substantial and temporary houses, and by the distribution of these different types of house upon the land.[2]

Family and Place in Ancient Ireland

I heard the term "home place" often in my field research in the vicinity of Ballyduff in the old Barony of Clanmaurice in northwest Count Kerry. As I began to examine the use of the term, I found that not everyone who had a home had a home "place," and that living at the home place was not the same as being *in* the home place.

A concept of place is rooted deeply in Irish history, tied to a time when the *rath* and its enclosed *lios* defined clearly upon the landscape the place of a particular family or cognatic kindred. The Irish countryside is still dotted with the remains of raths – the old earthen or low stone circles that were palisaded to enclose and protect the *lios* with its house and farm buildings as far back as the Bronze Age. The *dun* was the more substantial circular fortification of a chief or king. Significantly, one's home place was enclosed, while the lands surrounding it were left open, marked only by some natural feature or standing stone (*gallán*).

Land, for the Irish, was defined in terms of place. Saris writes that, even in the late twentieth century, the Irish landscape "exists as named places with remembered histories" (1996: 542).[3] Land was not a commodity, possession of large quantities of which made one a wealthy man. Wealth, in ancient times, was measured by productivity, and land was evaluated in terms of the numbers of cows or peasants it could support. Well into the twentieth century, a farm was quite likely to be described not as, for example, ten acres, but rather as "the grass of six cows." As a final bit of evidence for the superordinacy of the concept of place over the idea of land, let me submit the Irish word for land itself: the word is "*farran*," but it used to be written "*fearann*," which translates literally as "man there."

In ancient Ireland, the central social and political institutions, the *tuatha* (tribes or chiefdoms) and component *finte* (kindreds), were associated with core territories, but were not themselves exclusively territorial units. Within the *tuath*, all classes, with the exception of slaves, together "constituted the [tribe] in its territorial or general sense, and all bore in common the name of the *Flaith*" or lord (CPALII, *Ancient Laws*, Vol. IV, 1879: cxxix).[4] Thus, the *tuath*, although it was not a unilineal kinship group (i.e. an anthropological "clan"), was far more than a mere aggregate of neighboring families. It should not go unremarked that the English terms chiefdom, kingdom, or lordship – all of which may be found as glosses for *tuath* – all take their primary meaning from the leader (chief, king, or lord). The term *tuath*, to the contrary, meant "people (as opposed to ruler)" (Binchy 1979: 67) or "the laity" (Kelly 1988: 323).

In the *Crith Gablach*, a law tract of the early eighth century, the houses appropriate to men of varying ranks are specified. The house of the *ócaire*, a low-ranking young farmer with limited land and assets (Patterson 1994a: 216–17), is described as 19 feet in length, accompanied by a "back-house" of 13 feet (Binchy 1979: xiv). This back-house or outhouse is described as "big enough for him to divide his food in it and put aside the *bés*, the customary render due to his lord" (Patterson 1994a: 122).

The law texts point out that the house of the *ócaire* was larger than the *tig inchis* of 17 feet, which is "a house of small dimensions, built for an old man who gives up his land to his friends or pupils on the condition that they shall maintain him." An *aithech* (head of household) or *threba* ("tribe tenant in his paternal home") was entitled to a house of 20 feet, with a back-house of 14 feet. The *bóaire febsa* ("from cows his rank and honour price are derived") had rights to a house of 27 feet with a back-house of 15 feet, as well as a kiln, a barn, a sheep-pen, a calf-house, a pig-sty, and a share in a mill. The *aire coisring* (the "family-chief" who speaks for his people) could have a house of 30 feet and a back-house of 19 feet. The *rí* (king) of highest grade was entitled to a house of 37 feet encircled by a *dun* of "seven score feet," with a gate 12 feet wide (CPALII, *Ancient Laws*, Vol. II, Appendix II: 466–92, 508; spellings follow Binchy 1979: 39–109).[5]

The house of the *aire coisring* would compare favorably in size with the standard nineteenth-century Irish farmhouse described by Estyn Evans:

> Today nearly all Irish farm-houses are a simple rectangle in ground plan, anything from ten to twenty feet in width and of varying length according to the number of rooms they comprise, each room being the full width of the house. The normal developed house has three rooms, consisting of a central kitchen with a bedroom at the bottom end and another – the best room, called simply 'the room' – behind the chimney, which helps to warm it (Evans 1988: 44).

The latter room is the one described as the "west room" in Conrad Arensberg's account of County Clare farm families (1988). Its significance is discussed by Lawrence Taylor in this volume (Chapter 9).

The word "*bothach*," used in ancient law tracts to refer to a lowly class of cottiers, derived from the term *both*, meaning "hut" (Binchy 1979: 78). Patterson refers to these *bothachs* as "hutted" dependents of the higher-ranking farmers (1994a: 152). Used as an adjective, *bothach* came to mean "full of booths, tents, huts." The term *bothán* is still used in modern Ireland to refer to a shabby hut or small cabin.

Most of these dwellings seem to have been constructed of wattle and daub, with some variation possibly keyed to local availability of materials. Given the careful descriptions of food entitlements and, elsewhere, of types and colors of clothing appropriate to given ranks, the fact that no differences in entitlements are given regarding building materials can be taken as an indication that size and not composition was of most importance in distinguishing houses appropriate to the various ranks of society in this period of Irish history.

Although members of a given *tuath* or *fine* might be found living in localities at some distance from their places of origin,[6] the chief of the *tuath* or head of the *fine* did live within the tribal or kindred territory, and actively symbolized the tie between people and place. Séan O'Tuama has suggested that this spiritual tie can later be seen in the relations of any Irish family with its land. He writes of the "bonding of each free family group with its own particular inherited land" as a parallel to the ancient nuptial ties between chieftain and tribal place that were enacted in some parts of rural Ireland down to the seventeenth century (O'Tuama 1985: 23; Binchy 1970: 11–12). Even in the 1980s, the metaphor of farm ownership in north Kerry kept faith with this essential symbol. The farmer himself was said to be *in* the farm, while others who resided there were not so described.

The home places of chiefs as well as other mature farmers of noble grade were marked by substantial dwellings, farm buildings, and encircling walls. The house itself played an important symbolic role in this entire social and political complex. For example, in the complicated redistribution of *fintiu* (land inherited through *fine* membership) following the extinction of a *derbfine* (segment of a *fine*), an important final step was the setting up of house posts upon newly claimed land (Kelly 1988: 104). Hereditary serfs, followers who had "adhered to the family of a Flaith (lord) for three successive generations" were figuratively referred to as "*senchléithe*," a term translated as "old house posts" (CPALLI, *Ancient Laws*, Vol. II, Appendix II: 494; Binchy 1979: 105; Kelly 1988: 35ff.). Further, the chief himself could be known as "*an cléithe coitcheann*," which translates as "ridgepole in common" (Dinneen 1979: 204). Also of some symbolic significance were the ubiquitous gate-posts marking the entrance to a home place right into the twentieth century in Ireland. Evans notes that these gate-piers were sometimes "referred to as the man and wife of the house" (1988: 103).

The substantial sort of house associated with a home place – a *lios* or *dun* – was not the only kind of residential place upon the Irish landscape. There were also more temporary or ephemeral houses that tended to appear in clusters (Kelly 1988: 110). These cluster settlements, which came to be called *clachán* in the literature on Ireland, have been the subject of some debate. Burtchaell, for example, argues that *clacháns* were "one of the most recent facets of Irish settlement history" rather than sites of great antiquity (1988: 120–1).[7] Buchanan, in contrast, argues that, since the Bronze Age, Irish settlement pattern has been characterized by a combination of dispersed walled farmsteads enclosed by *raths* on the one hand and, on the other hand, clusters of less substantial structures housing a lower class (1970). The matter has perhaps been resolved by Patterson, who sees "no dichotomy between dispersed farmsteads and *clacháns*"; the two types of settlement "must be seen as stages in the waxing and waning of farming communities" (1994a: 102; see also McCourt 1971).

After the arrival of the Anglo-Normans in the twelfth century, stone came to characterize the "more substantial houses" while the majority of habitations still "were built on a timber frame . . . and walls were of clay and wattle or turf, on stone footings" (Buchanan 1970: 150). Building materials, of course, varied regionally with availability, and in areas such as the Burren of County Clare or the Dingle Peninsula of County Kerry the ready availability of ample quantities of stone, although a curse on agriculture, meant that even the poorest folk could build their houses of substantial materials. Nonetheless, the most substantial houses of all – and those definitive of the most important places – became the tall and rectilinear stone castles of the Normans.

During Norman times, the settlement occupied by the lower class on manorial lands was termed the *baile*. These "ballys" were probably house clusters "in the same settlement tradition as the bond settlements of the first millennium A.D." (Buchanan 1970: 150). Buchanan believes that "[i]n most parts of the country this settlement pattern survived throughout the medieval period" (1970: 150). Continuity of settlement form does not, of course, imply that individual cluster settlements were of any great antiquity. Smyth affirms the discrepancy in house types associated with these different types of settlement, noting that "[d]ispersed farm settlement was generally associated with the more substantial thatched and stone houses of the Down and Civil Surveys [1653–4] than with the 'straw cabbins'" (1992: 268).[8]

Through the eighteenth century the farm cluster settlement or *clachán* was associated with an infield–outfield farming system, which often entailed shifting, incomplete subdivision of land (rundale or *ronndáil*) and farming partnerships (*comaithches*). The occurrence of commons was also frequently associated with this traditional system, and a hierarchy of house types was a consistent feature.

Besides the substantial houses of the dispersed farmsteads and the smaller, more ephemeral houses of the cluster settlements, there was an even more temporary and peripheral type of house. This was the "booley" (*buaile*) house, which had been built from ancient times in the outfield areas to shelter the transhumant herdsmen (or, often, herdswomen – see Patterson 1994a: 136) during the shift to summer pastures. Booley houses known from archaeology (Gibson 1995) are invariably of stone, but this was not the typical case. Evans reports that such houses observed in the nineteenth century were "built of sods upon a foundation of earth and stones and were thatched with heath" (1988: 35). The tale of the life of St Senan demonstrates that such houses took only a day or two to construct (Patterson 1994a: 78). The English called such structures "hovels," characterized as "the squalid burrow of a representative of a regressive race" (Saris 1996: 545).

This crudest and most transient type of house was also important to the house system, not simply as a shelter for the herdsman, but also as a mark of the extent of a kindred's or lord's right of place. Any kind of house upon the land could be of critical importance to indicate that the land was being actively occupied.[9]

Continuity: Evidence from Ballyduff

The Ballyduff area, in the sixteenth and seventeenth centuries, likely was characterized by infield–outfield farming arrangements. Maps executed in 1697 for the Lord Barron of Kerry show such a settlement pattern (Map 4.1) for townlands bordering the Ballyduff area.[10] There were also large tracts of commons through this time period, occupying roughly all the modern townlands adjacent to the village of Ballyduff and surrounding the estates at Rattoo and Ballyhorgan. Petty's Survey map from 1683 shows commons covering a substantial acreage.

Ballyduff experienced enclosure and the break-up of cluster settlements progressively through the eighteenth and nineteenth centuries. Documents from the mid-eighteenth century and early nineteenth century indicate that field enclosures in the central townlands were not universally in use and were a source of controversy in some areas where they had been erected.[11] Map 4.1 shows the use of markers rather than fence or hedge enclosures to mark field and townland boundaries. The commons associated with the Burgesslands of Rattoo were officially divided in 1748 between the townlands of Ballyhorgan, Rattoo, Rahealy, and Benmore (see Map 4.2). An intense controversy over the identity and boundaries of Derryrabeg in 1797–1804 is well documented, and indicates clearly that ascertaining the extent of holdings often required the assistance of "old persons who can shew and prove the Mears or Boundaries."[12]

Partnership farming was still in evidence in several parts of the Ballyduff area as late as 1857. In the townland of Knocknacree, where there is reputed to have been a *sráid* or street (Cantillon 1989) (a feature often identified with *clachán* settlements), there was a farming partnership between families of Connors, Keanes, and Costellos. There was also partnership farming in the townlands of Ardoughter, Knoppoge, and Kilmore. The last, with its several partnerships, is the site of a late-surviving *clachán* known as Coole or *Comhall*.

The use of the herdshouse or booley house as a marker of peripheral lands can also be documented within the Ballyduff area. A manuscript documenting the 1797–1804 land dispute over the townland of Derryrabeg defends claims of possession by detailing how the owner had "made a ditch as a mearing and built an Herdmans Hut."[13] In Griffiths Valuation of 1857, it was still apparent that lands held by major landlords or first-level tenants but not let to resident tenants, were at least occupied by a herdshouse. A substantial house marked the home place, but even an insubstantial house provided some claim upon the land by human presence and human activity.

In short, the diversity of settlement and house types described by Buchanan and others as an ancient Irish characteristic found expression within the Ballyduff study area. We can infer the existence of the infield–outfield system and document the existence of commons, partnership farming, *clacháns* and herdshouses. The argument is not made here that these features had continued unchanged from great antiquity; rather, the existence of this set of forms is taken as evidence of the continuation of certain social and economic processes that generate the forms in question.

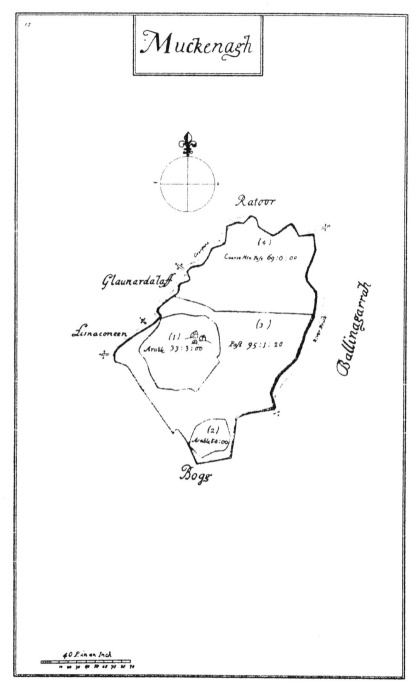

Map 4.1 Map of the townland of Muckenagh (McKenna), executed in 1697 for the Lord Barron of Kerry, from the documents collection of University College Cork. (Digitally enhanced by Brandon Duhon.)

Map 4.2 Map of study area, courtesy of Michael Murphy Department of Geography, University, College Cork.

A Model of Family System and House System

The family system that emerged from the ancient *tuatha* and *finte* is essentially congruent with the system described above for the stratification of house types. Each farming family had its center, its stem, which occupied and was conceptualized as being *in* the home place. Beyond this, however, a description of the articulation of the family system with the house system must depart from the traditional depiction of the Irish stem family, for it must account for those who depart from this center as well as those who remain within it.[14]

In my research in western Ireland since 1986, I have established that the family system of the Irish, ancient and modern, is considerably more complex than is suggested in the stem-family model derived from the work of Arensberg (1988) and Arensberg and Kimball (1940). Specifically, I have shown that neither unitary inheritance nor the dispersal of children not favored as primary heirs were goals of overweening importance to the people themselves (Birdwell-Pheasant 1992).

Figure 4.1 Substantial farmhouse. Pierse home place in Derrico (Photo credit Donna Birdwell-Pheasant).

Instead, the home place and *most of the land* went to one heir, while other land, houses, and resources were generally passed to the heir's siblings (see also Fitzpatrick 1983: 366–7; Guinnane 1991). In other words, the integrity of the home place was maintained, even while other children were allowed to settle upon the family land or to remain connected to it while living elsewhere. Although I have found significant differences in the family dynamics of farmers as compared to laborers and non-agricultural people, there is clear evidence for shared values with respect to these very notions of family and of place (Birdwell-Pheasant 1993).

The primary heir *in* the home place generally occupied a house of substantial construction and relatively commodious dimensions (see Figure 4.1). These *long-cycle houses* reflected substantial ties to place – relatively secure tenure, control over livelihood, and a high probability of supplying the next generation of heirs to the place.[15]

In Ireland, there was, in practice, a much broader access of kin to the home base than is found in some other European settings. Such a home place was not a site for nuclear retreat into privacy (Hareven 1991: 256), nor a mechanism for the practice of kin-exclusion through strict unitary inheritance (Birdwell-Pheasant 1998). Rather, it was a place where all those of the place – its descendants – could come together. It was a site for the enactment of the virtues of hospitality. All the children of the farm generally had rights to stay there forever, if they remained unmarried or childless and faithful to the integrity of the place under the designated heir. Only occasionally were their rights bought out by the primary heir. The grandchildren of the farm also had rights, mediated by the kind of relationship obtaining between the primary farm heirs and their own linking relatives. Where the farmer was unmarried or childless, such a grandchild of the farm might even inherit (Birdwell-Pheasant 1992: 216–18). The hospitality with which Yankee cousins and great-nephews are still received at the old home place is indicative of the continuing ties that can, within limits, be activated.[16]

Offspring other than the designated heir and unmarried siblings generally lived in houses of smaller dimensions and/or lesser quality. We might call them *short-cycle houses*, because their ties to place were more ephemeral and their construction more impermanent. This type of house is typified by the *bothán scóir*, an example of which is included in the exhibits at Bunratty Folk Park (Danaher 1985: 19). We have already noted that the term *bothán* referred to a simple hut inhabited by simple people. The adjective *scóir* derives from the verb *scóirim*, which means "I break up camp or house" (Dinneen 1927). Thus, the name given for this dwelling translates to mean something like "retirement cottage" or, more anthropologically, "fission house."

Where one's primary right of place derived from relations to people, inhabiting a more ephemeral house was not a sign of social or economic insecurity. These houses were occupied by people who were firmly tied to the family's center, but who would not themselves become centers. These peripheral families might supply the future heir to the place in times of demographic crisis; but this was not a usual expectation.

Finally, the offspring of these peripheral families would be even more distantly removed from the conceptual family center. Unlike the Portuguese case described by Brettell (this volume, Chapter 2), there was no *partilha*, in which formal division of property finally excluded peripheralized family members from further claims upon the patrimony. In Ireland, the status of various family members and their descendants was left more contingent, to be settled by time, need, and circumstance. The houses of these peripheralized branches were increasingly insubstantial and their ties to place more attenuated. The likelihood that the next heir to the place would come from their ranks was very remote. Their position was the social analog of the spatially peripheral booley house, which marked the outer extent of family influence. This is more than analogy, for in fact these peripheral families often occupied dwellings that were very like the temporary shelters described by Evans. This was especially the case as those who were the descendants of successive generations of non-heirs accumulated upon the landscape in the years leading up to the Great Famine of the mid-nineteenth century.

Changes in Relations of Family and Place

The ascendancy of English law initialized important changes in Irish relations to land and place. The role of land under the English system of values was radically different from that which had existed under the traditional Irish system. Land, to the Irish, was most important as a source of status and of livelihoods, and was measured in terms of the numbers of cows and peasants (*ceiles*) it supported. To the English, on the other hand, land was a commodity to be exploited for the profit of the landlord or bought and sold to the advantage of the yeoman farmer (Macfarlane 1987). The prevalence of toponymics in inventories of English family names suggests that places more often gave their names to people, rather than (as in Ireland) the other way around.

As English law gradually overwhelmed the native law of the Irish *brehons*, Irish farmers found that their tenure on the land was no longer secured by the force of shared custom and mutually respected contract under an essentially familial structure. This loss of security in contracts affirming one's place was, I believe, part of the cause of the upsurge of population that occurred between 1700 and 1847. The balance in the nexus of family and place shifted toward the family as the only reliable source of security. Furthermore, as agricultural markets changed, the labor needs of essentially English landlords also changed, and they responded readily by either creating attractive conditions for multiplication of small tenancies or else by wholesale clearances and evictions. The moving balance between population and resources, which had focused on livelihoods and which had been maintained so well under the traditional system, was lost.

Buchanan tells us that, in the early eighteenth century, "subdivision was countenanced by most landowners, many of whom left the conduct of their affairs to middlemen whose chief concern was to extract the maximum rent from a numerous tenantry" (1970: 153). In the first instance, this permitted the continuation of the shifting, impermanent form of subdivision characteristic of rundale. In time, however, landlords objected to the open-ended allocation of property under rundale, and were at times quite inclined to grant new smallholdings to several offspring of established farmers. This was especially the case in regions where willing workers could bring marginal land under productive cultivation, as in the townland of Ardoughter near Ballyduff.

Laws governing inheritance also encouraged the partition of farms. In 1704, a law was passed requiring Catholic farmers, at death, to divide their land among all their sons. If the eldest son should become Protestant, however, he would be permitted to inherit the whole estate intact (Doherty and Hickey 1989: 67; Birdwell-Pheasant 1998).

Landlords also came to favor a dispersed settlement pattern over the *clachán* clusters in which "the women and the men spent too much time talking and quarreling" (Smith 1962: 19–20). The compliance of the rural populace with landlord pressures to disperse may be attributed in some degree to a desire for upward mobility through emulation of the residential style of the better-off. Evans notes that, although the *clachán* had once been "the center of communal life and tradition," it came to be despised as "a symbol of squabbling poverty, and it is the wish of nearly everyone to have a house where he cannot be overlooked" (1988: 11–12). The families of partnership farmers certainly would have found a rich community life within the residential clusters; however, upward mobility entailed movement outside such a cluster and emplacement in a more substantial farm of one's own.

Tenants granted their own holdings in these efforts to disperse population were "almost invariably without capital, [and] land was let bare, frequently even a dwelling had to be erected" (Smith 1962: 17). This "extreme fragmentation of holdings led to destitution" through the early years of the nineteenth century, and to a "growing disparity of scale between the dwellings of rich and poor" (Buchanan 1970: 152–4).

The transformation of the rural landscape also entailed the enclosure of field-plots, which occurred at different times in different areas, but generally between 1750 and 1850 (Evans 1988: 20). As discussed above, Ballyduff fits this general pattern. This enclosure signaled a new type of relationship between people and place. The earthwork or stone wall that had once encircled the *lios* or *dun* as place had ceased to be constructed. Instead, stone walls or hedges now marked and thus "fixed" the boundaries of individual fields. For the Ballyduff area, comparisons of nineteenth-century maps with twentieth-century aerial photographs readily reveal the continuity of field divisions. It remained customary, as noted previously, to erect two great stones or, later, concrete pillars, to mark the entrance into the place (Evans 1988: 22). The farmhouse and assorted farm buildings continued to mark the center of each place.[17]

The breakdown of this complexly integrated pattern of family and place was linked to jural and economic change and constituted a profound disruption of the family-and-place nexus that had regulated the distribution of people upon the land for many centuries. As regulatory mechanisms failed, and as the people's sense of security of place declined, population rose. From fewer than 300 people in 1660, the population of the Ballyduff area had grown to nearly 4,000 by 1841.[18] Initially, much of the population increase was due to immigration, specifically from the strongly Irish Barony of Iraghticonnor immediately to the north, and, from a bit further to the north across the Shannon River, from County Clare.

Natural increase also played a role in the rising population. From 1783 to 1786, the Ballyduff area averaged 23.5 births per year. The average rose to 44 for the four-year period 1807–10, but had fallen again to 24.8 for 1827–30.[19] Beginning in 1833, however, there was a sharp upturn. Births soared to an all-time high of 132 in 1833, and exceeded 110 in every year but one through 1846, when the impact of the Great Famine reversed the pattern.

Through this prodigious population growth, there was an unprecedented proliferation of the kind of people who would be most likely to inhabit short-cycle, ephemeral houses. In theory, in each generation, the numbers of those inhabiting short-cycle houses could be expected to increase at an increasing rate. This was because the offspring of inhabitants of short-cycle houses could expect nothing better for themselves – or for their own children. Whereas only a few of the offspring of the inhabitants of substantial houses would end up inhabiting short-cycle houses, all the offspring of inhabitants of ephemeral houses were likely to end up inhabiting the same type of structures, or even poorer ones. These were also the people – according to Kevin O'Neill (and my data tend to support his conclusions) – who were likely to marry younger and have more children (O'Neill 1984).

The quality of houses was further depressed by the fact that where "the tenants built and repaired their own houses with, normally, no assistance from the landlord," it is observed that "there was little inducement to build houses to last longer than the lease of say 21 years" (Evans 1988: 43). By 1841, about 40 percent of all rural housing in Ireland consisted of one-room mud (or turf) dwellings (Buchanan 1970: 156); in County Kerry, the proportion was two-thirds (Evans 1988: 46). The houses that clustered along the Old Street at Knocknacree, precursor to the village of Ballyduff, were made entirely of earth (Cantillon 1989).

Within the Ballyduff study area, both size of holdings and security of tenure depended at least in part on who one's landlord was. On Thomas Anthony Stoughton's 15 tenanted townlands (excluding his demesne at Ballyhorgan) primary tenants accounted for more than 95 percent of his total tenantry of 110. Furthermore, 68 percent of his tenants held leases, while only 32 percent were tenants at will. By contrast, on Wilson Gunn's 11 townlands (only 4 in my study area proper), only 48 percent of his 146 tenants were primary tenants, and only 34 percent had leases; the other 66 percent were tenants at will.

To make matters worse, the farms occupied by Wilson Gunn's tenants were also very small. In his townlands within my study area, holdings ranged from a half acre to 7 acres in size. In Stoughton's townlands, only in Lacka East were any farms smaller than 2 acres. In Leagh the smallest was 4 acres (largest 80 acres) and in Knoppoge South the smallest was 5 acres (largest 30 acres). In other Stoughton townlands, farms were at least 10 acres, more often 20 or more.

Houses and Places through the Famine

In the Ballyduff area, in the decades before the famine, the number of houses in each townland was at least four times (and up to twelve times) the number of "places."[20] In other words, for every house marking a place, there were 4 to 12 houses not so situated. This suggests that the great majority of houses in the area were of the shorter-cycle, peripheral type.

Given this fact, it is not surprising that the greatest loss of housing in the famine was of the short-cycle type. Besides their predominance in terms of sheer numbers,

Table 4.1 Changes in Numbers of Places and Numbers of Houses as a Consequence of the Great Famine, in Selected Townlands

	No. of Places		No. of Houses			
	1830	*1857*	*1841*	*1851*	*1857*	*1891*
Stoughton lands:						
Knoppoge*	16	17	69	34	36	31
Ardcullen*	4	7	18	11	10	11
Leagh*	3	4	14	10	9	7
Gunn lands:						
Rahealy	3	3	38	12	9	12
Knocknacree 6	2	24	9	9	10	
Other lands:						
Cloghane	7	6	48	30	23	37
Kilmore	10	13	121	54	35	45
Ardoughter	15	16	89	56	56	67

* These designations include more than one townland. Ardcullen includes Ardcullen Marsh; Leagh includes Leagh Marsh; Knoppoge includes various designations of Knoppoge (e.g. Casey's Knoppoge in 1830 and Knoppoge North and South in 1857).

Sources: 1830 – Tithe Applotment Surveys of 1827 and 1834; 1857 – Griffiths Valuation; 1841, 1851, 1891 – official census data.

these peripheral houses also tended to be occupied by more vulnerable residents. Peripheral families and individuals were freer to migrate. Further, tenants with minimal resources were often the first to consume their cash crops and fall behind on the rent. Hence, they were also generally the first to be evicted (Kennedy 1973: 30). Eviction of the poorest tenants was actually encouraged by the amendment of the Irish Poor Relief Act in 1843 to "make the landlords of tenements and small holdings at and under a value of four pounds liable" for payment of the tenant's assessed Poor Law rate. As Helen Burke described the situation: "If a landlord evicted his tenants with a land valuation of four pounds or less and knocked down the house, he not only regained the use of the land himself but he also avoided paying the rate levied on him for the tenant's holding" (Burke 1987: 81). Therefore, it was the short-cycle houses of the poorest tenants that were most likely to be "knocked" by landlords.

The data for Ballyduff fit this general scenario. Although there was a decrease of 48.6 percent in numbers of people and a decline of 48.1 percent in total numbers of houses between 1841 and 1851 as a result of the famine, the numbers of places held remarkably constant, as did the families associated with these places (see Table 4.1). For example, in the townlands of Knoppoge,[21] the numbers of houses declined from 69 in 1841 to only 34 in 1851, a loss of more than half. The numbers of places, however, actually increased from 16 in about 1830[22] to 17 in 1857. And of the 16 families in places in 1830, 10 were still there in 1857. Two more families present in 1830 had acquired places in 1857. All four of the names coming in were already known elsewhere in the district; most of the names lost from the Knoppoges as occupiers of places continued strong in other townlands, which were likely their places of origin. The three townlands suffering the highest percentage decline in population between 1841 and 1851 were Knockananore, Rahealy, and Rattoo – townlands belonging to Wilson Gunn and, as noted above, characterized by smaller holdings and less secure tenure.

In the famine, then, there was an absolute loss of great numbers of insubstantial houses and the people who had inhabited them. Lack of housing may have encouraged further emigration in the years immediately after the famine. Places, however, not only maintained their integrity, but in some cases actually were enlarged (or new ones were founded) through the incorporation of abandoned smallholdings.[23] *As the periphery crumbled, the center held strong.*

House and Place since the Famine

After the famine, the long-standing, integrated pattern of centrally located, long-cycle houses accompanied by peripheral, short-cycle houses was transformed by several developments. These included housing programs administered by landlords and government as well as changes in the composition of the population and their cultural orientations. Despite such changes, the conceptual importance of the home place was still evident.

The house and other buildings defining a landlord's place often served as a focus of attacks during the long disputes fought in the idiom of land, an idiom understood by the English landlords so much better than the traditional Irish idiom of family and place. In Ballyduff, dissidents had burned the out-offices of Rattoo West, the place of the Gunn family, in 1829 (O'Connor and Quinlan 1989). During the troubles of 1919–20, attacks were directed against the great houses themselves, with the south wing of Rattoo House being destroyed by bombs, and the Stoughtons' estate house being "knocked" altogether.

Programs for the construction of more substantial housing for laborers guaranteed that the pre-famine pattern would not reassert itself. Laws passed in 1856, 1860, 1870, and 1881 were ineffectual in much of Ireland, but resulted in the construction of more than 7,000 cottages in Munster (Bourke 1991: 487). In 1883 the Boards of Guardians (regional administrators of the Poor Laws) began building houses for the poor, and later the County Councils (1898) built cottages for laborers and other rural folk (Buchanan 1970: 156). These new cottages (see Figure 4.2), with their block walls and slate roofs, were a far cry from the tenant-

Figure 4.2 Landlord-built house, early 1900s (Photo credit Donna Birdwell-Pheasant).

built *bothāns* of the pre-famine era. Indeed, it was believed that the "bright, cheery appearance" of the new cottages would "uplift children both morally and socially" (Bourke 1991: 487). Landlords in some parts of Ireland provided tenants with "precisely measured doors and windows" as well as sturdy iron gates as mechanisms of "improving and enlightening" the rural populace. The new rural cottage was meant not merely as shelter, but to "*organize the life* of those who depend on them [the landlords] for shelter and sustenance" (Saris 1996: 545).

We can gain an overview of the houses of Ballyduff for the early twentieth century by examining census records of 1901 and 1911. In the 1901 census, the criteria for describing the quality of houses were four: type of wall construction, type of roof construction, number of rooms, and number of windows on the front of the house. The first two criteria basically distinguished between walls or roofs built of what were considered to be durable materials (stone, brick or concrete for walls; slate, iron, or tiles for roofs) and what were considered perishable materials (wood or mud for walls; thatch for roofs). Apparently, something like the distinction made in this chapter between long-cycle and short-cycle houses was deemed relevant by Irish census-takers. The third criterion, number of rooms, is also of some traditional importance, while the fourth – number of windows on the front of the house – was more likely to be a measure of the extent to which a house was modeled on more modern standards of housing.[24]

Table 4.2 Quality of Housing in the Ballyduff Area in 1901 and 1911

Quality of Houses Occupied in 1901, by Occupational Category

Occupational Category	Quality of House			
	Class 1	Class 2	Class 3	Class 4
Strong farmers	4	40	10	0
Modest farmers	0	50	62	2
Non-agricultural	3	24	12	0
Laborers	0	17	49	11

Quality of Houses Occupied in 1911, by Occupational Category

Occupational Category	Quality of House			
	Class 1	Class 2	Class 3	Class 4
Strong farmers	4	48	4	0
Modest farmers	0	62	49	0
Non-agricultural	7	30	13	1
Laborers	0	28	51	2

A simple formula enabled the census-takers to place any house within a ranked fourfold classification. A Class 4 house was the poorest type, and could be a wooden or mud house with thatched roof and two rooms but no windows in front, or else one room with one window. To qualify as Class 1, a house had to be substantially built and have many rooms and many windows. In the Ballyduff area, the great houses of the two landlords easily qualified as Class 1 structures. Most people lived in Class 3 and Class 2 houses (see Table 4.2).

In 1901, of fifteen households occupying Class 4 houses, twelve were laborers' households, and three were elderly people in life-cycle poverty. Available evidence suggests that two of these were laborers' widows. In general, strong farmers were more likely to be in Class 2 houses and laborers were more likely to be in Class 3 houses. By 1901, there was also a strong association between substantial houses (Class 2) and non-agricultural occupations. Although the family pattern of non-agricultural people was distinctive – they showed the highest geographical mobility and greatest frequency of postmarital neolocal residence (Birdwell-Pheasant 1993) – they were the people who were most firmly linked into the cash economy. The quality of their dwellings reflected not a central position within a family structure – in fact, they tended to be more peripheral – but rather a greater control over expendable wealth.

Farmers, too, could avail themselves of grants and improve the quality of their houses. Some of the provisions affecting farmers explicitly discouraged bachelors as well as older farmers who resisted turning the farm over to the next generation.

This, too, tended to undermine the old associations, wherein the farmer who was *in* the farm remained central, even where he remained unmarried.

The Modern Landscape of Ballyduff

The modern landscape of Ballyduff is significantly different from the landscapes of the past. However, social diversity still finds expression in the more modern built forms.[25] A dispersed settlement pattern for farmers still prevails, although in this era of automobiles and tractors most have moved to the road rather than situating the farmhouse and buildings more centrally on their holding. In the townland of Kilmore, the old *clachán* at Comhal still exists.

Finally, in recent decades, the rural Irish have experienced a phenomenon dubbed "bungalisation" by one critical Irish journalist (Moore 1986). The term refers to a modern landscape "teeming with new bungalows that bear the stamp of poor planning and bad taste," although intended to reflect the residents' commitment to modern lifestyles (Moore 1986: 1). Their siting and often flamboyant architecture are perhaps symbolic of a new type and quality of linkage to place. These bungalows are clearly *on* the land, but are not *in* the landscape, not *of* the land in the way the old homes were.

Further complicating the look of the modern Irish landscape, the role traditionally fulfilled by the ephemeral tenant-built cabins has now passed to the caravans, mobile homes, and pre-fab cottages of a cash-based economy. On one farm, for example, the future heir to the farm occupies a small caravan with his wife and baby. On another, the farmer's bachelor brother occupies a tiny pre-fab cottage by the side of the road. Elsewhere, a returned migrant has situated his own mobile home on a corner of the family property. This phenomenon suggests that the loss of the old-style houses left something of a void in the rural Irish way of family life, which now is being filled by more modern elements. There is, after all, a certain logic to a system of substantial houses marking one's family place and the series of more ephemeral structures providing someplace for all of those who need it. The logic breaks down, however, when (as in one case in Kilmore) the returned emigrant builds an ostentatious bungalow on a small bit of land.

The transition to professionally built block and brick bungalows has had another consequence, as well. It has left across the land a collection of ghost structures, old houses whose stones will never again be pilfered and re-used to construct the houses and barns and fences of another generation. Crumbling stone houses stand mute watch over the changing landscapes of a new generation.

Where the old houses are maintained, it is often as a gesture to the old folks, who are still drawn to them. When I went to visit the Pierses (the Derrico Pierses, who have been in their place for centuries), I found old Mrs. Pierse not in the new family bungalow, but musing over some task or other in the spacious, flagstone-floored kitchen of the old house, where a turf fire glowed on the hearth. She was embarrassed at having been caught, as it were, out of time, in this old anachronism of a house when there was a fine, new bungalow less than a hundred yards away. I asked if she minded if I took some photographs of the old house. Wouldn't I rather, she asked, take photos of the new house? At least, she insisted, be sure and take a picture of it, too, on my way out.

It is not just that the new houses are less photogenic. Their message is different.[26] They do not signal the same sort of union with place that the old houses accomplished. Rather than marking a home place, a center around which successive generations revolve and return, these new houses are but copies of generically modern suburban structures found anywhere in the world. In the global field in which they seek a place, they are eminently peripheral.

Acknowledgements

The field research described here was begun in 1986 when I was a Fulbright Research Fellow associated with the Economic and Social Research Institute in Dublin, Ireland. Further research was funded by National Science Foundation grant BNS-8606731 and grants from the National Endowment for Humanities and Lamar University. I am grateful for this support. I would also like to thank Denise Lawrence-Zúñiga and Caroline Brettell for their helpful comments on this chapter, as well as Brandon Duhon for graphic design.

Notes

1. "House systems" may be defined as sets of interrelated processes governing people's access to and use of houses, house space, house premises, and domestic equipment throughout the life cycle and across generations. House systems include both material and symbolic dimensions of houses, premises, and furnishings.

   "Family systems" are sets of processes for ensuring both biological and social reproduction within a society, including (but not limited to) processes of marriage, kin-group affiliation, residence, inheritance, and child rearing (see Birdwell-Pheasant 1998).
2. This focus on consonant patterning in interacting systems draws on suggestions made by Mary Douglas in her discussion of Suzanne Langer's philosophy of "analogic structures" (Douglas 1991: 290–3).
3. The Irish term for this historical topography is *dinnseanchas*, and it has deep roots in Irish myth and story.
4. The translators of the *Senchus Mor* chose to use the term "clan" as the English gloss for *tuath*. However, descriptions of the composition and dynamics of the *tuatha* clearly indicate that they are more like what anthropologists understand

to be a tribe or chiefdom and not at all like the unilineal descent groups that we refer to by the term "clan." I have therefore substituted the term "tribe" for "clan" where the reference is to the people themselves, and the term "chiefdom" where the political organization is concerned. The best explanation of the meanings of these terms and of historical changes in the institutions to which they refer is found in Patterson (1994a, 1994b).

5. Scholars generally accept that the highly detailed specifications given in the *Crith Gablach* are idealizations; realities were probably more diverse and irregular. Charles-Edwards reminds us that the law texts were "written by lawyers for the professional instruction of other lawyers" and that "the law which is taught is not necessarily the law which is practiced" (1993: 17). The texts did not purport to describe what was actually done nor even prescribe what must be done, but rather set forth what one had rights to under the law (Charles-Edwards 1993: 19).

6. Where both ties of place and ties of kinship were broken or attenuated, people might "travel" for a while, and then take up residence and identity in a new place, often in partnership.

7. "The archaic feature of the '*clachán*' is its ideal of cooperative land utilisation rather than its occupation of ancient sites" (Burtchaell 1988: 121).

8. This was not a reference to the English-style cabin, which Saris describes as "the neat, progressive habitation of the yeoman (generally Protestant) farmer" (1996: 545).

9. Ancient law tracts have a special, derogatory term (*Midlach*) to refer to an individual who was "a non-resident; a man who has not occupied land or property, who does not work, or for whom there is no work done" (CPALII, *Ancient Laws*, Second Tract: 522).

10. Unfortunately, there are no such maps for any of the townlands included in this study. They were executed for the townlands under the authority of Lord Kerry, who was headquartered at the village of Lixnaw, less than ten miles from Ballyduff.

11. Several such documents are in the collection of Trinity Library, Dublin, and include MUN/P/23/613 and MUN/P/23/1532(1).

12. Trinity University Library Manuscripts, item MUN/P/23/1532(1).

13. Trinity University Library Manuscripts, item MUN/P/23/1532(1).

14. The stem analogy is not inappropriate for the Irish family, as Bouquet has suggested it may be for some non-European societies (1996). Charles-Edwards notes: "The standard metaphor for the kindred was that of the tree and its branches. It is a common metaphor in many societies, but the Irish liked to elaborate on it. There was the trunk, *bun*, with its branches, *gabla*. The trunk consisted of the common ancestors, whereas the branches were the collateral lines of descent, *gabla* stemming from the *bun*" (1993: 28).

15. The ties to one's immediate place of residence were sometimes overwhelmed by continuing ties to one's place of origin. Local historian Bertie O'Connor of Ardoughter, Ballyduff, highlights this by noting how generation after generation, despite long tenancy in a distant townland, the deceased would be returned to the burial plot in "their own clan lands . . . for interment in what was their only true property" (personal communication, January 1993). Gibson proposes that, historically, such attachment to the burial places of one's ancestors was associated with one of the three elements identified as marking the existence of a chiefly capital, namely "the inauguration mound . . . usually a man-made feature such as an Early Bronze Age burial mound said to be the resting place of some famous ancestor in the chiefly pedigree" (1995: 117).

16. Ballyduff's local historian points out that there was often another good reason to receive these distant cousins with open arms, in that it may well have been that cousin's ancestors who kept those in the home place going "in times of difficulty" through remittances from America (B. O'Connor, personal communication, January 1993).

17. The farmhouse may not always have been situated at the geographical center of the family property. Patterson notes that archaeological data suggest that "there was a relationship between a household's social status and its geographical location, with higher-status units tending towards the edges of the townland, lower-status units adhering to these, and middle-rank units scattered in the interior" (1994a: 102). Gibson, however, argues for a more central location for the dwellings of places (1995: 117). It seems likely to me that the position would be an artifact of the history of the place and family; where division had occurred, the location of houses and outbuildings would be near a common edge, which would have been the center of the undivided place.

18. Estimates for 1660 are very rough, relying on Pender's survey of 1659 and resting on the assumption that "numbers of people" really refers to numbers of taxable adults rather than a total population count. Smyth recommends a conversion factor of about 2.5 in calculating probable populations from these seventeenth-century data (1992: 245).

19. The odd time periods are an artifact of record availability. Parish birth records available for this area begin in 1782, but are incomplete for that year. There are no records for 1787–1805, and records for 1806 are again incomplete. There is a continuous set of records from 1807 onward.

20. The place was operationally defined for this study as a house that included both land and "offices," according to census documents. The term "offices" referred to farm buildings such as barns and sheds.

21. For this analysis, I have grouped all townlands whose names include the designation "Knoppoge" under a single category, because the actual designa-

tions and the boundaries thereof have shifted from one census to another. The total area designated "Knoppoge" has remained more constant.

22. Tithe applotment data are available for some of the townlands for 1827, and for other townlands such data are available for 1834. I assume here that both sets of data have a high probability of being correct readings for the year 1830.

23. Glassie found this to be the case in Ballymenone, as well. "From a landscape crowded with hamlets and little farms," he writes, "to a landscape of separate homes and big farms, the depopulated land shifts to provide privacy and enable individual success" (1982: 604). However, depopulation was apparently a more persistent problem in Ballymenone than in Ballyduff.

24. This last criterion also acted, at times, as an unexpected disincentive to home improvements. In the townland of Clashmelcon, when a rather substantial old farmhouse was being "knocked" during my fieldwork in 1986 to make way for a newer structure, workers found that several windows across the front of the old house had been filled with blocks of turf and plastered over. That was because taxes in the late nineteenth and early twentieth centuries were assessed according to, among other things, the numbers of windows in the house. Fewer windows meant lower taxes.

25. This appears to contrast with the situation Glassie describes for Ballymenone, where the "old houses do not materialize the community's differences but express one-ness" (1982: 331). I believe the contrast between Ballyduff and Ballymenone may be explained by two factors: first, Ballymenone experienced a more profound, continuing population decline (1982: 603), which undoubtedly affected the poor and peripheral more significantly than it did the central families; and, second, Ballymenone had ready access to locally manufactured brick, which enabled even a modest structure to share attributes of the "long-cycle" house. Even stone is hard to come by in quantity in Ballyduff.

26. In Blanton's terminology (1994), their indexical message emphasizes contrast with the old-fashioned cottages of the poor, while their canonical message announces the householders' commitment to a modern lifestyle.

References

Arensberg, Conrad M. 1988 [1937]. *The Irish Countryman: An Anthropological Study*. Prospect Heights, IL: Waveland.

Arensberg, Conrad M., and Solon T. Kimball. 1940. *Family and Community in Ireland*. Cambridge, MA: Harvard University Press.

Binchy, D. A. 1970. *Celtic and Anglo-Saxon Kingship*, The O'Donnell Lectures for 1967–68. Oxford: Clarendon Press.

—— (ed.). 1979 [1941]. *Crith Gablach*, Mediaeval and Modern Irish Series. Dublin: Institute for Advanced Studies.

Birdwell-Pheasant, Donna. 1992. "The Early Twentieth Century Irish Stem Family: A Case Study from County Kerry." In *Approaching the Past: Historical Anthropology Through Irish Case Studies*, ed. Marilyn Silverman and Philip Gulliver, pp. 305–47. New York: Columbia University Press.

———. 1993. "Irish Households in the Early Twentieth Century: Culture, Class, and Historical Contingency." *Journal of Family History* 18(1): 19–38.

———. 1998. "Family Systems and the Foundations of Class in Ireland and England." *History of the Family: An International Quarterly* 3(1): 17–34.

Blanton, Richard E. 1994. *Houses and Households: A Comparative Study*. New York: Plenum.

Bouquet, Mary. 1996. "Family Trees and Their Affinities: The Visual Imperative of the Genealogical Diagram." *Journal of the Royal Anthropological Institute (Incorporating Man)* 2(1): 43–66.

Bourke, Joanna. 1991. "Working Women: The Domestic Labor Market in Rural Ireland, 1890–1914." *Journal of Interdisciplinary History* 21(3): 479–99.

Buchanan, R. H. 1970. "Rural Settlement in Ireland." In *Irish Geographical Studies in Honor of E. Estyn Evans*, ed. Nicholas Stephens and Robin E. Glasscock, pp. 146–61. Belfast: Department of Geography, Queen's University.

Burke, Helen. 1987. *The People and the Poor Law in 19th Century Ireland*. West Sussex, England: Women's Education Bureau.

Burtchaell, Jack. 1988. "The South Kilkenny Farm Villages." In *Common Ground: Essays on the Historical Geography of Ireland (Presented to T. Jones Hughes)*, ed. William J. Smyth and Kevin Whelan, pp. 110–23. Cork: Cork University Press.

Cantillon, Kathleen Houlihan. 1989. "My Search for the 'Old Street.'" *Ballyduff Magazine* 2: 47–9.

Charles-Edwards, T. M. 1993. *Early Irish and Welsh Kinship*. Oxford: Clarendon Press.

CPALII (Commissioners for Publishing the Ancient Laws and Institutions of Ireland). 1879. *Ancient Laws of Ireland*, Vol. IV. *Din Techtugad*. Dublin: A. Thom & Company.

Danaher, Kevin. 1985. *The Hearth and Stool and All!* Cork: Mercier.

Dinneen, Patrick S. 1979 [1927]. *Foclóir Gaedhlge Agus Béarla: An Irish–English Dictionary, Being a Thesaurus of the Words, Phrases and Idioms of the Modern Irish Language*. Dublin: Irish Texts Society.

Doherty, J. E., and D. J. Hickey. 1989. *A Chronology of Irish History Since 1500*. Dublin: Gill and Macmillan.

Douglas, Mary. 1991. "The Idea of a Home: A Kind of Space." *Social Research* 58(1): 287–307.

Evans, Estyn. 1988 [1957]. *Irish Folk Ways*. London: Routledge.

Fitzpatrick, David. 1983. "Irish Farming Families Before the First World War."

Comparative Studies in Society and History 25: 339–74.

Gibson, D. Blair. 1995. "Chiefdoms, Confederacies, and Statehood in Early Ireland." In *Celtic Chiefdom, Celtic State: The Evolution of Complex Social Systems in Prehistoric Europe*, ed. Bettina Arnold and D. Blair Gibson, pp. 116–28. Cambridge, UK: Cambridge University Press.

Glassie, Henry. 1982. *Passing the Time in Ballymenone: Culture and History of an Ulster Community*. Philadelphia, PA: University of Pennsylvania Press.

Guinnane, Timothy. 1991. "Re-thinking the Western European Marriage Pattern: The Decision to Marry in Ireland at the Turn of the Twentieth Century." *Journal of Family History* 16(1): 47–64.

Hareven, Tamara. 1991. "The Home and the Family in Historical Perspective." *Social Research* 58(1): 253–86.

Kelly, Fergus. 1988. *Early Irish Law Series*, Vol. III: *A Guide to Early Irish Law*. Dublin: Institute for Advanced Studies.

Kennedy, Robert E. Jr. 1973. *The Irish: Emigration, Marriage and Fertility*. Berkeley, CA: University of California Press.

McCourt, Desmond. 1971. "The Dynamic Quality of Irish Rural Settlement." In *Man and His Habitat: Essays Presented to Emyr Estyn Evans*, ed. R. H. Buchanan, Emrys Jones, and Desmond McCourt, pp. 126–64. New York: Barnes and Noble.

Macfarlane, Alan. 1987. *The Culture of Capitalism*. New York: Basil Blackwell.

Moore, Sarah. 1986. "The Bungalisation of the Rural Landscape." *Farmers Journal* 1 (May 31): Section 1, 6–7 (Dublin).

O'Connor, Bertie, and Séan Quinlan. 1989. "Ballyduff: A Place in the Kingdom of Cíar." Ballyduff, Ireland: Rattoo Heritage Society. [Video.]

O'Neill, Kevin. 1984. *Family and Farm in Pre-famine Ireland: The Parish of Killeshandra*. Madison, WI: University of Wisconsin Press.

O'Tuama, Séan. 1985. "Stability and Ambivalence: Aspects of the Sense of Place and Religion in Irish Literature." In *Ireland: Towards a Sense of Place*, UCC-RTE Lectures, ed. Joseph Lee, pp. 21–33. Cork: Cork University Press.

Patterson, Nerys Thomas. 1994a [1991]. *Cattle-lords and Clansmen: The Social Structure of Early Ireland*. Notre Dame, IN: University of Notre Dame Press.

——. 1994b. "Clans Are not Primordial: Pre-Viking Ireland and the Modeling of Pre-Roman Societies in Northern Europe." In *Celtic Chiefdom, Celtic State*, ed. Bettina Arnold and T. Blair Gibson, pp. 129–36. Cambridge, UK: Cambridge University Press.

Saris, A. Jamie. 1996. "Mad Kings, Proper Houses, and an Asylum in Rural Ireland." *American Anthropologist* 98(3): 539–54.

Silverman, Marilyn, and Philip Gulliver (eds). 1992. *Approaching the Past: Historical Anthropology Through Irish Case Studies*. New York: Columbia University Press.

Smith, Cecil Woodham. 1962. *The Great Hunger: Ireland 1845–9*. Glasgow: Collins.

Smyth, William J. 1992. "Making the Documents of Conquest Speak: The Transformation of Property, Society and Settlement in Seventeenth-century Counties Tipperary and Kilkenny." In *Approaching the Past: Historical Anthropology Through Irish Case Studies*, ed. Marilyn Silverman and Philip Gulliver, pp. 236–92. New York: Columbia University Press.

Part II:
Houses and the Construction of Family Life

–5–

Reconstructing Sexual Geography:
Gender and Space in
Changing Sicilian Settlements
Sally S. Booth

To talk about the family and the house in Sicily is to talk of men and women and changing patterns of sexual geography. In the past, women were generally restricted to domestic space of the home and the adjacent courtyard, while men were free to enter the public space of the street and the cafe, the center of local economics and politics. The reconstruction of western Sicilian towns damaged by the 1968 earthquake precipitated significant transformations in domestic architecture and settlement. Changes in the design of houses and towns have been accompanied in turn by changing ideas about men and women and the spaces they inhabit. In the past twenty years, the traditional sexual geography of the Mediterranean agrotown has been both reinforced and challenged. In this chapter, I treat transformations in architecture in the reconstructed settlements and the inhabitants' reactions to these changes as a vantage point on contested ideas concerning gender, morality, and space.

Urban geographers have incorporated issues of power and stratification into analyses of the built environment, producing important and theoretically valuable research. While there has been great emphasis on class as a dynamic aspect of urban process, investigation of how class and gender intersect in the transformation of space has been minimal. Thus, here I treat the relationship between changing domestic space and women's experience in both waged and unwaged work.

After discussing patterns of gender segregation in traditional dwellings and agrotowns of the western Sicilian interior, I focus on new housing forms built after the earthquake. Reconstruction following the 1968 earthquake coincided with emerging feminist ideas regarding women's work and role in the public realm, as well as changing ideals of privacy. Planners of the new towns disregarded the different ways men and women traditionally inhabited public and private space. Furthermore, they overlooked some important social functions of different types of spaces in the old settlements.

In the dramatically transformed architectural context of the new towns, men and women find themselves more isolated, both from each other in the home and from other men and women outside the home. While the architectural design of the old towns emphasized the contrasts between the community of men and the community of women, in the new towns the focus shifted to the nuclear family. Notwithstanding class variation in housing, the barriers between male and female spatial domains and, subsequently, between different families have in fact increased in post-earthquake housing built by the state. It is from this perspective that I examine the reactions of inhabitants – particularly women – to the constraints associated with new housing, as they challenge the gendered spatial arrangements designed by architects and planners hired by the Italian state.

In general, women find the new housing designs of the post-earthquake reconstructed settlements restrictive and inconvenient. The majority of Sicilian women are inclined to use the dwelling space for production of foodstuffs and for domestic chores associated with child care and family maintenance. To facilitate these tasks many invest a sizable portion of family income and great effort to alter the new dwellings. There are two major types of alterations: (1) poorer families with women involved in home production redesign the space of the new house to mirror house design prior to reconstruction – that is, they reposition the kitchen work space to adjoin semi-public areas such as the courtyard or street; and (2) richer women, often professionals working outside the home, are beginning to reject altogether the urban row housing of the agglomerated settlement in favor of resettlement in detached suburban villas in the surrounding countryside. These two different responses reflect new ideas regarding domesticity and changing patterns of housework as influenced by economic necessity and status considerations.

Different responses to housing change in Sicily indicate new residential alternatives sure to affect future settlement patterns significantly. While the question of domestic space in contemporary Europe is often phrased in the dichotomous terms of traditional versus modern housing, the Sicilian material forces us to reconceptualize the model and recognize the linkages between gender ideals, work requirements and class expectations. The dynamics of changing domestic space reflect women's needs and aspirations as much as the intentions of architects and planners. Recognition of this dynamic has theoretical and policy implications relevant to planned housing projects generally.

The Traditional Agrotown

Before the earthquake, the settlement pattern in the Belice Valley of western Sicily was relatively uniform and stable. In the two major historical periods of settlement formation – the medieval Arab colonization of the twelfth century and the feudal expansions of the 1600s conducted under the aegis of the Spanish crown – towns were built as agglomerated settlements with small narrow streets lined with contiguous housing, broken up only by courtyard entrances, churches, and small shops. Like the settlement architecture of Mediterranean villages throughout North Africa and Europe, western Sicilian towns give the feeling of enclosure; long expanses of walls with few openings characterize residential streets (Oliver 1987: 119, 202; Valussi 1968: 38). In western Sicily, the agrotown remained the dominant settlement type until the investment of emigrant remittances in housing in the 1960s and the state reconstruction projects of the 1970s and 1980s. The traditional house type of the agrotown was established in the 1600s and 1700s, and some suggest the only change in Sicilian housing between then and the postwar period was a continuing decline and impoverishment of the original form (see e.g. Renna 1979: 59).

Several factors account for the extraordinary stability of settlement type and housing design from the seventeenth to the twentieth century. Agglomerated settlements on hilltops had ecological implications, since inhabitants feared the malaria associated with the lowland countryside. The crowded settlements had political ramifications as well. Landowners found it easier to mobilize and control the peasant labor force in a relatively confined urban area, while peasants were less likely to lay claim to the land they worked while living distant from it (Smith 1976: 248). Banditry in the countryside and the absence of infrastructure and public services outside of towns also impeded dispersal and settlement (Blok 1969; Schneider and Schneider 1976: 34–6). In short, the long duration of feudal conditions in western Sicily assured the continuity of the agrotown until the latter part of the twentieth century (Valussi 1968: 183).

The typical Sicilian settlement was organized around a public core area in the town center. This was surrounded by rings of older, then newer housing. Cultivated fields and the rocky, uncultivated countryside lay beyond. The traditional agrotown was traversed by a central corridor or boulevard, the *corso*. Shops, offices, municipal buildings, bars, men's clubs, and *piazze* were located along this axis. This area was considered the center of male public space, the area where men could and were expected to move freely to work, shop, and socialize. As such, it was the site of much business and political activity, both formal and informal, and thus the central locale of expressions of civic culture (see also Silverman 1975).

Yet the public character of this central zone was never absolute; instead its public–private patterning varied by time and function (Sciama 1993: 88). For instance, the public nature of coffee bars was variable. Theoretically open to all, they were nevertheless informally segregated by class and occupational groupings, as well as by gender.[1] The public functions of the *corso* also shifted according to time and context. While normally the exclusive domain of men, on summer weekends and during religious festivals the evening *passeggiata* (promenade) was enlivened by women. All dressed up and accompanied by their families, they paraded up and down the *corso*. At other times women would deliberately avoid the downtown area. During the ordinary business day, for instance, they avoided the *corso* by having men do the shopping and other tasks. Or they might have brought along their children to chaperone them in the male areas.[2]

Finally, the most private of all public places on the *corso* were the men's clubs, the *circoli*. Membership in these store-front clubs was formally divided by class and occupational group. Each town in western Sicily had a number of *circoli*; e.g. a club for the *civili* (or bourgeois) class, a fishermen–hunters' club, a leftist workers' club, and a sports fans' club. The *circoli* were, by definition, restricted. Women were not welcome as members, nor were they comfortable entering these clubs to communicate with their menfolk. Young boys, employed by the nearby bars, acted as go-betweens, delivering coffee, drinks, and messages to the men in the *circoli*.

Despite the varying public–private quality of town space, the geographic distribution of different areas in a town can be viewed as a continuum of public and private zones of male and female activities. While the *corso* was used by the outside visitors and the male population of the town, the adjoining neighborhoods were more exclusively the domain of residents. Both men and women frequented the neighborhood streets, which were lined with entrances to houses and courtyards and interspersed with small shops. Women used these streets to work, socialize, and move through the town. When visiting kin or friends across town, women would often take indirect routes through side streets in order to avoid the *corso*.[3] Women used the side streets as work space during the weekdays. There, with better light and, more importantly, the company of neighborhood women, they watched children, cooked, sewed, and socialized outside their doorways. Occasionally men helped with domestic tasks in this semi-public area, usually with special projects associated with harvesting and food processing.

The most significant semi-public space for women in the traditional agrotown was the courtyard, or *cortile*. The courtyard has been a defining feature of western Sicilian settlement since the medieval period of the Arab colonization (roughly between the ninth and fourteenth century), and has displayed a remarkable continuity with past urban structure due to its enduring functional utility in the daily life of agriculturalists (Casamento *et al.* 1984: 6). In a comprehensive study of pre-earthquake residential patterns in Sicily, Giorgio Valussi argues that the most characteristic element of the house, both in town and in the country, was the courtyard, the terrace, or the alcove on the side street; that is, it was the semi-public workspace of women that characterized the Sicilian house (Valussi 1968: 184).Enclosed by houses on three sides and by an often gated entryway on the fourth, the courtyard served as an extension of semi-public space communally shared by the surrounding houses. The *cortile* was commonly linked to the house by the kitchen entry, and it was considered the primary workspace for women. While men stored equipment, animals, and transport vehicles in the courtyard, it was women who inhabited the space. They used the area to clean and prepare agricultural goods, visit with neighbors, cook, feed family and seasonal workers, wash and dry laundry, and collect rain water (Valussi 1968: 44). Architecturally, the *cortile* gave light on to the interiors of surrounding houses. Importantly, as the "center of all agricultural and family movement" the courtyard was the physical form of "social protection," providing a sheltered workspace for women, invisible to the passing public (Valussi 1968: 44).

Houses in the Traditional Agrotown

The divisions of town space into continua of male–female and public–private were reiterated in the divisions of house interiors. And, as in town space, class differences complicated the patterns of gender segregation of household space.

Great regularity characterized housing form for poor and middle-income peasants in the traditional agrotown. Made of the same materials (tufaeous rock), they varied in size, structure (number of rooms), and number of stories. The typical, single-story, one-room house of a poor landless peasant family had four separate areas for storage, stall and hayloft, a kitchen at the entrance, and an elevated alcove for sleeping in the back of the unit (see Figure 5.1). The common two-story house of a poor peasant family had areas for storage, stall and hay on the ground floor, and sleeping space upstairs. The kitchen area of this home was often part of an outside alcove in the courtyard or on the street (e.g. Valussi 1968: 37; Salomone-Marino 1981: 51). The typical, two-story, two-room house of a richer landowning peasant family (*burgisi* or *civili*) was composed of a ground-floor entry hall, a kitchen-dining area, stall and hay room, and a storage area for transport vehicles and goods. The upper floor was divided into bedrooms, a dining room, a living room, a kitchen, and a storage area (see Figure 5.2). More often than not the *burgisi* house had two kitchens – one on the ground floor for daily cooking and feeding of harvest laborers, and one upstairs reserved for family use and special occasions (e.g. Valussi 1968: 43).

Residences in the traditional agrotown were divided between day and night spaces.[4] Women's work, agricultural and socially reproductive, occurred in day space centered around the kitchen. The kitchen area, especially in smaller, poorer houses, was either outside or linked to the outside by an entryway. Thus women, especially poorer ones, worked in kitchen areas that frequently spilled out into the semi-public space of the courtyard or street. Night space, on the other hand, was restricted to the family and was shared by men, women and children for sleeping. In houses of the richer *burgisi* and *civili*, men and women also shared sleeping areas, but were well-segregated for other activities. Here women worked in an upstairs kitchen for at least part of the time. While removed from contact with the street and courtyard, these kitchens frequently opened on to balconies, which faced the street and neighboring balconies. In more elaborate houses, a separate study and living room allowed richer men exclusive areas in which to conduct business or entertain.

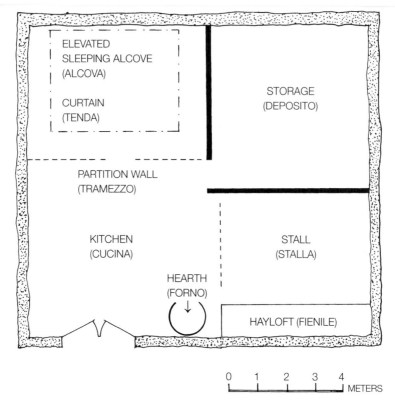

Figure 5.1 Typical house of landless peasant family (Drawn by Brian Stadler).

To summarize, then, the architecture of gender in the traditional agrotown operated on two different physical and conceptual levels. First was the town space external to the house, access to which varied most significantly by gender and secondarily by class and occupation. All men, local and outsider, rich and poor, had free access to the public center, the *corso*, where they socialized, conducted business, or negotiated employment. Moving between the public, semi-public, and private spaces of the town, men were able to act as "mediators" for women, transferring information between the outside world and the domestic one (Schneider and Schneider 1976: 102). Only neighborhood men had free movement in the semi-public side streets, where they stored agricultural goods and tools and occasionally assisted with domestic work. Most rigidly circumscribed of all external areas was the *cortile*; only men from the surrounding houses had full access to this most private of public areas. But for special occasions, women did not have free access to the *corso*. Their movement around town was limited to the side streets, which were used as traveling routes and work spaces. The *cortile*, the most

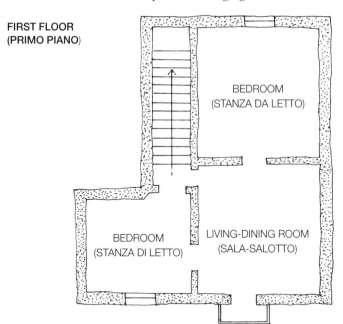

FIRST FLOOR
(PRIMO PIANO)

BEDROOM
(STANZA DA LETTO)

BEDROOM
(STANZA DI LETTO)

LIVING-DINING ROOM
(SALA-SALOTTO)

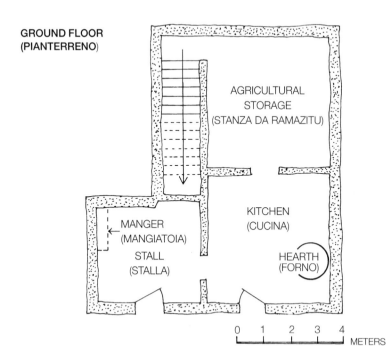

GROUND FLOOR
(PIANTERRENO)

AGRICULTURAL
STORAGE
(STANZA DA RAMAZITU)

MANGER
(MANGIATOIA)

STALL
(STALLA)

KITCHEN
(CUCINA)

HEARTH
(FORNO)

0 1 2 3 4
METERS

Figure 5.2 Typical house of a landowning peasant family (Drawn by Brian Stadler).

exclusive of women's exterior spaces, functioned as an extension of the kitchen, shared only by kin and the nearest female neighbors.

The ambiguous nature of the courtyard brings us to the second level of gender segregation in the traditional western Sicilian settlement, the house. Day space, comprising the kitchen and the courtyard, was the focal point of women's activities. While shared by poorer women, the day space was separated in an upstairs area in the homes of richer women. Lacking easy access to the courtyard, these women used kitchen balconies as extensions of the workspace and for socializing with neighbors. While men had access to all domestic space, they spent much less time in or near the home; only richer men had exclusively male space in which to work inside the house.

The implications of these spatial patterns of gender segregation bear on larger aspects of stratification. The findings from Sicily corroborate the cross-cultural research of Daphne Spain (1992), who found women's low status consistently linked to high levels of spatial segregation. Where women have only limited or no access to places of socially-valued information – such as the workplace, the school, or places in the house or town associated with business and politics – there is little possibility of gender equality. By contrast, in societies where socially-valued information or space is accessible to both men and women, there tends to be more parity between the sexes (Spain 1992).

This theoretical framework relating spatial domains to gender equality and inequality is well suited to explain the Sicilian material. In the traditional agrotown, men had easy access to socially valued information in the town center, walking along the *corso*, gathering in the bars and *circoli*, or passing time in the *piazza* (White 1980: 150). In these areas business, politics, and social life were discussed, contracts mediated, exchanges arranged, jobs secured, and prices negotiated. Women were excluded from the news exchanged in the town center; their access to socially valued information was limited to the communally shared areas of side streets and courtyards. But it is important to remember that the nature of the information valued by men and women differed. While not publicly recognized as powerful, women of a neighborhood or shared courtyard exercised a measure of social control over important spheres of Sicilian private and public life – namely the household economy (home production and social reproduction) and the social reputation of townspeople, neighbors, and kin. Marriage ties, family status, personal standing, and honor were all discussed, negotiated, and determined in the course of women's talk (Schneider and Schneider 1976: 93–4, 207). The spatial domain of this talk was women's work spaces, the kitchen and the courtyard.

Overall, access to the semi-public space of the side street and *cortile* provided women the wherewithal to work communally and to exchange information. But class differences intersected the spatial patterns of gender in the agrotown. Like the bourgeois house of nineteenth-century England and of the United States (Spain

1992: 113), the houses of rich Sicilians were more spatially segregated by gender than those of the poor. Because they could afford to build separate rooms for the separate activities of men and women, as well as two kitchens (one spatially removed from immediate contact with the *cortile*), the spatial barriers around richer women were more imposing and ultimately more isolating. Thus, private space was more absolute; semi-public areas were not shared by neighborhood women as in the more popular quarters, but were instead restricted to the use of family women alone. Use of the balcony to exchange information only partially mitigated the isolation of the wealthier women.

There is little question that Sicilian society was characterized by unequal relations of patriarchy. In southern Italy "a woman was good if she was a selfless wife and mother subordinating herself to husband, family, church, and society" (Birnbaum 1986: xv). More importantly, women's work of child care and house-work was not highly valued, either socially or financially. Clear illustration of Spain's model correlating levels of gender segregation with sexual stratification is found in the agrotown, where relations of patriarchy were supported by the spatially segregated work of men and women. Men dominated with control over legal, economic, and political aspects of local life. They controlled spheres of influence by means of their easy access to the public areas of interaction – men's interaction. Richer men in professional occupations could move in the most exclusive public places – the elite bars and *circoli* – and could so preserve and enhance their elite position with their hold on the more restricted and most valued information. Women had little or no access to the economics and politics of the public sphere, and thus little social power *vis-à-vis* men.

Yet the semi-public nature of women's work in poorer quarters complicates this issue. By virtue of their shared work spaces near or in the courtyard or side street, these women did have access to relatively important social information (White 1980: 150). While male workspace was inaccessible to women, female work space of the poorer classes was by necessity used by men to pass through, to store their goods and tools, and to work.[5] In short, poorer women had occasion to share information both among themselves and with men; they had greater access to and more control over social information than was available to their middle-class counterparts. This potential imbalance between the classes, with poorer women exercising a degree of power over information inaccessible to richer women, was mitigated by the Mediterranean ideologies of honor and shame. Because their houses afforded rich women work spaces of minimal exposure and visibility, these women enjoyed a higher status; they were socially compensated for enduring political obstacles associated with their housing. By contrast, poorer women compromised their social honor; they ran the risk of bringing shame upon themselves and their families by being observed while engaged in domestic tasks and in contact with non-family men.

Sicilian Society Transformed

The social and economic convulsions associated with the "economic miracle" of the 1950s and 1960s formed the backdrop for the massive physical upheaval caused by the destructive earthquake of 1968 in the Belice Valley. In fact, the earthquake often serves as a historic watershed in popular thought, marking the irrevocable transformation of conservative Sicilian society. Modernization, the economic and cultural integration into national society, and particularly the feminist movement, would dramatically and permanently impact Sicily.[6] This changing society inhabited new forms of domestic and public space in the towns reconstructed by the state after the earthquake.

Italy of the late 1960s and 1970s was characterized by an "extraordinary period of social ferment" (Ginsborg 1990: 298). Emerging out of the student uprisings of the universities and the militant labor organization of northern factories, collective movements associated with the progressive Left affected all segments of Italian society. Routines and expectations of daily life in western Sicily were profoundly transformed by these trends. Even more than the mobilizations of students and workers, the feminist movement had explosive consequences in Sicily, where male–female relations were extremely conservative and strongly patriarchal.

The economic miracle refers to the linked processes of dramatically declining agriculture in the South and rapidly developing industry in the North. In Sicily, the great exodus from the land and flight to the North of the male labor force meant that towns were "feminized." They became "women's colonies," populated overwhelmingly by women, children, and the elderly (Birnbaum 1986: 241). Despite the great number of female-headed households, feminism itself faced many major obstacles in the South, especially in Sicily.[7]

The formidable barriers confronting the feminist movement in southern Italy were linked to the conservative social and political climate. Women were legally and economically subordinate to men (Birnbaum 1986: 13) and "imprisoned" by traditional family structures (Schneider and Schneider 1976: 93). The dominant institutional powers in Sicily – the Christian Democratic Party, the Catholic Church, and the Mafia – all resisted progressive social change promoted by the feminists (Hellman 1987: 183, 167). In Italy, politics was "almost exclusively the domain of men" until the 1970s (Ginsborg 1990: 366). The political climate for women's participation was particularly "brutal," with political parties from both the Right and Left reacting to the mobilization of women with "obstruction, isolation, and ostracism" (Hellman 1987: 168, 169). Significantly, the absence of public space for democratic participatory politics, especially the politics of women, further hindered the feminist movement in the South (Hellman 1987: 126).[8]

Despite these impediments to women's mobilization, the feminist movement has enjoyed remarkable success in the Italian South. The passage of important referenda (legalizing divorce in 1974 and abortion in 1981), the well-organized resistance to the nuclear base at Comiso, and the ongoing struggle to establish women's service centers and clinics demonstrate the continuing relevance of feminism in the South. More significant has been the changing consciousness of southern women; women have attained the "skills that gave [them] the confidence to act in the public sphere and to redefine 'women's personal problems' as public issues" (Hellman 1987: 206). Consequently, women have entered the public sphere in ways unimaginable in the past in the traditional agrotown.

The most striking change has occurred in the realm of education. Co-education for elementary grades has signalled the end of sex segregation of children. Traditionally, women's education was cursory and brief in Sicily. But during the watershed years since 1968 more inclusive rules of access have greatly affected women's opportunities for university training. By 1968, a full third of all university students were women (Lumley 1990: 55). Middle-class women received higher education, and many trained for professions outside the home.[9] These are the women who spearheaded the feminist movement in the South. They now work as clerks and professionals outside the home, entering previously restricted spaces of work such as offices, schools, clinics, and town halls. In fact, many jobs within the bureaucracy set up for earthquake reconstruction (e.g. building departments and housing offices) were set aside specifically for educated women.

Although poorer, less educated women have been less directly influenced by the feminist movement, they too have been more active in the market economy since the earthquake. The Sicilian economy is characterized by underdevelopment, where emigrant remittances and state entitlements subsidize a consumer economy that lacks a significant productive base (Schneider and Schneider 1976: 207). As a result of this lopsided economy, many Sicilians work in unregulated illegal jobs. *Lavoro nero* (literally "black work," or unregistered employment) taps the reserve of the unemployed, or more specifically, the working unemployed, who are often women engaged in housework. While factory work is still rare in western Sicily, there has been a marked increase in *lavoro nero* among poorer Sicilian women since the nation-wide recession of the 1970s. *Lavoro nero* frequently depends on local resources and seasonal variations; in different towns of western Sicily it includes jobs in embroidery, sewing of clothes or rugs, flower-tying, and fish processing (Birnbaum 1986: 242). Domestic space is utilized for *lavoro nero*, at no cost to the merchant or middleman, for the piecework production of market-based goods. This kind of home-based work is highly exploitative; because of its private nature, neither state regulations nor benefits and services apply to the workforce. Thus, since the earthquake and the changes associated with social movements, poor women in western Sicily are more involved with the national and international markets. Ironically, this involvement has meant the increasing privatization of women's daily lives, as the low-paid piecework of *lavoro nero* is added to the unpaid routines of housework and child care.

In short, the feminist movement and the recent economic changes have had varying consequences for the different classes of western Sicilian women. Middle-class women with college educations and professional jobs have challenged the gender-segregated patterns of the traditional agrotown by entering the public space of formerly male workplaces. By contrast, poor women have been forced by economic necessity to retreat further into the private zone of the house, combining domestic work with market-based production. While an increasing number of women (21 percent in 1973 to 28 percent in 1983) are working as domestics for families of professional women (Hellman 1987: 207), most women are responsible for the double duty of unpaid housework and child care in addition to their paid work as professionals or pieceworkers. It is in these contexts that women and their families have reacted to the new structures of domestic space provided by the state in the course of reconstruction after the earthquake.

New Housing in Reconstructed Towns

A powerful earthquake struck the Belice Valley on January 14, 1968. It registered eight on the Richter scale and was followed by nearly a hundred aftershocks. Fourteen communities were destroyed or badly damaged, affecting a population of almost 97,000 (for population figures of the 1961 census, see Renna 1979). In terms of physical damage, initial assessment showed that 32 percent of the total real estate holdings were leveled and another 24 percent were rendered uninhabitable without extensive repairs (Caldo 1974: 53–7). These figures are now known to be underestimates. As reconstruction proceeded, many more inhabitants claimed house damage and applied to the state for financial assistance. Reconstruction of well over half of all real estate brought about significant changes in the expectations and experiences of settlement and housing for the inhabitants of the Belice Valley towns.

The new form of settlement does little to reiterate the overall form of the traditional agrotown. Reconstructed towns and neighborhoods instead recall English New Towns and American postwar suburban developments, because they were planned with these models in mind (for Italy see Gregotti 1968: 80; for the Belice see Renna 1979: 104 and De Bonis 1979: 121, 137). While the basic functional components of the old towns – churches, schools, shopping districts, government buildings, infrastructure, and housing – are found in the new, the reconstructed towns are arranged without reference to the traditional patterns of public–private and male–female space of the agrotown. Dramatically altered are the arrangements of social space, such as main streets and *piazze*, where men exchange news, network for jobs, and pass the time. Furthermore, the neighborhood streets and *cortili* in which women work, pass along information, and watch children, are unrecognizably changed or absent altogether.

In the reconstructed settlements the architecture of gender is influenced by the new arrangements of public institutional buildings. Once dispersed up and down the *corso*, the youth clubs, party headquarters, museums, and civic organizations are now centralized in or near municipal offices. Men's clubs, which are uncommon in the reconstructed areas, are no longer located in the shopping areas of the main *corso* of the new towns, no longer integrated into the public space of men's experience.

Patterns of gender-segregated shopping areas of the old towns have not been reproduced in the new commercial districts. The new commercial zones are set apart from the residential areas and favor access by automobile. These business areas are closed in on themselves, more like the strip-malls of suburban America than the agrotown's *corso*, with its continual flow of pedestrian and car traffic. While the shopping area of the *corso* had many functions, the commercial centers of the new towns are solely commercial; they only function as locales to market manufactured goods.

This singularity of purpose is expressed architecturally. Structural design and stylistic details of the new zones act as barriers that inhibit easy movement and social interaction. In the commercial center of Montevago, for instance, the closed cement walls surrounding the center are perforated only by an occasional window, tiny and high over one's head (for photographs, see Renna, De Bonis and Gangemi 1979: 297–8). Within the block is a dense forest of reinforced concrete pillars, topped by a low, imposing, checkerboard ceiling of concrete. Needless to say, this area is rarely used, and then only for shopping. Men spend little time in these shopping blocks, perhaps because the defining activity – consuming – is so spatially circumscribed. It is thus difficult to combine shopping with socializing, networking, and seeing and being seen, as well as with passing through to other areas. Further complicating the uses of the commercial zone is the accessibility afforded by the automobile. As women are considered more protected and freer of movement in a car, they more easily can and do enter the new public space to consume. Like men, they enter and leave again immediately, after completing the given task.[10]

These towns were each planned as a total unit, as ensembles, so to speak, with little room for individual variation. They all had standardized housing projects made of reinforced concrete, which were more similar to housing estates on the peripheries of cities of the Italian North than to those Sicilian towns they were built to replace. While these towns were long anticipated by those affected by the earthquake, the inhabitants had little input to their structure or design. It is therefore not surprising that it was this form of integration into the national architectural and planning patterns represented in the reconstructed towns that Sicilians, especially Sicilian women, challenged and resisted.

The extent of reconstruction varied according to the degree of devastation and the political will and power of the local officials. While some towns were rebuilt completely, in others only certain neighborhoods were reconstructed. New housing was of three basic types, roughly differentiated by financing arrangements, architectural styles, and locations within the reconstructed areas. Highly uniform housing projects were planned and built entirely at state expense for the poorest residents. These tenants had no say whatsoever regarding the design or location of their new houses. (See Figure 5.3 for a typical *casa popolare* or public housing unit.) A second type of housing is the state-subsidized cooperative, entered into by middle-class clerks and professionals. Different architects were hired to design these housing projects, and there is more architectural variation among them. Residents can usually decide their own configuration of a standardized set of architectural components. (See Figure 5.4 for a common cooperative unit.) The third type of housing is private construction to which the state contributes a significant percentage of financing. This kind of housing, although subject to less stringent regulations, demonstrates a remarkable degree of regularity, probably because of the common standardized models used.

People's reactions to the new housing in the reconstructed towns and neighborhoods vary according to their levels of participation in determining the design of their domestic space. Thus, there is less satisfaction with the popular housing and more with the private housing, with the cooperatives falling somewhere between.

Curving boulevards with houses set back behind iron-grill gates and driveways into dusty yards give the reconstructed towns and neighborhoods an expansive look. They seem huge, open and empty.[11] In other areas of the new settlements, apartment blocks squat on eight-foot-high concrete pylons. The shadowy ground floor is reserved as parking areas for cars. While the old towns were built on a scale suitable for pedestrians and beasts of burden, the movement and storage of the automobile in large part determine the design and dimensions of the new towns.

The planners who designed the new towns and established the building codes and zoning regulations used an urban middle-class model of domestic space, a model that presumed the outside employment of women and consequently precluded the home production of domestic necessities. The new house, urban and bourgeois in tone, emphasizes the privacy of an isolated nuclear family. Its domestic spatial arrangements differ in significant ways from the earlier housing designs of the agrotown. The courtyards and front street areas, formerly the central locales of women's neighborhood networking and domestic production, are entirely absent in the new towns. They have been replaced by individually gated yards, enclosed entryways, and parking zones, all separating the house from the street. Private domestic space is increasingly detached from the surrounding semi-public space; entry and exit between these two areas is no longer a simple question of stepping

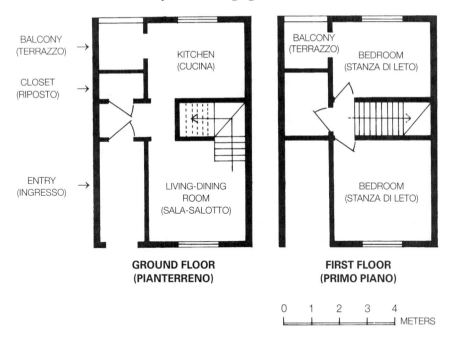

**GROUND FLOOR
(PIANTERRENO)**

**FIRST FLOOR
(PRIMO PIANO)**

0   1   2   3   4
└───┴───┴───┴───┘ METERS

Figure 5.3 Typical public housing unit. (Drawn by Brian Stadler).

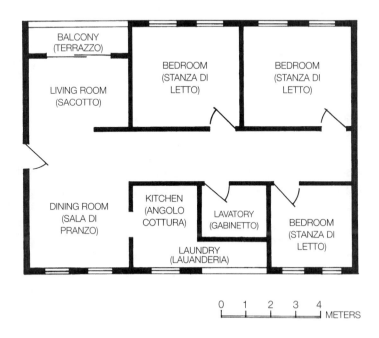

0   1   2   3   4
└───┴───┴───┴───┘ METERS

Figure 5.4 Typical cooperative housing unit (Drawn by Brian Stadler).

between kitchen and courtyard or street, but of crossing horizontal and vertical obstacles of gate, yard, entryway, stairs, and parking area.

Tasks that were once done cooperatively in the semi-public areas adjoining the house can no longer be achieved communally in the new towns and neighborhoods. The balcony, formerly a kind of elevated courtyard, is now placed at odd angles facing away from other balconies, making simple conversation between households all but impossible. Kitchens in the new housing projects are very small, aptly called "cooking corners." These are placed at the back of the house, remote from the public activity of the street. As a result of these architectural changes, women in the new settlements find it difficult to use semi-public space and find themselves more confined to the private interiors of the house.

The reconstructed settlements were not designed with the customs and traditions of the earthquake victims in mind. I would argue that the planners hired by the state did not intentionally subvert the patterns of male–female space of the traditional agrotown. In fact, in most cases, they did little to understand or acquaint themselves with the socioeconomic conditions and settlement patterns of the inhabitants of the damaged towns (De Bonis 1979: 139). Instead, the planners, mostly men from northern Italy, had little experience with the Mediterranean codes of gender segregation and honor and shame. They overlooked the historical spatial patterns associated with gender segregation, with social interaction, and with men's and women's employment (or lack of it) inside and outside the house. They used models designed for bourgeois inhabitants in northern Europe and the United States. The famous architect, Vittorio Gregotti (1968) argues that planners everywhere in Italy had as their overarching goals to standardize house form, improve "taste," and increase consumption by the masses (Gregotti 1968: 79). The radical trans-formation of the dimensions and arrangements of public, semi-public, and private space in the new Belice settlements appears to be an unintended consequence of these goals.

In the new towns the public space of business is no longer open to the back-and-forth traffic of daily routines so important to men's politics and social life. Instead, business space has become exclusively commercial, with physical bound-aries decisively marking its limits. Likewise, the semi-public spaces of women's work and social exchange are absent or inaccessible in the new towns. The new houses were in fact designed for employed women who would fulfill domestic requirements on the market, consuming manufactured household products, clothes, linens, and processed foodstuffs. In all respects, the new towns have been planned for small families in which both parents work outside the home, but neither in agriculture. The new housing was designed for a small, urban, middle-class family as a place to consume, retreat from work and relax from the pressures associated with secure, daily employment.

Women's Different Reactions to New Housing

The housing of the reconstructed towns and neighborhoods was problematic for the inhabitants, especially the women, of the agrotowns of western Sicily. Both housewives and professional women found it unsatisfactory, although for different reasons. Its design precluded home production for housewives and its uniformity and rules prohibiting modifications failed to fulfill the goals of professional women for housing that was simultaneously a place of privacy, leisure, and display of class status. While the first group of women found it necessary to modify the state-provided housing, professional women took the more dramatic and unprecedented step of rejecting the agglomerated settlements entirely and moving to the countryside.

I discuss the two reactions in turn. Many non-professional women who have moved from housing in the old agrotown into the modernist reconstruction projects have rejected the increasingly privatized domestic space. They have modified their houses in an attempt to reconstitute a spatial environment conducive to home production, communal work, and the social interchange of neighborhood networks. These women still must work at home, making the year's supply of tomato sauce, drying and processing nuts and fruits for Christmas sweets, embroidering sheets and pillowcases for daughters' trousseaus, or, increasingly, turning out piecework in the market for *lavoro nero*. More importantly, their social power rests, in large part, on the community of women constituted in the courtyards or street fronts of the agrotown. They still want to discuss the village news with neighboring women, since their access to the male space of the *corso* remains limited by their work requirements and their moral codes of proper female behavior. As most modifications are prohibited in public housing projects, many risk fines to transform street-level garages into second kitchens for everyday use, storage, and seasonal home-production activities. With their corrugated steel doors open, these kitchen-garages become semi-public spaces like courtyards; passing women pull up chairs, talk, sew, watch children, engage in piecework, and prepare food together.

Other aspects of the new space in the reconstructed towns are also considered objectionable. For instance, the middle-class nuclear family (parents and one or two children), which the planners expected to inhabit these housing estates, does not conform to the western Sicilian reality. Often the married couple is joined by more children or a grandparent. Many inhabitants in the state housing projects have closed in the new, rarely-used balconies (located off bedrooms) to increase their limited interior space and provide additional sleeping areas. Transgressing the rules of the government housing office for the sake of propriety, inhabitants claim the need for separate bedrooms for children of different sexes and grandparents. Alternatively, some have used the balcony areas to increase the size and prestige of the formal day areas of living or dining rooms.

Home modifications in the housing projects also bear on conceptions of gender and space. A working-class informant, Giuseppina, lives with her widowed father and younger brothers. She has installed a hot plate and a sink in the garage to adapt it better for cooking. Tired of sharing a bedroom with a brother, she has had a corner balcony closed in to make a private bedroom for herself. Her attempt to carve out her own space appears odd, however, since she owns a house in the same state housing project two doors down, the right to which she inherited from a grandparent. When asked why they risked fines and legal troubles for the modifications of her father's house, she referred to the moral code regarding women and space. "Daughters and windows are always in danger," (*Figlie e vetri son sempre in pericolo*), she said, quoting a proverb about women's vulnerability. She added, "It wouldn't be right to live all alone." When pressed, she agreed she was worried less about her personal safety in that crowded and therefore well-supervised neighborhood than about people criticizing her and her father for improper behavior. Living alone would indicate her potential sexual freedom and her father's and brothers' lack of concern regarding her honor. The house two doors down will sit empty until she marries.

Another informant, Carmela, lives with her young sons, husband, and mother in a second-story apartment in the reconstructed zone. She too has transformed the garage into a kitchen, but uses it primarily for storage and seasonal food preparation. Although she worked for years in a cafe before marriage, she now avoids leaving the house, to the point of buying most of the family food from travelling vendors whose goods she hoists up in a basket to her second-story apartment. She explained, "It doesn't seem right. I have a family to care for; people would think I was neglectful if I went traipsing about town."

Aside from the majority of women who work at home and live in the new housing projects, a minority of women have received university education and work outside the home, often in the new jobs associated with reconstruction in local government offices. These women discuss their entry into the public spaces of offices, the *corso*, and even the cafes (social clubs remain strictly off-limits to women) in terms of a conscious challenge to past cultural norms regarding the exclusivity of male domains. They see themselves as the local forerunners of the feminist movement. "We brought feminist consciousness to this tiny town," proclaimed one proudly. They recount the insulting remarks made to them by men and women alike, reassuring me that only the poor, uneducated, and provincial would stoop so low as to criticize their courageous conquest of public space.

These are the women who, with their families, have begun to reject town residence in favor of dispersed settlement in the countryside. Although this alternative was not offered as part of the state-provided plans for reconstructed settlements, it is a possibility permitted by the territorial zoning plans and by the recent provision of rural infrastructure such as roads and electricity lines.

The residential dispersion has occurred in two phases. Since the late 1970s, the upper-middle, and then the middle classes have begun in earnest to build country houses for summer residence. Prior to the earthquake, farmhouses were being abandoned throughout the Sicilian countryside. The typical rural house at that time was little more than a tool shed – twenty-five to thirty square meters, without windows or plumbing (Caldo 1974: 53). Now most old and new towns are closely ringed by dispersed villas in areas previously devoted to agriculture. In these villas, professionals and their families enjoy a few months of privacy and selective appreciation of the peasant heritage. While architecturally these villas often imitate elements of rustic buildings, with wooden archways and wood-burning bread ovens, these houses are specifically designed for non-agriculturalists in pursuit of leisure, free from the social control exerted in the crowded neighbor-hoods of the town. This new pattern of settlement – a winter residence for work and town living, a summer residence for recreation and country life – served as the precedent for the more dramatic, yet still uncommon, move to relocate permanently in the countryside.

Professional women and their families were the first to move out of town. This group of women may make and store tomato sauce or embroider in their spare time, not out of economic necessity but to savor the authentic experience of home production. They need not participate in labor exchange networks with other women, as they can easily purchase housework, child care, commercially prepared foodstuffs, and linens. They have access to social information from the public sphere by virtue of their professional jobs outside the home. They do not need the conditions of communality afforded by housing in the agglomerated settlement. Nor do they need to modify this housing to take better advantage of domestic work space and neighborhood networks.

It is in this context that professional women and their families have moved out of the centralized towns to the suburban rings around them. It is ironic that these women, most influenced by feminism and thus more likely to be working for wages, are not linked to the communal networks of women promoted in the feminist program. Instead, they have retreated into the more isolated and privatized nuclear family, an institution eschewed by the feminist thinkers.

The decision of a professional couple to settle permanently in what was once the unpopulated agricultural hinterland, together with the opposition they encount-ered from friends and family, indicate slowly changing conceptions of residence, at least among a small segment of the population. As an informant, Giovanna, explained, she strove for the comforts associated with classic suburban living – gardens, privacy, quiet, and safe play areas for children. Working in town, both she and her husband were tired of constant contact with people by the end of the day. She found particularly appealing the "privacy" (they use the English word, indicating the foreignness of the concept in the agrotown) of their country house.

Coming home from work she was assured peace and quiet, freedom from the surveillance of the town gossips, and relative safety from impromptu visits from neighbors and conversations across balconies. She and her husband had no intention, however, of returning to the peasant occupations of their parents and grandparents. For this couple, the country no longer connoted hard work in lonely fields, but a new residential alternative. They saw themselves linked to an international culture of suburban living by virtue of their particular housing preference. As a consequence of their professional employment outside the home, they were propelled to relocate away from the concentrated settlements.

Conclusion

In this chapter I have discussed ways in which settlement transformation and variation in women's employment opportunities have influenced notions of male and female space. Most of the residents of the state housing projects in the reconstructed towns come from the class of poor agriculturalists. They have modified their housing to better accommodate the requirements of women's work and social space. They view the urban character of the old and new concentrated settlements as an essential feature of civility, and their ideas of how men and women should occupy space in town are important in the conduct of their everyday lives. Women of the lower classes still attempt to avoid male public space – the *piazza* and the *corso* – whenever possible. They often criticize the upper-middle-class women for working outside the home and entering these spaces on a regular basis. Professional women are occasionally accused of flaunting themselves in male arenas. Furthermore, outside employment is viewed by some as a form of family neglect.

It remains a question whether poor women sanction professional women as an expression of resentment at their own lack of job opportunities outside the home. A complex irony is that poor women have now achieved the traditional norms of female honor set by the middle class in the traditional agrotowns prior to the earthquake, while contemporary professional women are in fact patterning their lives in ways similar to those of poor women in the past. Prior to the economic miracle, lower-class women were forced to compromise their honor by working outside the home as field hands, domestics, midwives, or herbalists.[12] Although the countryside was considered dangerous, especially for women, many often passed part of the year in the rural farmhouse (the *baglio* or *massaria*). Others did work that spilled easily out onto the street or the courtyard. Only with the prosperity of the postwar period did lower-class women return to the confines of the house for work. Women's work just for one's own family in one's own home was viewed as a way to restore and maintain the family honor.

The move to the countryside of professional women and their families is incomprehensible to many poorer women. The countryside is still seen by most as a place of male agricultural employment. Furthermore, it is considered distant from the important networks of female kin, neighbors, and friends. Guiseppina and Carmela, like many poor women living in the new public housing projects, view themselves as the true bearers of an authentic cultural tradition. They denigrate the more educated women for being seduced by what they see as foreign, superficial, and ultimately destructive urban moral codes.

As educated women have begun to enter the workforce, they have contradicted the ideals of male exclusivity in public spaces. These women see their conquest of public space as a model to be emulated by less educated poorer women. They think it their responsibility to introduce and enact modern ideals of sexual equality to provincial people living under a shadow of outmoded moral codes. These women encourage their daughters to enter the public arenas of the town and scoff at women who restrict their daughters' movements in these actions, in these places.

These professional women and their families are pursuing a new residential option in the Belice Valley by settling permanently in the countryside. They are leaving the agglomerated agrotowns and reconstructed areas because they find their lives there constricted. They have not only contested the moral codes regarding sexual geography, they have also physically removed themselves from the particular settlement formation associated with these codes, in their attempt to establish new patterns of social behavior in new spaces.

In contemporary western Sicily we find two different responses to the moral codes regarding gender and space, both associated with specific class positions and possibilities. Using modifications, poorer women have challenged the bourgeois arrangements of domestic space provided by the architects of the state, but have accepted the model of public–private restrictions on gender assumed in the past by the middle class. While professional women claim to challenge the patterns of sex-segregated space, they have chosen to abandon this space to establish their domestic life outside the town. Thus, the attempt to challenge and transform the architecture of gender in the western Sicilian settlement has ultimately resulted in patterns of increased class segregation, with both stylistic difference and geographical distance further separating the poor and the middle classes.

This chapter points to the serious issue of how class intersects with women's work and changing domestic space to perpetuate segregation. Recognition of this unintended yet nonetheless important dynamic in the social process of spatial transformation will better inform the policy and design of planned housing.

Notes

1. Sanctions against women entering the male space of the coffee bars were rigid. A neighbor worked in a bar as a young woman and ten years later still remembers with bitter resentment the way she was snubbed by townspeople

for engaging in work located in such an exclusively male place. She is poor and uneducated, and sees her foray into the workforce as a humiliation of poverty, not gender.

For important analyses of the symbolic components associated with class and with gender in the Mediterranean agrotown, see Gilmore (1980) and Giovannini (1981), respectively.

2. Children could act as chaperones, perhaps because women with children symbolically declare their status as mothers to onlookers, a role that makes them both less aggressive and less vulnerable in male space.

3. Recalling the Arab settlement, Fernea (1965) tells of Iraqi women demonstrating sexual modesty by using the same roundabout routes to avoid entering the male space of the town center. For narratives on women's experiences of avoiding male areas in Sicilian towns, see Booth 1988.

4. This division of houses into "night" and "day" spaces is a local conceptualization shared by residents and architects.

5. Ernestine Friedl (1975) correlates gender stratification with work patterns to point out that in societies where men and women work in close contact there tend to be relatively higher levels of gender equality than in societies where men and women work apart and where gender inequality is more pervasive. From this, we would expect relations between men and women in Sicilian middle-class families to be more patriarchal than relations between men and women in poor families.

6. Denis Mack Smith points out the uneven nature of this modernization in western Sicily. While mafia interests blocked industrialization, fearing the development of an educated proletariat, those same mafia interests were deeply involved with the speculative building boom of the 1960s, where planning rules and building codes were ignored in the tremendous explosion of construction in cities and agricultural towns. Yet Mack Smith concedes that the large-scale social changes of the 1960s associated with feminism, emigration, and increased communications did interfere with the hegemonic hold of the mafia over western Sicily (Mack Smith 1968: 539–42).

7. Judith Hellman, in a study of Italian feminism, claims that while northern cities each had its own specific problems in mobilizing women, in the South the feminist movement faced all the problems found in the North combined, plus others (Hellman 1987: 184).

8. An eccentric gadfly in a small town in western Sicily wanted to reach women, who he thought would be more sympathetic to his criticisms of the entrenched powerholders. He complained that they did not hear his speeches in the main *piazza*, so to reach them he marched into every *cortile* and sidestreet, stood up on the table he carried under his arm, and held forth. While many thought he was crazy, his point on the location of female audiences was valid and accurate.

9. There has been a steady decline in fertility and family size since the Second World War in Italy, which might be correlated with the increased numbers of women working in the labor force.

10. One can only speculate how this commercial space will be used in the future. Will it become a place of men's information and exchange? Will it retain its singular function as a space of consumption? It remains a question as to how the inhabitants will use and change it.

11. In fact, the population density of the newly reconstructed towns is much lower than that of the old towns.

12. At the end of the last century, poor women's occupations were more varied yet. In an 1897 survey of women's work, medical healing and witchcraft, public mourning and weeping, trousseau appraisal and matrimonial mediation were mentioned along with agricultural work, reproductive intervention, and petty commodity trading (Salomone-Marino 1981).

References

Birnbaum, Lucia C. 1986. *Liberazione Della Donna: Feminism in Italy*. Middle-town, CT: Wesleyan.

Blok, Anton. 1969. "South Italian Agrotowns." *Comparative Studies in Society and History* 11: 121–35.

Booth, Sally S. 1988. "Dove Sono le Donne?" *Labirinti* 1(4): 4–11. (Gibellina, Italy.)

Caldo, Constantino. 1974. *Sottosviluppo e terremoto: La valle del Belice*. Palermo: Manfredi.

Casamento, Aldo, Pina di Francesca, Enrico Guidoni, and Adalgisa Milazzo. 1984. "Vicoli e cortili: Tradizione Islamica e urbanistica populare in Sicilia." Catalog for the Biennale di Venezia. Palermo: Edizione Giada.

De Bonis, Antonio. 1979. "La vicenda allo Specchio." In *Costruzione e progetto: La valle del Belice*, ed. Agostino Renna, Antonio De Bonis, and Giuseppe Gangemi. Milan: CLUP.

Fernea, Elizabeth W. 1965. *Guests of the Sheik: An Ethnography of an Iraqi Village*. New York: Doubleday.

Friedl, Ernestine. 1975. *Women and Men: An Anthropologist's View*. New York: Holt, Rinehart and Winston.

Gilmore, David D. 1980. "The Social Organization of Space: Class, Cognition, and Residence in a Spanish Town." *American Ethnologist* 4(3): 437–51.

Ginsborg, Paul. 1990. *A History of Contemporary Italy: Society and Politics 1943–1988*. London: Penguin.

Giovannini, Maureen. 1981. "Woman: A Dominant Symbol Within the Cultural System of a Sicilian Town." *Man* 16: 408–26.

Gregotti, Vittorio. 1968. *New Directions in Italian Architecture*. New York: Braziller.

Hellman, Judith A. 1987. *Journeys Among Women: Feminism in Five Italian Cities*. New York: Oxford University Press.

Lumley, Robert. 1990. *States of Emergency: Cultures of Revolt in Italy from 1968 to 1978*. London: Verso.

Mack Smith, Denis. 1968. *A History of Sicily: Modern Sicily After 1713*. New York: Viking.

Oliver, Paul. 1987. *Dwellings: The House Across the World*. Oxford: Phaidon.

Renna, Agostino. 1979. "La Costruzione Della Città e Della Campagna." In *Costruzione e Progetto: La Valle del Belice*, ed. Agostino Renna, Antonio De Bonis, and Giuseppe Gangemi. Milan: CLUP.

Renna, Agostino, Antonio De Bonis, and Giuseppe Gangemi (eds). 1979. *Costruzione e progetto: La valle del Belice*. Milan: CLUP.

Salomone-Marino, Salvatore. 1981 [1897]. *Customs and Habits of the Sicilian Peasants*, ed. and transl. Rosalie Norris. Princeton, NJ: Associated University Press.

Schneider, Jane, and Peter Schneider. 1976. *Culture and Political Economy in Western Sicily*. New York: Academic Press.

Sciama, Lidia. 1993. "The Problem of Privacy in Mediterranean Anthropology." In *Women and Space: Ground Rules and Social Maps*, ed. Shirley Ardener. Oxford: Berg.

Silverman, Sydel. 1975. *Three Bells of Civilization: The Life of an Italian Hill Town*. New York: Columbia University Press.

Smith, C. T. 1976. *An Historical Geography of Western Europe Before 1800*. London: Longman Group.

Spain, Daphne. 1992. *Gendered Spaces*. Chapel Hill, NC: University of North Carolina Press.

Valussi, Giorgio. 1968. *La casa rurale nella Sicilia occidentale: Richerche sulle dimore rurali in Italia.* Florence: Leo Olschki-Editore.

White, Caroline. 1980. *Patrons and Partisans: A Study of Politics in Two Southern Italian Comuni*. Cambridge, UK: Cambridge University Press.

Suburbanizing Rural Lifestyles Through House Form in Southern Portugal

Denise Lawrence-Zúñiga

At first blush, Vila Branca appears as any other rural southern Iberian castle town, with its whitewashed houses and their red tiled roofs clustered tightly together atop a defensible hill. At one end sits the twelfth-century Reconquista castle, at the other is the main church. Quaint and traditional – until one sees the grid-like arrangement of shiny new suburban-style homes spread around the western base of the hill. One of the most significant changes in Western family life during the nineteenth and twentieth centuries has been the increasing importance of the material aspects of home in relation to family life, a trend largely associated with the growth of the industrial bourgeois classes. Nineteenth-century European middle-class urbanites in particular began promoting house form not only as a means for improving physical standards of living, especially in early industrial cities where housing was notoriously lacking in hygienic provisions, but also as a vehicle for intentionally changing the values and behaviors of working-class families. The appropriation of bourgeois and later modern house forms in rural areas, including the suburban-style detached house, signifies a major shift in rural family lifestyles and values.

Over the last hundred years, and especially since the late 1970s, rural Portuguese communities have witnessed notable transformations of their physical environments as changes in residential forms, construction technologies and planning ideas have taken hold. These material transformations have also had powerful effects on family and community life. This study explores the impact of changing house forms, most recently detached and semi-detached suburbanized housing, in a rural agrotown in southern Portugal, and traces some of its effects on family life. It investigates the power of material culture as an agent of change and contemporary house form as an instrument for shifting the significance of the rural home from a center of work and family sociability to a container for the pursuit of family and individual privacy. Further, it explores some of the competing ideals of home and domesticity that find somewhat anomalous expression in local built forms, which fragment and recombine meanings and uses of urban models into new and unanticipated configurations.

The Power of Built Form

In a general sense, the power of the built environment rests in the notion that the material expression of a cultural idea can have lasting effects on people long after the original construction. The physical boundaries found in the arrangement of walls, ceilings and floors, and permeable elements such as doors and windows, constrain as well as provide opportunities for human behavior, shaping continuously activity and meaning. But the fundamental power of the house rests in its capacity as a cultural model to represent and guide appropriate behaviors and sentiments. The form housing takes, then, acts as both behavior setting and mnemonic for idealized concepts of the domestic unit that resides within, the family. The spatial order of the house represents a moral system of domestic values and relationships encoded, in the case of Europe, at specific historic junctures. The suburban home, now being built throughout rural Southern Portugal, has its most recent roots in the bourgeois and modern housing reform movements of the late nineteenth and early twentieth centuries.

Although the modern suburban house formally originated between the wars, its historical antecedents can be found in nineteenth century bourgeois concepts of domesticity that emphasized a rational order of bounded spaces, each specialized by function and intended to nurture and ensure the privacy of the nuclear family and its individual members (Hareven 1991; R. Lawrence 1986). The bourgeois home of the late nineteenth century, whether a single suburban house or an urban apartment, organized daily life into a hierarchy of spaces that separated the intimate life of the family from formal areas used by visitors and work areas used by servants. The first areas encountered when entering the house were, at minimum, the hall or entry, adjacent to which was a parlor or sitting room and a formal dining room. Ideally, one bedroom for the married couple and one for each child or, at minimum, two children's bedrooms to keep genders separated, were located to the rear or on a second story. These spaces were intended to ensure sexual propriety as well as foster the development of individual autonomy (Rybczynski 1986). On the ground floor, strictly separated from the "front-stage" parlor and dining room, were the "back-stage" and less presentable kitchen, where domestic servants prepared meals, and service areas such as the laundry. The plan assumed that visitors would be greeted in the entry hall or foyer, and entertained in the parlor or salon and dining room, but would not be allowed to penetrate into the more private areas of the home (Guerrand 1990). Although these formal spaces were used to present a self-consciously constructed image of the family, they also served the family collectively for daily activities. Overall, the plan of the bourgeois house was aimed at ensuring the reproduction of the "modern family," in which sentiments ideally bind family members together through adult romantic love and choice of marriage partners, mother–child relations that glorify maternal love and put children's welfare above that of adults, and family intimacy and individual growth that require physical separations (Shorter 1977: 17).

During the late nineteenth and early twentieth centuries bourgeois reformers sought to address urban working-class housing problems, such as overcrowding and unsanitary conditions, which they believed were responsible for what they perceived as a dysfunctional family life. By introducing a modest version of their own homes, with a parlor or living room, they believed they could encourage family togetherness and help wives steer their husbands away from the tavern and bring children in from the street. Whether by intentional reform or imitation, working-class families often did set aside such a room for best, but used it instead as a symbol of their respectability (Lofgren 1984). Most of the housing reforms during the twentieth century soon focused on incorporating scientific and techno-logical innovations in standardized schemes that could be used to mass-produce healthful housing solutions for the working and the rapidly growing middle classes. Ideas for designing modern, efficient kitchens and bathrooms received a lot of attention; but mass implementation of more technologically sophisticated schemes had to wait until after the war. Most postwar urban housing schemes were built in the form of apartment buildings clustered together in "new towns" near major cities; but rural housing largely remained self-built by owners in areas where land was more plentiful, and single homes like those found in the early bourgeois suburbs provided the model.

As rural residents seek to improve their housing by emulating the earlier bourgeois homes, building with modern construction materials, or acquiring the latest technological amenities to improve their standard of living and comfort, they adopt and adapt housing models originating in urban areas to their own needs and produce unique local forms. Rural bourgeois houses were already widespread before the lower classes could afford to borrow their features early in this century; but recently modern suburban houses have appeared in profusion, making signifi-cant improvements in rural standards of living. When families acquire new house forms, however, they do not necessarily intend to acquire all the behaviors and meanings encoded in the forms as they were originally produced. Rather, families appropriate new forms because they promise a desired experience, but families also bring to bear their own understandings grounded in their particular historical and social experiences on the actual use of new housing (Grumann 1976; Korosec-Serfaty 1985). Their appropriations may generate some new behaviors, but are also likely to produce hybrid forms, or local adaptations, as more customary behaviors blend together with new material forms. The social relations produced and reproduced as a result of local adaptations may be an unintentional, and even unconscious, but acceptable consequence of the appropriation (Bourdieu 1977; Giddens 1984).

This research explores the changes in house forms and family behaviors represented by three successive types of housing in a rural southern Portuguese community. It describes each of the forms and its encoded pattern of family life, and the physical and behavioral adjustments and modifications made as a result of residents' appropriations of newer house forms. The study particularly focuses on the recent introduction of the suburban-style single-family house and its impact on living in older housing in the local community. It examines the extent to which family behaviors, lifestyles, and values have changed to fit the new house forms, especially in relation to issues of family privacy and respectability. This study is based on longitudinal field research beginning in 1976–7 and on periodic visits since that time, with a longer-term stay in 1993.

Vila Branca

Vila Branca is a small agrotown in the Alto Alentejo with a population of about 600 residents. Traditionally, the latifundist landholding pattern organized inhabitants into a class system of large and small landowners, tenant farmers, and landless laborers; a small class of landowner-merchants and crafts people were also present (Cutileiro 1971). Because of declining agricultural activity after the Second World War, many people left Vila Branca seeking employment in large urban centers such as Lisbon, or overseas in the former African colonies. This process severely depopulated the community, leaving behind a disproportionate number of elderly residents. Since that time, however, some local sources of employment have developed or stabilized in the nearby marble quarries and construction trades and in the expansion of local civil and public services. Although most young people must still leave Vila Branca to find employment, a number of young families have been able to find steady employment in the local area. In addition, many older couples who had migrated earlier to urban areas now look at Vila Branca as a possible site for retirement and have held on to family homes as a resource for eventually accommodating these plans.

The organization of family life in Vila Branca is based on the nuclear family, with couples ideally seeking to establish an independent household at marriage. The average age at marriage has declined in recent years for males (those over 50 married at 27 years of age and those under 50 at 24.5) and for females (those over 50 married at 23.7 years of age and those under 50 at 21.4). The ideal number of children is two, preferably a boy and a girl; but the number of children per couple has been declining, with older couples averaging between three and four and younger couples now averaging two. Although many young couples have left Vila Branca in search of employment, those who stayed behind or returned endured a shortage in available housing before the late 1970s. This shortage consisted not only in a reduced number of units, but also in a standard of living below acceptable levels, including the lack of indoor bathrooms and insufficient bedrooms for family members. Families who had moved to urban areas but retained houses in the local community for vacations created part of the shortage, but a good part was also created by the lack of available land and resources to construct modern homes until the most recent development began.

The physical organization of Vila Branca reveals the town's long history and its previous status as an important administrative center. Situated between the Reconquista castle and the Igreja Matrix (main church) is the Rua Direita (main street), along which the former centers of government and the Misericordia church and hospital, now in ruins, are located. This was once the most prestigious part of town, boasting many fine homes owned by wealthy landowners and several social clubs. Now it is inhabited mostly by elderly couples and widows, a few individuals and families, and tourists. In 1990 a recently arrived entrepreneur opened an inn in the lavishly remodeled two-story home of a former wealthy landowner, and a restaurant, serving those tourists, on the Rua Direita. In addition, several homes have also been purchased by the same entrepreneur for tourism purposes, and a number of other old homes have been bought and renovated by the Dutch and Portuguese for weekend and vacation visits to Vila Branca.

The bulk of Vila Branca's permanent population, however, resides beyond the old historic center of town in the surrounding lower areas or *arrabalde* (outskirts). As many as three distinct phases of development characterize the settlements in the *arrabalde*. The first of these seems associated with the construction of housing for dependents near some *montes* (isolated farms) belonging to the wealthy, which by now have been incorporated into the town through conurbation. Although many of these houses were constructed before the twentieth century, additional houses were added at the end of the nineteenth century and the beginning of the twentieth by residents who applied to the local town government, the *Junta da Freguesia*, to grant them land for house construction. The most recent phase began in the 1970s after the so-called Marxist revolution of 1974. In both phases, land utilized for housing purposes was converted from the town's *baldio* (commons) and subdivided to accommodate housing needs and other uses. In the first instance, construction consisted of rows of houses arranged in linear fashion along streets radiating out from the old center of town; each house directly abuts the street without a setback, although each house has a small yard or *quintal* at the rear. In the 1960s, electricity and water lines were installed to serve each house, and by the early 1970s a sewer system had been completed. The most recent housing development, the *urbani-zação*, consists of subdivided lots organized according to a grid pattern of connected streets; each lot is designed for a detached or semi-detached single-family home with a front and back yard and a garage. Construction in this latest development began in the late 1970s through the auspices of a governmental agency that took responsibility for planning the subdivision, creating minimum housing standards, and providing design assistance to families wishing to construct homes.

The "Traditional" House

The oldest cluster of houses in Vila Branca is strung along three parallel streets that connect the castle and church. In addition to a number of large homes formerly owned by wealthy families there are rows of simple houses that are distinguished by a single major room, the *cozinha* (kitchen), that fronts directly onto the street. Simple houses typically have one or more rooms to the rear and sometimes above in a type of loft; these include *quartos de dormir* (bedrooms), *dispensas* (pantries or storage areas), or, in the past, the *cavalariça* to house the family mule (Figure 6.1).

Traditionally, these homes were occupied by landless laborers, sharecropping families and small landowners, who used the *cozinha* as a workspace for agricultural activities as well as a living area. The dominant architectural feature of the *cozinha* is the *chaminé* (chimney), a large walk-in fireplace used for a combination of functions including heating, cooking, and smoking meats, and for intimate social gatherings of family members and close friends. The *chaminé* is truly the hearth – the center of family life; but its multiple functions are also dirty and malodorous. Cooking and heating with kindling and charcoal, even in the best-ventilated *chaminés*, leaves clothing, skin and hair covered with a smoky residue, and interior walls must be frequently whitewashed to keep them clean.

With the *chaminé* typically located next to the front door, these houses created an imposing whitewashed exterior facade, which, traditionally, was not punctuated by any other openings such as windows. The houses were clustered tightly together, each sharing common walls with its neighbors. Most houses had a *quintal* (garden) in which to grow vegetables and to keep small animals such as a pig, a goat, a lamb, rabbits or pigeons. In addition, the *quintal* was often used for toilet activities, and in the summer months might serve to accommodate bathing. As late as the 1980s families and elderly residents used the narrow streets almost as often as the interiors of their houses for living activities; in general, the street in front of each house was considered an extension of living space. On warm days women gathered in the streets, sitting on small chairs, to gossip, sew, or prepare food for meals while their children played. Although much of this activity has decreased in recent years because of depopulation and an increase in television watching, some elderly people still gather together in front of the old Misericordia, or in public spaces near the church and castle, to chat in the cool morning and evening hours on a summer's day.

New Houses

Just around the turn of the twentieth century, a new type of house began to appear in the lower areas surrounding the old historic center of Vila Branca. These houses,

UPPER LEVEL

GROUND LEVEL

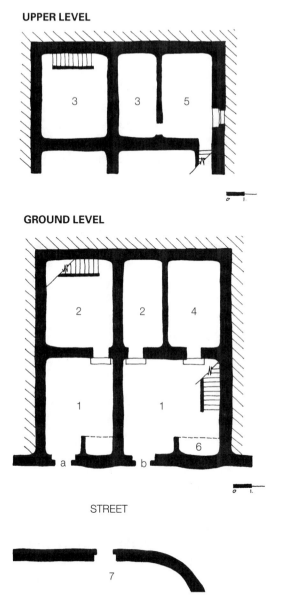

STREET

1. Cozinha – Kitchen
2. Quarto – Bedroom
3. Dispensa – Pantry or storage
4. Cavalariça – Stable (later converted to a quarto)
5. Sala – Parlor (was once a storage room)
6. Chaminé – Chimney
7. Quintal – Garden
a. Entry to first house
b. Entry to second house

Figure 6.1 Two traditional houses (Drawn by Dana Hendrix).

consisting largely of row houses, were built by a class of newly affluent local merchants, artisans and small landowners in a style that imitated the bourgeois house. The houses featured a *casa de entrada* (entry hall or entry room), which opens directly onto the street and serves as a corridor connecting the main rooms. At the rear of the house is a *cozinha* with the traditional *chaminé*, which continues to house most family life, and directly outside behind the *cozinha* is a *quintal* where toilet functions were originally located (Figure 6.2).

In addition to a new form of spatial organization, the *casa de entrada* introduced the concept of the semi-private space where residents could engage in conversations with casual visitors beyond the view of their neighbors' prying eyes. These houses also boasted a *sala* (salon or parlor), usually a *sala de jantar* (dining room), which faced the street, adjacent to the *casa de entrada* but separated from the kitchen, and which was intended for entertaining and visiting with friends and family. Like the salon described by James and Kalisperis in Greece (Chapter 7, this volume), the *sala* was meant to be a room set apart from ordinary uses, reserved primarily for entertaining guests. A family used this room to display itself, to present itself formally to others with its best furnishings, china, silver, and family mementos and photographs. Movement beyond this formal area into the kitchen at the rear, however, was restricted to the more intimate relations of close family and friends.

Suburban Houses

The most recent housing development in Vila Branca began construction in 1977 and consisted of a number of two-story detached single-family houses and one-story semi-detached single-family houses. Since that time approximately 28 new houses, including some one-story detached single-family homes, have been constructed. Although the homes are built by individual owners, each must conform to government standards in terms of minimum room sizes and overall size and plan, sanitary and safety features, minimum number of bathrooms and bedrooms, construction techniques, etc.; house plans are sometimes provided to home builders, who adapt them with government assistance and approvals to their own needs. The houses typically include a modern kitchen, in which the traditional *chaminé* has been replaced by a stylized vent over the stove, and which frequently accommodates a refrigerator, washing machine, freezer and other appliances. Houses are organized around a "T"- or "L"-shaped corridor or hall that connects two or more bedrooms, one or more *salas* (*sala de jantar* or *sala de estar* – "living room"), a *dispensa* for storage, and one or more bathrooms (Figure 6.3).

The front yards of these suburban-style houses are a standard size, since setbacks from the street are regulated by the government. House façades may be symmetrical or asymmetrical in organization, but include one or more windows in addition to the front door; usually the front entrance contains a *varanda* or *marquise* (uncovered

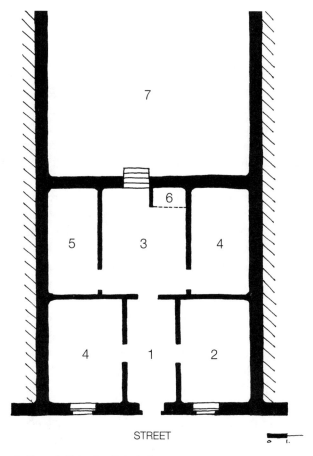

7

6

5 3 4

4 1 2

STREET

1. Casa de Entrada – Entry hall
2. Sala – Parlor
3. Cozinha – Kitchen
4. Quarto – Bedroom
5. Dispensa – Pantry
6. Chaminé – Chimney
7. Quintal – Garden

Figure 6.2 A new house (Drawn by Dana Hendrix).

and covered veranda, respectively) which serves as a semi-private space for greeting visitors. Each house is also surrounded by a short wall, which contains a large metal gate for the driveway and a small gate leading to the walkway and the front of the house. A taller wall of about one meter separates one neighbor's yard from another's. Each house includes sufficient space in the rear for a *quintal* and a garage to park the family automobile and store equipment. Curiously, constructed alongside or attached to most garage structures is the familiar traditional *chaminé*, which had been found only inside the kitchen of the previous two types of housing.

The *chaminé* is often the very first structure completed on a subdivided lot, and it is usually functional before construction on the actual house begins. In fact, many families inhabit the structure while they are in the process of building their own houses. This structure is called a *casa de matança* (house for pig killings), or a *cozinha alentejana* (Alentejan kitchen) if its use is more general. The ostensible reason given for its construction is to house activities for the annual family pig killing, a ritual event that takes place over the course of several weeks and to which family members are invited for their labor and to feast. The traditional way to preserve the pork is to make sausages and hams, which are salted and smoked in the *chaminé* for two or more weeks. Although the killing of the family pig is a single event, many residents use the *cozinha* throughout the cooler months, and sometimes throughout the year.

The *cozinha alentejana* typically contains much more than just the *chaminé*, and often includes a dining table and chairs, some small chairs for sitting around the hearth, and a propane stove for cooking. Running water and electricity for a refrigerator are also found inside, and many families move the television there so that the *cozinha alentejana* can be used year round for cooking, eating and socializing with the family. Some families who have a *cozinha alentejana* never use the formal kitchen inside the house, and sometimes the kitchen has no appliances at all. Residents admit embarrassment if asked about the two kitchens, but explain that they prefer to cook in the *cozinha alentejana*, rather than dirty the house, and it is easier and less expensive to heat with traditional kindling and charcoal than with more expensive fuels. Although the *cozinha alentejana* is the locus for extended family activities, not everyone in each family necessarily concurs with its usage. Sometimes only one or two family members use the *cozinha*, just because they like to sit by the fire with friends or by themselves, while others use the house.

New Lifestyles, Old Forms; Old Lifestyles, New Forms

Although only 28 new houses have been constructed in the *urbanização* since the 1970s, many other houses in Vila Branca have been at least partially renovated. The most significant renovation in almost every case has been the installation of an indoor bathroom, while room additions and modernization have also occurred as a matter of course. In the houses built at the turn of the twentieth century, adding a bathroom and modernizing the kitchen and other rooms has not been difficult, since houses are relatively spacious and the rear *quintal* affords additional room in which to expand. Many owners of these houses have added a garage to the rear of the *quintal* with an attached *cozinha alentejana* similar to those of the houses in the *urbanização*, and they have modernized the interior kitchen.

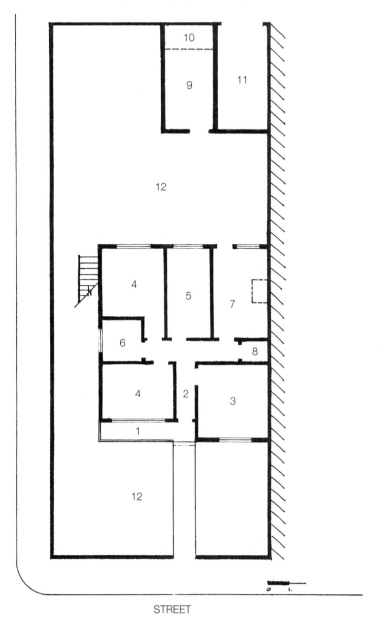

STREET

1. Marquise – Porch
2. Corredor – Corridor or entry hall
3. Sala de Jantar – Dining Room
4. Quarto – Bedroom
5. Sala de Estar – Living Room
6. Casa de Banho – Bathroom
7. Cozinha – Kitchen
8. Dispensa – Pantry
9. Cozinha Alentejana – Alentejan kitchen
10. Chaminé – Chimney
11. Garagem – Garage
12. Quintal – Garden

Figure 6.3 Suburban house (Drawn by Dana Hendrix).

More dramatic are the renovations of houses in the old center of town, which often lack the space to expand. Owners of these houses are most likely to add bathrooms by situating them in the large space provided by the *chaminé*. Several reasons are given for this strategy, but the most important is the ease of, and therefore the lesser expense involved in, making connections to water and sewer lines located at the front door near the *chaminé*. In addition, other rooms within the house may already be assigned to other functions, and it often seems unreasonable to residents to take away precious bedroom space, for example, when family members need places to sleep on occasional visits. Further, the size of the *chaminé*, with its deep and high interior, often provides sufficient space for constructing the straight walls that allow for a tub, toilet, bidet, and sink, without protruding too far into, or "robbing" (*roubando*) too much space from the *cozinha*. Evidence of this transformation, however, can often be detected in the exterior façade by the disappearance of the chimney top and the appearance of a small window for ventilation in the middle of an otherwise blank whitewashed wall.

A somewhat surprising secondary effect of the construction of the bathroom within the *chaminé*, however, is the frequent conversion of the *cozinha* to a *sala* and the addition of a *cozinha alentejana* in the *quintal*, if there is one, at the rear or side of the house or across the street. In the *quintal*, the new structure housing a traditional *chaminé* and a fully functioning kitchen operates as it once did inside the house; here is where the family gather to cook, eat, warm themselves and socialize, although they return to the interior of the house to sleep, bathe or use the toilet, and, increasingly during the summer, to watch television. Of course, many of the houses in the old center of town have been purchased and renovated by outsiders for touristic purposes, or remodeled by retired former residents, to include a modern kitchen and a bathroom as well as living areas, bedrooms and verandas. These residents have found other places for the bathroom and have retained the old *chaminé*, using them now principally as *lareiras* (fireplaces), a decidedly bourgeois custom.

In appropriating new house forms, the residents of Vila Branca have changed some of their behaviors and familial relationships, but they have also adapted house forms to reproduce other behavior patterns, many of which are unlikely to have been anticipated by the original house designers. The shift in the location of the kitchen to the rear of the house, away from the street, and its recent modernization have concentrated food preparation in one space, when it is used, while excluding activities formerly conducted in the *cozinha*, such as sewing, which now occurs in the *casa de entrada* or the *sala*. Many residents have, however, continued to maintain a complex of hearth behaviors, including cooking, eating, warming, and socializing, in the space occupied by the *chaminé*, wherever it might now be located. But leaving the house to use the *cozinha alentejana* is entirely consistent with the previous pattern in which residents left the house to use the quintal for toilet functions. In all houses, most women have shifted to the use of gas stoves to cook; but in old houses they often locate their stoves inside the *chaminé*, using it to vent cooking odors. Those who do not cook inside the *chaminé*, or who remove their stove to smoke sausages, may use the *chaminé* to build a fire for warmth during the winter months, although they also use electric heaters elsewhere. It is not unusual to find the family in the *cozinha alentejana* in the evening, gathered around the fire, watching television after eating the evening meal. The new combination of architectural forms and characteristic Alentejan behaviors creates some fascinating moments for the ethnographer.

On several occasions I have been invited to lunch or dinner at the home of a couple who were among the first to build a new house in the *urbanização*. The house has two stories; on the first floor is a metal workshop with a bathroom and a small market, and on the second is the family residence, consisting of a *sala de estar, sala de jantar, cozinha, casa de banho* (bathroom), and three *quartos de dormir*. In the *quintal* is a *cozinha alentejana* with *chaminé*, dining table and chairs, running water, sink, stove, and refrigerator; all the cooking, eating and family life in general is centered in this space. On most occasions, including important holidays, I have been entertained in this space as well, but on one occasion when I was accompanied by an American friend we were served lunch in the kitchen, not the dining room, both of which are located upstairs in the house. The meal had been prepared in the *cozinha alentejana* in the *quintal* and carried platter by platter upstairs to the second floor. The family explained that they do the same thing when they use the *sala de jantar* for special family occasions, preparing all the food in the *cozinha alentejana* and carrying it inside, one course at a time, to be eaten. When I asked why they did not use the inside kitchen, the wife replied that she had never used it and was more comfortable cooking in the space outside.

This apparent anomaly is repeated in the homes of a number of residents in the *urbanização* and now in other parts of Vila Branca, although perhaps not in quite as extreme a form. In one home, the kitchen remains an empty but decorated space, with a large potted plant resting in the space eventually intended to accommodate the stove, while the *cozinha alentejana* is completely furnished and continuously used. Not everyone, however, follows these patterns of behavior. Some women insist on cooking and serving meals to their families in the kitchen inside their houses and use electric heaters for warmth. In another case, a wife prefers to cook and serve meals inside the house where, afterwards, she spends her evenings watching television while her husband retires to the *cozinha alentejana* to sit by himself in the *chaminé*. Another family, which had remodeled a very large house inherited from the wife's family, had the luxury of having two *chaminés*, one of which was converted to a *lareira*, while the space in which it had been located became a *sala*; the other, located in a space that served as both garage and kitchen, served the family on a daily basis.

In contrast to the modern kitchen, the modern *casa de banho* does get used, and gratefully, by those who have installed one. By the late 1970s, when the first houses in the *urbanização* were being constructed, the number of fully functioning indoor bathrooms in Vila Branca was around twenty. Bathroom functions, including washing hands, using the toilet, and bathing were carried out in different spaces. In older homes a washstand stood next to the door by the *chaminé* in the kitchen. Residents describe bathing as inconvenient, requiring arduous labor to heat water and fill tubs, which were often located in the *dispensa* or the bedroom; toilet functions were often carried out in an outhouse in the *quintal*, or by using a bucket for dumping in open fields.

Residents argue that in former times wealthy landowners were the only ones able to construct *casas de banho* in their private yards and hire servants to assist with their baths. Poorer residents describe their own personal hygiene with embarrassment and a tinge of shame, because they lacked the resources to carry out these activities easily, frequently, or in complete privacy. Bathing, at best, was a once-a-week affair, and a visit to the toilet could involve leaving the house to go to the *quintal* in full view of the neighbors, or walking from one's house with a bucket to dump in the fields on the other side of the castle. In addition to convenience, one of the great advantages of indoor plumbing, then, has been to secure individual privacy for hygienic activities within the home. One resident explained that before building an indoor bathroom, she was not convinced it was necessary – *uma vaidade* (a vanity) – but now felt she could not live without it, especially in the middle of the night.

Although just about everyone can afford the privacy and convenience of bathroom facilities within their own homes, not everyone acquires them for their own personal needs alone. In fact, older people do not seem to bathe any more frequently than they did in the past, although young people do. Many families living in the older section of town feel pressed to find space for a bathroom to accommodate the needs of family members or others who visit. One woman said her daughter, who lived and worked in Lisbon, refused to come home for visits unless the family built a bathroom. Since the daughter often brought friends home with her, she expected her family to enable her to be a good hostess by providing the same conveniences she enjoyed in the city. Another suggested that it was embarrassing for her son to bring his wife and children to visit her because they were used to having a bathroom at their house in the city. She argued that she would not spend the money to put a bathroom in her rented house, however, until she was able to buy it from her cousin, who had so far refused to sell.

Appropriating the New House Forms

Until the introduction of the suburban house with its obligatory interior bathroom, the most significant addition to a "traditional" Alentejan home was a *sala* and, space permitting, an entry – rooms which recall the first bourgeois innovations during the nineteenth century. Elements of this spatial order, appropriated before the early twentieth century by local families of moderate affluence, eventually found their way into many of the homes of rural sharecroppers and landless laborers. One resident in the old center of town boasted a *sala* in the second-story loft in her home – an almost inaccessible space for family members, since most activities were conducted in the *cozinha*, and certainly out of reach for visitors. Although it was furnished with a sofa and family pictures, she admitted she really never used it; "but at least she had one, and with it came respectability." Another woman demonstrated her plans for dividing the old *cozinha*, which went largely unused after the construction of another kitchen, into a *casa de entrada* and *sala de jantar*. This renovation would allow her to secure a space in which to present the family formally and to buffer contacts between the family and visitors. Even now residents continue to modify their homes, appropriating "respectable" archi-tectural forms in order to learn, practice, and realize their encoded behaviors and meanings by moving through them.

Other family values and behaviors that continue to evolve through interactions with built forms are linked to lifestyle ideas introduced in the nineteenth century. The notion that the kitchen and, more specifically, the *chaminé* are dirty and malodorous are concepts that live in full force in Vila Branca. Relocating the *cozinha alentejana* with its traditional *chaminé* in the *quintal* is an act intended to remove the polluting elements and preserve the cleanliness of the interior of the house. Appropriating the new modern kitchen with its vented stove, however, has not necessarily eliminated fears about foul odors from cooking. In most new houses, as well as in older ones, the kitchen and the *sala de jantar* are separated by as much distance as possible; open kitchen–dining room combinations have been rare. This separation occurs even when the *cozinha alentejana* is located in a free-standing building outside and even if it is the primary site for everyday cooking and eating.

Although most families have long stated a preference to provide a private bedroom for each child, the resources to accommodate these desires have not always been available. At minimum, opposite-sex siblings should sleep in different bedrooms; but if only one room is available, one child, usually the girl or the youngest, sleeps with the parents; boys are often given less desirable spaces for sleeping, such as the attic or *dispensa*. Same-sex siblings almost always share a bedroom; in one family this economy of bedrooms permitted the construction of a *sala de estar* in the extra space when a new house in the *urbanização* was built. Children's behaviors differ somewhat in different parts of town, however, with those in newer houses more often using their bedrooms to study or to visit with friends, while those in the old center use the kitchen to work and the *sala*, if there is one, to visit. The idea of children's privacy and individual development, then, is more firmly expressed in the housing built around the turn of the twentieth century and in later suburban-style houses, but continues to be worked out as remodeling and new construction occur in other parts of town. These differences are due to variations in family income, education, and class; those with more income and education are more likely to realize their architectural aspirations in spaces supporting the growth of children as individuals.

Most recently, the passion for the modern bathroom has dominated residents' interests in shaping their houses and lifestyles. Secure in the idea that these facilities do not introduce unwanted odors into the interior of the house, as they once did with less efficient technology, residents have placed them in a variety of places. In constructing and renovating newer houses, residents have been able to incorporate bathrooms easily into plans, most often near bedrooms, and residents of houses built before the 1970s have attached them to the rear of the house or converted a *dispensa*. But residents of the oldest houses have had the biggest problem, because of a lack of space. In converting the *chaminé*, but without the construction of a separate *cozinha alentejana*, cooking, dining and social functions continue in the most public area of the house adjacent to the bathroom, a private space intended for personal hygiene; this adjacency provides privacy of access for neither visitors nor family members. This new arrangement seems awkward to many families, who complete the transformation of the old kitchen into a *sala* and build a new kitchen elsewhere.

Most appropriations of new built forms in Vila Branca – the *salas, casa de banho*, and modern kitchen – are given perfectly rational explanations that relate to improving standards of living, personal hygiene, comfort, and general household cleanliness. But residents' reasons only partially conform to the intended benefits encoded in new house forms by designers. The anomalies in built form and behavior expressed in maintaining two kitchens – one which is often used as the traditional hearth and the other a modern decorative possession, or the spatial substitution of the *chaminé* for the bathroom in remodeling an older house, are issues generally unexplored by residents. A giddy laugh or a reassurance that there is no other reasonable way to build is intended to dismiss the question. Although residents are aware of the awkwardness in their new lifestyles brought about by disrupting previous adjacencies between kitchens and bathrooms and other domestic spaces, they focus on the improvements, emphasizing that exiling the dirty *chaminé* from the increasingly sanitized house still allows them to live in two worlds, the modern and the traditional.

In spite of these anomalies, however, the replacement of the old hearth, the former social center of the home, by a private space, a bathroom, used principally by individuals, is an idea that is more than just ironic. It signifies a transformation in the fundamental meaning of the Alentejan home and physically represents the potential of material forms to complete the anticipated and desired behavioral transformations by channeling and shaping daily activity. The suburban southern Portuguese house has transformed the meaning of home from a rural collective workplace, a simple, earthy and sometimes smoky place that enhanced the sociability of family members, into an increasingly sanitary leisure space modeled after bourgeois and modern ideals intended to nurture individual privacy and personal growth.

Conclusion

Vila Branca residents of all classes have invested heavily in the material conditions of their home life throughout the twentieth century. What began as modest attempts to acquire respectability by appropriating the bourgeois *sala* and entry hall have now given way to more elaborated schemes to acquire comfort and become modern with the latest construction technologies and amenities. Rural working classes, in particular, have been especially concerned with acquiring a sense of security by purchasing or building homes, and advertising their new levels of respectability by transforming through new construction and renovation traditional domestic practices into modern ones. Indeed, the acquisition of new domestic forms has brought about many of the desired changes, benefits intentionally encoded by designers and sought by residents, such as spaces in which to entertain or gain individual privacy, and the conveniences of indoor plumbing and amenities. But the interest in maintaining some aspects of previous home life patterns has also produced some new built forms, such as the *cozinha alentejana*, which plays an active role in reproducing traditional sentiments and behaviors. In the new houses, the modern kitchen no longer accommodates previously integrated functions of the hearth such as cooking, heating, eating and socializing, but fragments and recombines them with other activities. Rather than getting warm in the *chaminé* in the company of others, residents use an electric heater and watch television, alone or sometimes with others, in the *sala*. The desire to continue the combination of hearth functions in the *cozinha alentejana*, however, has institutionalized a new built form, an alternative to the modern kitchen. By way of contrast, previously fragmented and socially embarrassing toilet and bathing functions, which were relegated to the *quintal*, bedroom, kitchen or *dispensa*, have now been consolidated and brought inside to accommodate hygienic needs, encouraging the development of individual private behaviors.

Although Vila Brancans have certainly been intent on modernizing their houses and changing the way they live by acquiring new domestic forms, they have done it in their own way, adapting contemporary urban forms and creating a synthetic local version. Despite the intentions of designers and reformers throughout the twentieth century to program changes in behavior by encoding house forms with specific meanings, the residents of Vila Branca have interpreted these forms according to their own logic and selectively adapted them to local custom. While consolidating and sanitizing previously fragmented functions now found in the modern bathroom and bringing them into the house, and exiling the traditional hearth to the exterior, residents continue to place what is most polluting outside. This strategy may unintentionally diminish the importance of traditional family sociability, but it also brings with it a new measure of respectability. The bourgeois *sala*, because it was set apart, brought respectability to many local families; now exiling the dirty kitchen to the exterior in exchange for the bathroom makes the entire house respectable. And while it may seem that the creation of the *cozinha alentejana* is just a local adjustment, or form of resistance, to the modern suburban house, and will eventually disappear as families convert to more modern lifestyles, one note should be made. In recent years, the *cozinha alentejana* has made an appearance in the back yards of upper-middle-class professionals and middle-class suburbanites living in the nearby large city of Evora. These *cozinhas* seem to serve primarily men, who find them an escape from a home often dominated by women; but the kitchens do not support everyday cooking activities nor the full range of hearth activity. Rather, these *cozinhas* are used for ritual occasions – to smoke meats from an occasional pig killing – or to gather socially with friends on the weekends or in the evenings. The *cozinha alentejana* has achieved its own status as an institutional entity apart from, but referencing, its traditional and essential domestic functions, and has been reintroduced into modern suburban life from local rural communities.

Acknowledgements

The research presented in this chapter was sponsored in part by a grant from the Wenner-Gren Foundation for Anthropological Research. A slightly different version of the article is published in Portuguese as "Casas Suburbanas e Estilos de Vida Rurais no Sul de Portugal" in *Trabalhos de Antropologia e Etnologia*, Vol. 37 (3–4): 197–218. This work has benefited from the insightful and helpful comments of Donna Birdwell-Pheasant, Brian Juan O'Neill, and Francisco Ramos, whom the author wishes to thank. The author also wishes to acknowledge with deep gratitude the efforts of Cal Poly Pomona architecture student Dana Hendrix, who enthusiastically drew and redrew countless versions of the house plans illustrating this article.

References

Bourdieu, Pierre. 1977 [1972]. *Outline of a Theory of Practice*, transl. Richard Nice. Cambridge, UK: Cambridge University Press.

Cutileiro, Jose. 1971. *A Portuguese Rural Society*. Oxford: Clarendon Press.

Giddens, A. 1984. *The Constitution of Society: Outline of the Theory of Structuration*. Berkeley, CA: University of California Press.

Grumann, Carl. 1976. "The Concept of Appropriation (*aneignung*) and Modes of Appropriation." In *Proceedings of the Third International Architectural Psychology Conference at Louis Pasteur University (June 21–25, 1976)*, ed. Perla Korosec-Serfaty, pp. 113–25. Strasbourg, France.

Guerrand, Roger-Henri. 1990. "Private Spaces (Scenes and Places)." In *History of Private Life: From the Revolution to the Great War*, ed. Michele Perrot, transl. Arthur Goldhammer, pp. 359–450. Cambridge, MA: Harvard University Press.

Hareven, Tamara. 1991. "The Home and the Family in Historical Perspective." *Social Research* 58(1): 253–86.

Korosec-Serfaty, Perla. 1985. "Experience and the Use of the Dwelling." In *Home Environments*, ed. I. Altman and C. Werner, pp. 65–85. New York: Plenum.

Lawrence, Roderick. 1986. *Le Seuil Franchi*. Geneva, Switzerland: George Editeur, S.A.

Lofgren, Orvar. 1984. "The Sweetness of Home: Class Culture and Family Life in Sweden." *Ethnologia Europea* 14: 44–64.

Rybczynski, Witold. 1986. *A Short History of an Idea: Home*. New York: Viking.

Shorter, Edward. 1977. *The Making of the Modern Family*. New York: Basic Books.

−7−

Living Spaces in Transition:
From Rural to Urban Family Life in Serbia
Judith A. Rasson, Mirjana Stevanović and Vladimir Ilić

Introduction

Family formation processes have a material as well as a non-material aspect. Families create living spaces and adapt them to their needs, which change over time as the family develops and as the wider social context changes. They do this within the confines of available material resources, and within available cultural models for appropriate housing, living arrangements, and amenities. Houses are a compromise between family needs, resources and structures.

In every society, families and households interact with architectural forms. The family form and its place in the developmental cycle, subsistence needs, cultural influences and/or cultural requirements all affect architecture, but architecture affects them, too. Architectural influences on family size can include the type and amount of building materials available, family finances, the architectural construction skills of family members, the kind of skilled labor available, the availability of suitable building sites, and the regulation of housing by governmental authorities.

The built form is a compromise between cultural expectations and personal ideas people have about how housing should be and the resources available to construct it. In the case of Serbia (a republic of former Yugoslavia), social and legal regulation of housing, particularly in urban locales, has had a significant impact on compromises between family needs and wants and the opportunities for achieving them.

Many residents of Beograd (also spelled Belgrade), the capital of Serbia, live in government-owned apartment houses, following Serbian cultural habits inherited from their ancestral villages although they work in industrial settings. There are many factors that influence the way people live in city housing, including cultural expectations about the nature of a home and domestic activities; government regulations on apartment size and access to urban housing through social institutions or family finances; the physical setting – floor plan and dimensions of the apartment; and the internal dynamics of the family as a unit with a developmental cycle of its own. Our intention in this chapter is to discuss some changes in family uses of household space that affect and are affected by these factors. The patterns discussed here also have much in common with those in other cities in former Yugoslavia.

In the case described here, the most interesting feature is the adaptability of households in a society that changed from mainly subsistence farming to industrial production at the same time that it changed from capitalism to socialism/communism. The impact of both these changes, which were largely concurrent, was to reorient an entire society socially, politically, and economically. Despite these changes, not all old cultural behaviors were swept away. People retained many (perhaps most) cultural ideals and behaviors and applied them to new contingencies. Changes in the built environment mirrored new social situations and were met with new behaviors grounded in old cultural expectations.

Research Strategies

Addressing urban development in former Yugoslavia is difficult because the region is not well-represented in anthropological literature; Halpern (1963, 1965), Hammel (1969a,b) and Simić (1973, 1988) are virtually the only foreign authors who have addressed urban anthropological questions. Urban life has been the purview of sociology (Burić-Čuković 1968, for example); but a great deal of sociology in former Yugoslavia was devoted to Marxist theory rather than to field investigations.

Traditionally, anthropologists studying peasant society (Lockwood 1975; Halpern and Halpern 1972; Halpern 1958; Lodge 1941) concentrated on village life. Indigenous ethnologists and folklorists also concentrated on village life, focusing mainly on such themes as folk beliefs, rituals, and practices. Investigations of the built environment focused on the formal dimensions of architecture (Deroko 1964, 1968). Most of the information on questions surrounding the built environment comes from historic preservationists (for instance, Pavićević-Popović 1975; Nenadović 1975; Krunić 1980), limited by the nature of their discipline to historical structures that predate the urban growth spurt since the Second World War. The urban spatial aspect of the postwar rural–urban transition has been largely ignored, certainly since Simić's review of urban housing (1973: 94–107).

The research presented here is based partly on the life experiences of the authors.[1] Data in this paper were not collected in the field with the research goal in mind. Rather, we decided to evaluate housing and the domestic cycle retrospectively and in the literature through the theme of the symposium that formed the basis for this book. For the historical discussions of rural life we relied on published sources. For the discussions of recent times we assembled anecdotes and experiences from our friends and acquaintances as well as from our own lives. The data in our examples are weighted in favor of professionals of modest means, because these are the circles we move in. Neither the poorest nor the richest nor the politically best-connected sectors of society are well represented. We believe that the qualitative data presented here are representative of many people's experiences in Serbia and to a certain extent of those of people in other regions of former Yugoslavia.

Background

Serbia, located along the Danube south of Hungary and west of Romania and Bulgaria, is a patchwork of fields and forests that lie on rolling hills and mountains in an area of Continental climate. Serbia was home to agriculturalists as far back as 6000 BC; agriculture remained the most common occupation even as the region later came under the sway of the Romans and later still became a dukedom. The Turks added it to their empire in the fourteenth century, and it remained so until the nineteenth. It produced wheat and has been particularly famous for pork products. Agricultural pursuits occupied most inhabitants even when it became a monarchy. In 1941, the government fell to the Nazis. After the Second World War, a communist government came to power and agriculture began to be replaced by industrial production as the primary occupation of the inhabitants. This meant a rapid transition from a predominantly peasant society into a developing urban-industrial society (Trouton 1952; Halpern 1958).

The transition from rural to urban has been viewed mainly as a part of the modernization process (Burić 1976; Simić 1973; Hammel 1969a,b; Halpern 1963, 1965, 1967). Some change is attributable to influences outside the family, but influences also arise from within, and changes are complex and interact with each other and with the histories of individual families. External forces that have affected families and households are: the change from the family as production and consumption unit to mainly a consumption unit; the shift to a money economy; industrialization; and government policies. Internal changes include increased education, a shift in family decision-making processes, migration, fertility rates, and inheritance practices.

The larger social, economic, and political context of society impacted individuals, the family, and the household. Yanagisako found that, although external demographic and economic processes do affect domestic groups, such groups maintain some control over their affairs (1979: 166–75). She cautioned against seeking a single developmental trajectory through which all families pass, ignoring social variability and masking historical change. These are points well taken with regard to domestic groups in Serbia, where not every family was part of a joint or extended family and where some elements of household and family organization made the transition from rural to urban lifestyles. Modell and Hareven (1978: 245–69), adopting a life-course perspective, suggest that families and the individuals within them have choices about the timing of life transitional events such as splitting up a collective household. Hammel (1969a), in a study of social mobility associated with industrialization in the Beograd area, discovered that the timing of workforce entry was an important variable under family control, with important subsequent effect.

The transformation from the patriarchal family to a peasant–industrial family has been viewed by both Serbian and foreign scholars as an economic process. The traditional multi-generational *zadruga*-type family (discussed below) was transformed into smaller family units with only two generations living together. These families often moved to new areas or abroad, but still preserved some traditional forms in the economic activities of the family (Nikolić-Stojančević 1989).

The Spatial Transition from Rural to Urban Family Life

The spatial transition from rural to urban family life can be discussed by looking at three loosely defined residential social environments – villages, towns, and urban centers. An overlap can be seen between villages and towns, and some (although fewer) similarities between towns and cities. Villages have been characterized by a mix of older joint-family, open-plan houses and newer single-family dwellings. Towns were characterized by a predominance of single-family dwellings, but at present many towns also incorporate urban-style apartment buildings. Urban housing is characterized almost entirely by multi-story apartment blocks. The processes of adaptation within these three residential environments have been taking place over the last several decades. Some of the social processes correlate with changing spatial patterns within and between households.

In some instances the change in predominant housing type was gradual, but in some instances more abrupt. Gradual change is exemplified in the transition from the simplest dwellings with an open plan to houses with more rooms that can be closed off. The houses with more rooms became the predominant type of housing in towns, but were also constructed in villages, where they predominate today. More abrupt change in housing type occurred with movement from the village open-plan house and single-family dwelling to the multi-apartment building. This abrupt change profoundly affected inter- and intra-family/household relationships. The move to urban apartments had both intended and unintended effects.

The changes from a village-like or town-like type of housing to city multi-apartment buildings is not proposed as some sort of evolutionary sequence. All three house forms were in use at the same time. This continues to be the case, as both town-style and urban apartment-style dwellings are in use and new ones are being built. Only the simplest form of one-room structure has gone out of use in most places.

Rural Dwellings and the Zadruga

Historically, outside the urban areas many people lived in *zadruga*s,[2] a form of joint family, usually related in the male line, and a prominent feature of rural society. A *zadruga* is defined by Mosely as "a household composed of two or more biological or small-families, closely related by blood or adoption, owning its means of production communally, producing and consuming the means of its livelihood jointly, and regulating the control of its property, labor, and livelihood communally" (1976 [1940]: 19).

There are other terms for *zadruga*: *kuća* (house), *domaćinstvo* (household), *čeljad* (household or members). *Zadruga* literally means "cooperative." The term was first imposed by historians, ethnographers and folklorists, but later adopted by the peasants themselves (Stahl 1986: 51; Hammel 1968: 13). Also, the term *zadruga* was adopted for government farms after the Second World War, presumably to emphasize collectivity. In a comparative framework, a *zadruga* can be seen as "a family with a longer developmental cycle than the ordinary European family, a basic property-owning group among Yugoslav peasants" (Hammel 1968: 13). Traditional definitions emphasize kinship and co-residence; Filipović emphasized "economic cooperation in production and consumption" (M. Filipović in Hammel, Ehrich, R. Filipović, Halpern and Lord 1982: 1). Such communal families may date back to the twelfth century (M. Filipović in Hammel *et al.* 1982: 3) and many remained in operation well into the twentieth century.[3]

The rural-to-urban transition began earlier in Slovenia and Croatia, where Austro-Hungarian influence was stronger than in Serbia, where Turkish influence fostered different patterns. There were few urban centers in Serbia, and settlements tended to be isolated from lines of communication and transportation (Erlich 1966: 367–8). In Serbia, the real transition from rural to urban life started with Communist rule in the period after the Second World War.

Although some evidence suggests that the *zadruga* was not as ubiquitous as commonly has been believed (Hammel 1980), the *zadruga* is a powerful ideal image of a household that has been of interest to both indigenous and other ethnographers. Part of the fascination with this form of family probably arises from its flexibility, lending families the ability to adjust to changing political, economic, and social conditions over centuries. Some cultural and social elements of the *zadruga* family form even made the transition to urban-industrial life.

In Serbia, basic terminology provides a key to social organization. The word *kuća* – house (grammatically feminine) - does not signify a dwelling only, but is a term for an extended family in which two to three generations of *kućana* (house members) live together (Simić 1973: 46). Ethnographers used the folk category of *zadruga* (Hammel 1984: 29) and substituted the term "house" for household, ignoring the spatial dimension of the *zadruga*, i.e. the house itself. Houses were only analyzed as containers for families and households. Hence, the material and spatial correlations of the *zadruga* are not well documented. There are brief descriptions of the size and variability of the dwellings in some *zadruga*s (Halpern 1958: 98–9; Durham 1910: 284; Evans 1867), but there are no spatial analyses that stand alone or supplement other analyses. Even though houses figure significantly in the definition of the *zadruga*, the house itself has never been a primary focus of social scientific research.

The *zadruga* was a collective with strong continuity despite periodic fission. If interpersonal conflicts arose, a *zadruga* could split and new *zadruga*s or individual families could continue (Balikci 1965). The *zadruga* was an efficient agricultural unit, providing a flexible and effective workforce for subsistence and limited market production. Each *zadruga* as a corporate unit owned land, buildings, stock, and other property. The residential areas of several *zadruga*s formed a village or hamlet surrounded by outlying fields.

The aspects of *zadruga* organization important to this chapter are several, including large household size (both in terms of membership and space occupied) and the relative simplicity and openness of interior spaces, the organization of which afforded privacy for the family if not for the individual members of the family. Multiple sequential uses of space were determined by the time of day and season of the year. Labor was communal, organized by gender and age. Women cooked, washed, and looked after children, gardens, bees, and chickens. Each woman was responsible for clothing her own family, which meant spinning, weaving (looms were personal, not communal, property), knitting and sewing as time permitted. Men worked farther from the house, tending stock and laboring in orchards and fields. Women sometimes worked in the fields, too, mainly at haying and harvest times.

Many of these activities, in addition to the obvious farm chores, took place outdoors. Women could knit or spin in the door-yard or as they tended sheep, as well as in the house. Laundry and animal slaughtering were done outside. In summer, the wood-burning stove would often be moved to an outdoor kitchen (observed in 1969 in a village near Kragujevac), keeping the main house cooler and better accommodating big cauldrons of food that was being put by for winter. Each *zadruga* was largely self-sufficient economically and could exist by buying almost no subsistence items except sugar and coffee, which played an important role in hospitality rituals (M. K. Gilliland-Olsen, personal communication, 1993).

The architecture of a *zadruga* responded to the needs of agricultural production and storage, available building materials, terrain, and traditional local ideas of style (Findrik 1980; Nenadović 1975; Deroko 1964: 12). The men of a *zadruga* built simple structures for their family's use, while the construction of complex structures was done by the owners in conjunction with specialist contractors, as witnessed by inscriptions occasionally built into archways or basements.[4]

The main building of the *zadruga* was the home of the heads of the household – the father or senior male (*starešina*; *domaćin* is used for the male head of any household (Halpern and Halpern 1972: 147)) and the mother or wife of the senior man (*domaćica* (Lodge 1941: 319)). Halpern and Halpern noted that architecture was made to respond to flexible *zadruga* membership, emphasizing that "it is the kin unit which appears to have been the central dynamic, with focus on the nature of the household social structure as the primary variable, the dependent variables being the landholdings and physical homestead" (1972: 44).

Outbuildings were constructed as needed by the members of the *zadruga* and could be converted to different uses as needs changed. Each house lot was fenced and had a gate. The gateway (*kapija*) was sturdy, large enough for a farm wagon to pass through, often with gateposts of brick contrasting with the picket or paling fence around the household/farmyard area. Even the poorest holdings had a *kapija* marking the transition from public space to space controlled by the household. Houses were situated in a courtyard (*dvorišta*), rather than facing a street. The courtyard made it possible to use exterior space for some housekeeping tasks and helped to demarcate the family's private space.

An early depiction of a Slavonian *zadruga* composed of thirteen families (Evans 1867: 57) shows a group of structures enclosed by a fence of palings, opening onto an orchard and cornfield bordered by hedges. Outbuildings included a stable, a corn crib on stilts with wagon storage underneath, a pig sty, a distillery for plum brandy (*šljivovica*), a cow and goat shed, and a goose house. A well and a free-standing oven were also present. Two houses were located at the back of the enclosure – a "common dwelling house" and a "summer dwelling house." The summer dwelling was single-story, with a roofed porch running the entire length. The "common dwelling" was two stories, incorporating stairs to the second story at one end, with a roofed, arcaded porch running the length of the front. The first (ground) floor was divided into three spaces: a central kitchen with three open hearths, a "common hall" for dining, and a bedroom (with a bed) for the "house-father" (*domaćin*). The dining area and bedroom were furnished with stoves. The upper story was reserved for unheated bedrooms, each with a separate entrance onto the porch or narrow hallways (Evans 1867: 59). A loft above the bedrooms served as storage.

The large house described by Evans had the same elements as more modest homes. He noted that the three-room arrangement of the first (ground) floor was usual in "ruder cottages" of the region (Evans 1867: 59). The spatial arrangements of households showed consistency and longevity. Deroko's (1964: 23) simple houses have the same elements as Evans' large house (see Figure 7.1). In a single-room house, where all activities would necessarily have been compressed, the hearth was near the middle of the room, offset from two facing doors in opposite walls. In a two-room house, one room with a hearth and exterior door was called

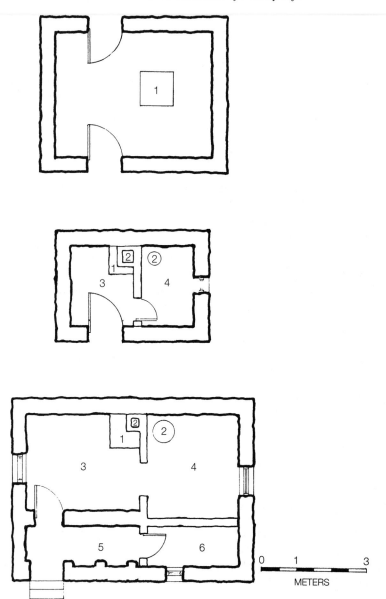

1. Hearth
2. Stove
3. House 'Kuća'
4. Room 'Soba'
5. Porch 'Trem'
6. Storage 'Ostava' or 'Klet'

Figure 7.1 Floorplans of simple houses (Redrawn by Chunni Tai from Deroko 1964).

"the house" (*kuća*); the adjacent room, with a stove, was called simply "room" (*soba*). A more elaborate two-room house added a porch (*trem*) and storage area (*ostava* or *klet*) along the front of the same two rooms.

Research in the 1930s documented continuity with earlier periods. The house was still built in a fenced yard that encompassed a garden, dwellings and out-buildings. The basis of the house was one or more rooms, often with a porch or veranda along one side. A passage sometimes separated the living room and kitchen from smaller storage or bedrooms. The kitchen was sometimes in a separate building, "perhaps merely in a shed," most often with a packed earth floor (Lodge 1941: 71). Although Lodge does not specify the season of use, it is likely that the separate kitchens may have been used most often in the summer.

In some regions, each married man and his family had a separate structure (*vajat* or *klet*) for sleeping and storing their personal possessions. In other areas each family had a room in the common structure, which was modified by additions, according to occasion and family finances (Lodge 1941: 59–60, 70–1, 90; see also Stahl 1986: 60, citing Laveleye 1886: Vol. 1: 129). The families' private rooms were unheated, "the only fire . . . [being] in the main room where food is prepared, where the heads of the group, and eventually the older people and younger aged children, sleep" (Stahl 1986: 60). This served as a symbolic statement that the united family had only one hearth. In a village in the Sandžak region in the 1930s, Lodge found that in the reorganization of a *zadruga* following the death of its old *domaćin*, "three new domains had each to be provided with a separate entrance for their different communal living-rooms and subsidiary rooms" (1941: 74).

In the 1930s, as earlier, some homes had open rafters in the rooms, but most had finished ceilings, which created a loft for storage or sleeping. Floors were commonly wood, except perhaps for the kitchen. Houses had walls plastered with mud, usually whitewashed inside and out. The whitewash was sometimes tinted, and some homeowners decorated walls of the main living room with stencilled patterns (Lodge 1941: 71). The houses in the nineteenth century and into the twentieth had small window openings, if any, often covered with paper rather than glass; such windows were not always made to open (Lodge 1941: 64, 71).

Rural dwellings contained little furniture, as it inhibited use of living space for multiple functions. Hearths were a raised platform, often placed away from walls, with a suspended chain and pothook to hold pots for cooking (see Halpern 1958: 106). Free-standing stoves replaced hearths, beginning in the nineteenth century (Lodge 1941: 71). Beds were rare, even into the twentieth century. Flat-woven woolen blankets or rugs (*ćilim*) were used as bed coverlets and on the floor for those without beds. Storage for clothes was provided earlier by wooden chests, later by armoires.

The Serbs are Orthodox Christians, but houses rarely had well-marked sacred areas, as was the custom among some Orthodox Christians in Romania.[5] In Serbian villages, some homes display a lithograph or icon of the family's patron saint in the corner of the main room. Before the Second World War, each room was blessed by the priest with holy water every year (Lodge 1941: 62). A lighted candle and icon or reproduction of the family saint's picture was displayed during the family *slava* (patron saint's day) celebration (Lodge 1941: 227–31).

Since *zadruga*s engaged in subsistence farming, foodstuffs had to be preserved and stored to last through the year. Thus, spaces dedicated to food processing and storage often were found in or near the kitchen and in a basement (*podrum*) or cellar (Lodge 1941: 70–4). A fruit spread, often made without sugar *(pekmez)*, pickled cucumbers and peppers, as well as sauerkraut (*kiseli kupus*) were for everyday subsistence. Sugared fruit preserves (*slatko)* were universally important for hospitality.

Kitchens provided multi-use space. Old people and children often slept there because it was warm. Visitors were entertained in the kitchen if no parlor was available. This was the case in south central Serbia near Kragujevac, and in Slavonia (part of Croatia, along the Sava River) (Gilliland-Olsen 1989). Out-buildings included sleeping rooms for sons and their families, sheds for storing tools and stalls for housing animals of various kinds, a corn crib, and special-purpose sheds such as those for making cheese. Stacks of hay and straw for animal feed and bedding and stacks of reeds used in construction were also inside the yard. Privies were rare as late as the 1930s (Lodge 1941: 59–60, 70–1, 90).

The relative wealth of the family as well as the number of members affected the sleeping arrangements. As noted above, sons and their wives might have bedrooms in the main house rather than in a separate structure. Among poor families at the turn of the twentieth century there was often only a kitchen/living room and one room for sleeping. In a Bosnian Serb family from the Bihać (Bosnia) area, an elderly woman informant reported that as a bride and young mother she slept in one room with her husband and children, her two brothers-in-law with wives and their children and her in-laws. She had eight children by the time she was twenty-seven (Gilliland-Olsen 1989). Rural life was not the bucolic existence that it is sometimes believed to have been. Under such circumstances it is no wonder that some people welcomed migration to the city (M. K. Gilliland-Olsen, personal communication, 1993).

Although many traditional subsistence patterns survived in villages, *zadruga*s were rare in the 1990s, especially since industrialization and urbanization after the Second World War. Major elements in their decline include population increase and consequent decrease in the availability of arable land; government policies on landholding and collectives; increasing production of cash crops; and an increasing reliance on a money economy, including a demand for industrially-produced products, especially textiles, farm machinery, and sewing machines. Although the *zadruga* in its strictest form did not transfer to urban areas, some traditional behaviors, attitudes, and values from rural lifestyles did survive the transition.

As noted above, not everyone lived in *zadruga*s even in the nineteenth century. For nuclear families that lived alone as a unit there was a slightly different use of space. The single-family detached dwelling was and is constructed in villages and towns to house single families or segments of former *zadruga*s. In towns it was and is the primary housing type after apartment blocks, because *zadruga*s are almost exclusively a rural phenomenon.

Town and City Dwellings

Single-family town dwellings housed fewer people than the number that formed a typical *zadruga*; there was a larger area per person inside the structure, there was more personal privacy, and the space allowed for communication with both residents and non-residents. Houses had a parlor for receiving neighbors and other non-family members, a kitchen, a storage room or closet (*špajz*), and one or more sleeping rooms (Figure 7.2). At the end of the twentieth century, most city dwellings had indoor plumbing, but even into the 1960s many town dwellings also had a privy in the yard (Lodge 1941: 90–1).

In towns, single-family dwellings are usually sited near the back of the lot, which is fenced, although the gate is not usually as elaborate as a rural *kapija*. The space in front of the house is used for a vegetable and flower garden. Town dwellings make use of fewer types of outbuildings, mainly those for storage or for chickens and occasionally pigs. A garage is a common addition in recent times.[6]

Urban development of cities like Beograd was under way by the turn of the twentieth century. By the 1930s, urban dwellers were living in apartments that were different from village housing. Figure 7.3 illustrates an apartment occupied in the 1930s by an engineer and his family.[7] The family's private rooms were segregated from more public spaces used for receiving guests or the large and semi-public kitchen area used by servants as well as by the family. There are two storage cupboards, one available to the household help in the kitchen and one controlled more closely in the private area by the housewife. Although this apartment was larger than postwar apartments, it is similar in that little space was devoted to hallways. This not only maximized the living space available in rooms, but also allowed easy communication between spaces.

Apartment dwelling was rare in Serbia until after the profound changes attending the end of the Second World War. Older apartments were divided to house more people, and ownership passed to the state. New apartment blocks were constructed for the working class and did not include such spaces as servants' quarters. They reflected the ideas of urban planners and social theoreticians more than the ideas of their occupants, many of whom were newly arrived from the villages.

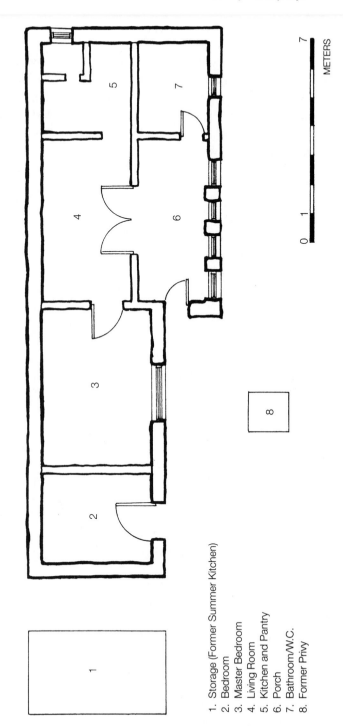

1. Storage (Former Summer Kitchen)
2. Bedroom
3. Master Bedroom
4. Living Room
5. Kitchen and Pantry
6. Porch
7. Bathroom/W.C.
8. Former Privy

Figure 7.2 Single-family dwelling in Smederevska Palanka, built between First and Second World Wars (Drawn by Chunni Tai).

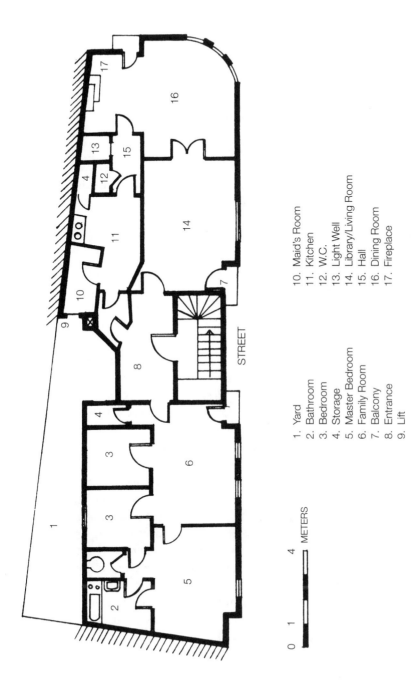

1. Yard
2. Bathroom
3. Bedroom
4. Storage
5. Master Bedroom
6. Family Room
7. Balcony
8. Entrance
9. Lift

10. Maid's Room
11. Kitchen
12. W.C.
13. Light Well
14. Library/Living Room
15. Hall
16. Dining Room
17. Fireplace

Figure 7.3 Floorplan of a Beograd apartment in the 1930s (Drawn by Chunni Tai).

Developments since the Second World War

In Serbia, many social, economic, and political changes occurred simultaneously after the Second World War, all touching individual households. Concomitant with political change came social and economic changes attendant on developing an industrial economy. A significant alteration of pre-war patterns was the growth of urban centers through migration from rural areas. Most migrants moved from villages, bringing with them traditional expectations about families, households, and housing. In the years since 1945, these families and their offspring have created new accommodations between rural and urban life patterns and between socialist and pre-socialist sociopolitical ideals. As in all situations of social change, some social and cultural elements changed while others maintained a stable connection to the past.

Urban growth after the Second World War meant a greater need for urban housing (Djurović 1966: 180–1). One of the avowed goals of the new government was to provide adequate housing. This goal went hand-in-hand with the goal of increasing industrialization and modernization, including urban growth. Other influences on behavior were institutionalized Marxist ideals of the equality of men and women, and the right of access to goods and services, including health care and education as well as housing.

Political leaders, seeking to reconstruct war-damaged industrial and commercial infrastructure, chose three development goals. The first was to create a proletariat through the urbanization of much of the peasantry, who were expected to oppose communism according to Marxist theory (Mladenović 1958, cited in Halpern 1967: 109–10). Peasant landowners were to be replaced with collective farms. A second intent of planned change was to satisfy the needs of the Partisans who had fought in the Second World War and who felt that they had the right to participate in the power structure of peace as they had in egalitarian communist war councils. A whole ideology of worker self-management arose from the attempt to reconcile management from the top with input from the bottom of the economic hierarchy (Djurović 1966: 124–39). A third goal of planned change was to create multi-ethnic populations in the cities by moving the population in from the villages (Djurović 1966: 238–9). Cities would ideally become microcosms of the ethnic mix of the country as a whole.

These goals of development, implemented by the federal government, were successful to a large extent, but entailed some unintended social changes. One such unintended consequence, which we examine here, was the continuation of *zadruga*-like family and household patterns at the same time that federal policy-makers were trying to direct social change toward patterns that they perceived as more modern.

In the immediate postwar years, the goal of urban construction was to provide adequate, no-frill housing, to create a modern material world fit to house a working Marxist state. Reinforced concrete, in use since the 1930s (Kojić 1979), was the construction material of choice. Urban planners and architects were heavily influenced by the theories of the International Congresses of Modern Architecture (CIAM), an urban planning forum of the 1930s. The doctrines of this group were influenced by the Swiss-French architect Le Corbusier and others such as the German Bauhaus group.

The style championed by these architects and planners was called the International Modern or International Style, and emphasized functionality and modernism and a break with previous architectural styles. It was supposed to be "serviceable, reliable, and cheap" (Gropius 1925–6 cited in Roth 1993: 10). International Modern style, however, has been shown to have its problems. "The most pervasive [fallacy] was that function in architecture was simple and therefore . . . easily analyzed . . . circulation as a primary social function of architecture was . . . undervalued" (Roth 1993: 481).

In Yugoslavia, a large percentage of everyone's salary went to the general building fund (*stambeni fond*). From that fund, flats were built; it was a revolving fund, so eventually everyone was supposed to get an apartment. Housing shortages, however, have been endemic, leading to the construction of entire suburbs like Karaburma, Banjica, Banovo Brdo, and Novi Beograd, made up of large blocks of flats.

Ownership of apartments was not vested in individuals privately (Arandjelović 1967). The apartment structure itself was owned and maintained (trash pick-up, steam heat boiler, roof, all public use areas, the elevator) by the "common building" (*društveni stan*) and managed collectively following self-management principles. Residents had a life-long lease as long as they continued to live there, and this lease was transferred to their children for as long as they lived there.

A person's place of work controlled apartments and maintained waiting lists for new places; the unemployed had no chance of an apartment. Many couples waiting for an apartment lived as tenants. Workers with seniority and families with children had priority. These two elements co-varied, as older workers tended to have both longer job tenure and children. A family could be on two lists if both partners worked, but once they got an apartment they had to give up their spot on the other list. Membership in the Communist party could also move a person up the list. The amount of floor space per family was regulated by law: a studio was for a single person or a couple, maybe even with children; a one- or two-bedroom flat was for a couple with children. A three-bedroom apartment was rare.

Because they were designed by planners and not by the residents themselves, new urban structures did not duplicate village houses or pre-war apartments. In the new apartment blocks, spatial aspects differed both from the traditional village/ *zadruga* dwelling and from the single-family dwelling of the town or village. New patterns in the use of space developed in apartment buildings as people adapted to new spaces.

The most apparent change in living conditions was the detachment of social life and daily activities from the natural ground level and their removal into an artificially-created elevated level. This made it difficult for residents to carry out a traditional mix of indoor and outdoor activities and inhibited social interaction. Private spaces for individuals became common. Communication was focused on family members, while communication with non-family members was restricted by architectural forms. The basic social unit was reduced to the nuclear family, separated from its traditional context and brought into relationships with neighbors assigned by chance. Communication with neighbors and other non-family members was re-established to a certain extent by establishing common gathering-places, sometimes marked by park benches, at ground level. People gathered in spaces in front of apartment houses to chat, play chess, do needlework, and so on.

Patterns in the use of space changed also because of the separation of home and workplace, but the use of space within the home contained a number of continuities with the past. Despite changes in subsistence patterns, including greater reliance on purchased than on home-grown food, patterns of food preparation and storage changed less than other work-related aspects of home life. A woman was still responsible for homemaking chores such as cooking, cleaning, and laundering, but to these responsibilities was added her new outside wage labor. Women's wages were pooled in the family income, allowing the family to buy consumer items. A state-sponsored study conducted in the late 1960s revealed that nearly every family had an iron, and many had a hot plate. Fewer had a heater or stove, and under 3 percent (of a sample of 206) had a vacuum cleaner or refrigerator. Only one family in the study had a washing machine (Burić-Čuković 1968: 74).

The same study also examined the changing relations between husband and wife, hoping to find that "the role of the working wife makes faster the process of transformation of the traditional family into the new, modern one," found instead that "a considerable number of working wives . . . perform domestic activities in the old-fashioned way, but have egalitarian relationships with their husband, i.e. enjoying their assistance, but all the time both of them think how it was better before" (Burić-Čuković 1968: 183).

Women held well-developed views on what constituted a well-furnished apartment (Burić-Čuković 1968: 69–70). A room, or apartment, was considered well-furnished if it was "complete," which meant that all items of furniture had to be present and that they had to match. Families furnished one "complete" room at a time, but often deferred purchases until they felt they had sufficient living space. A "complete" living room (also called a "combined room" (*kombinovana soba*)) contained a couch that made into a bed; an armoire for storing clothes, linens, books, and alcoholic beverages; a table with a crocheted tablecloth; chairs; and a table for the television or radio. Some later buildings, put up in the 1970s, had built-in closets, but they remain rare and are considered a luxury. An ideal "complete" bedroom was furnished with two beds with long silk pillows, two nightstands, a dressing table with full-length mirror, and two armoires or a double armoire. Furnishing a "complete" kitchen required a table, chairs and stools, a woodbox, and a *kredenza* (kitchen cupboard) with one glassed-in compartment (Burić-Čuković 1968: 69).

Essential to apartment life was the *špajz*, practically and symbolically the wife's domain. The *špajz* – a walk-in pantry – was often designed with an exterior vent to keep food cool and well-ventilated. Pantries served for all food storage until the 1960s, when small refrigerators with limited freezer space came into use. After the late 1970s, large freezers came into more general use and constituted a labor-saving device when freezing replaced the canning of foods. Through the 1960s, women canned fruit (*compot)*, made *pekmez, slatko, ajvar* (a chili-sauce-like relish), and *kiseli kupus*.[8] In practical and cultural terms, storing food for winter is still an important activity for women. In symbolic terms, the *špajz* represents a critical aspect of being a good housewife. Female identity and virtue were linked to providing the best, that is, the freshest, homemade, food for one's family (M. K. Gilliland-Olsen, personal communication, 1993).

In urban apartments, the most heavily used rooms were the living room and kitchen. The main room was the living room, which could also be a bedroom, but in that case it had to be transformed to a bedroom after all other daily functions were completed. In the absence of a parlor, formal guests were received in the living room. Socializing with friends was mostly transferred to the kitchen in older apartments. In apartments built in the early years after the Second World War, the kitchen and dining room were combined and fairly large. The elderly and/or young slept there, as they had in the village. It is possible, also, that postwar apartments had large kitchens as a continuation of pre-war urban patterns. Frequent guests liked to go to the kitchen to drink coffee and visit; it made them feel more like members of the family. By the early 1970s, kitchens were smaller and dining space was reduced. Later still, a dining area was reintroduced, but as a separate space from the kitchen. If an urban Serbian family maintains the custom of displaying a representation of the family patron saint, it is usually hung in the dining room.

Entryways and indoor toilets were largely urban innovations. Village houses might have porches, but the house door opened directly into a room, usually the kitchen. Urban apartments almost always had an entryway (*hodnik*), a small area just inside the apartment off the common hallway. From a practical standpoint, the entryway keeps dirt and snow from being tracked on carpets and provides a storage area for shoes, coats, and umbrellas. The entryway became a public space/ private space transitional zone into and out of the apartment, with the door to the rest of the apartment preserving family privacy. Apartments were built with indoor plumbing consisting of a toilet, a bathtub, and usually a sink. Generally, all these items were in the same room, although some apartments had a toilet cubicle separate from the sink and bathtub.

In urban life there was less space altogether, and especially scarce was outside space for messy jobs. Most apartments had a balcony, which provided a storage area for large objects like furniture. The balcony could be used to grow pots of flowers and greenery, to hang out laundry, and even to keep the *kiseli kupus* barrel. Some apartment blocks had a lockable storage area for each apartment in the basement. Balconies seemed underused as outside space, perhaps because they tended to accumulate grime from the street and droppings from birds, and were noisy.

In the village, periodicities of work were such that people spent much of their time outdoors. In the urban setting, most people worked indoors and spent less time outside. In an apartment there were some things that could only be done in the living room, such as watching television or reading. There were no outside chores such as would be performed on a farm, except perhaps looking after the family car. Many apartment blocks in areas such as Novi Beograd provided parking lots for the residents' cars; in older urban areas people were forced to park on the street or rent a garage.

The composition of the family remained much the same as in the rural household, especially in the first generation to move to the city. Often in the new urban dwellings, married sons lived with their parents. This was partly an old *zadruga/* village pattern and partly for new reasons (Gilliland-Olsen 1989). Economically, a family could save money by living together; newlyweds needed to save for a down payment on an apartment, furniture, and household goods, so it was cheaper to live with their parents for a while. Although the Yugoslav socialist system meant to provide housing for everyone, housing was not free. In the 1990s, new couples were more likely to want their own place sooner, but housing was still hard to find, especially in desirable areas close to the center of town.

It was not uncommon for a grandmother – especially the mother of the husband – to live with an urban family. Culturally, a man had a duty to his mother (Hammel 1967), especially when she was widowed. A grandmother could make a significant material contribution to the family by providing childcare, which was costly and hard to find. Also, she had company. "There is an especially warm relationship between grandparents and grandchildren, with much kissing, stroking, and verbal manifestation of affection. Often a child and grandparent share a bed, for warmth and security as well as for convenience" (Halpern and Halpern 1972: 89).

In a case from Beograd in the 1970s, the husband's mother lived with the family in a two-bedroom apartment (Figure 7.4). In this situation, the family arranged it so that the grandmother had one room and another room was furnished as a study for the parents, who were professionals. The study also served as a guest room.

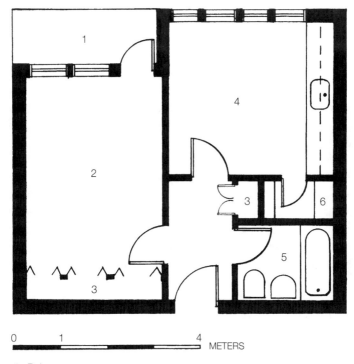

0   1   4 METERS

1. Balcony
2. Living Room/Bedroom
3. Closet
4. Dining Room/Kitchen
5. Bathroom
6. Storage

Figure 7.4 Floorplan of a Beograd apartment before remodeling (Drawn by Chunni Tai).

The parents and children all slept in the living room (male informant from Beograd, 1992).

In the first wave of urban migration, personal privacy was not regarded as a problem (except possibly by courting couples). To the contrary, the main cultural or social issue was the daily deprivation from social contacts through isolation in the urban apartment. People who used to expect to spend time together for coffee and conversation now watched television. For young people especially, going out (in same-sex groups) away from home helped avoid crowding, facilitated peer interaction, and provided social variety. More recent privacy concerns seem to be the result of a rising standard of living; young people have come to expect more personal privacy.

When a family reached maximum size in the developmental cycle, they were likely to split up because of crowding. Married children tried to get their own places, leaving their elders in the original apartment. In the past, older people did not often live alone. This was not always a matter of choice – although cultural beliefs emphasized family life – but rather a product of the shortage of apartments. In the villages, private space for the elderly was not provided and furnished no precedent. Parents who helped their children get their own apartments could end up alone. If an apartment was held by a widow or widower, one child (and his/her spouse, perhaps) stayed in residence, or a renter came, often a family from the householder's village of origin.

There were laws against holding an apartment without living in it. The way to deal with this problem was to trade. Families could consolidate several small apartments and trade for one larger, or vice versa (divorced people, too). Apartment trading was a type of accommodation to socialist, not free market, rules of housing. The trade was based on a number of factors, not all easily quantifiable, including floor space, location, quality of the flat, and possibly the exposure. Not all families followed the same path toward altering and/or expanding their living space. Some families saved up money to buy land and build a new house, often as an upstairs/downstairs duplex. It could then be used as a rental unit or for married children, in a persistence of older patterns.

Sometimes, instead of moving, people modified their living spaces rather than merely re-arranging them. In apartments with post-and-beam construction the concrete columns, beams, and slab floors bear the weight of the structure, and there was freedom to move interior walls. With shortages of space, most remodeling was aimed at trying to expand, although the net effect of rearranging the interior was to sacrifice storage space. A common apartment alteration was to enclose the balcony, making it part of the interior space. If the balcony was off the kitchen, as it commonly was, combining the spaces could yield a kitchen–dining area. Or else a large kitchen with a dining room could be remodeled to a small kitchen and a bedroom for a child or a grandparent (see Figure 7.5).

In a new pattern that developed in the mid-1980s, middle-aged people bought small parcels of land where they could raise a garden and freeze the produce.[9] Besides a garden plot, often there was enough land to build a weekend house (*vikendica*) as well.

A cultural pattern of migrants has been to maintain ties to the village, which had social importance because of the significance of family. The ties were also of economic importance because of access to resources, especially food. Sharing food also creates an important social bond, seen in rituals such as *slava* feasts. Relations between urban and village residents were not a one-way exploitation of village resources. Urban relatives provided a place to stay if family members had business in the city. Students going to technical schools or the university could find lodging with relatives. The relationship was and is a two-way conduit for goods and services as well as affective ties.

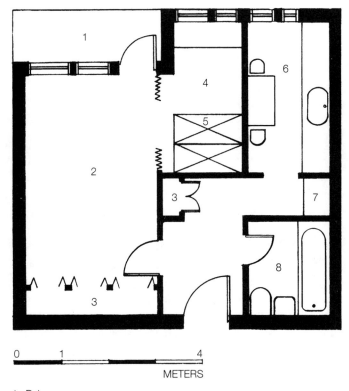

1. Balcony
2. Living Room
3. Closet
4. Study
5. Bed
6. Kitchen/Dining Room
7. Washing Machine
8. Bathroom

Figure 7.5 Floorplan of a Beograd apartment after remodeling (Drawn by Chunni Tai).

The traditional *slava* (family saint's name-day) ritual now plays a new role among the Serbs. In the past, it was the day to celebrate the memory of the family ancestors. Nowadays it is more like a family reunion, an opportunity for the entire family to get together. Family members return from all over the region where they have gone to find work or for other reasons. Thus the old role of the *slava*, the religious–magical communication of the living with dead ancestors, has faded and been replaced by communication among the living. The *slava* has become the symbol of kin-ties, drawing the larger family together with more strength than family surnames, which have traditionally been prone to changes for purposes of taxation and other administrative reasons, and thus are not strong enough as a family or kin symbol (Nikolić-Stojančević 1989). The *slava* survives among immigrant families even in the United States (Simić and Blank 1989).

Conclusions

The *zadruga*-type household has transformed over time in Serbia by splitting up into smaller units. The result of this was the formation of extended households that consisted of parents living together with their married children and sometimes with their married grandchildren (Šabanović 1982; Bojanić 1986: 131–2). The trend toward the gradual break-up of *zadruga*s would probably have continued into the era after the Second World War were it not for the introduction of communist ideology. The volume and speed of the transition from rural-agrarian or market-town lifestyles to urban-industrial lifestyles was greatly accelerated.

The economic and social survival of an individual in the past required attachment to a bigger household unit. Communist ideology in Serbia for the last fifty years embraced the modernization of society, urbanization, industrialization and the formation of a working class, as well as minimization of the power and responsibility of the peasants as a potential anti-communist force. The goal of governmental policies seems to have been to embed the individual in the state rather than in his/her family. Households accommodated to some influences while maintaining many earlier beliefs and behaviors. A larger number of people than were planned for (up to three generations) ended up living together in urban apartments. This was partly because the number of available apartments continually lagged behind the number of eligible families, but was also due to the persistence of cultural values of providing housing for elderly parents or married children.

Migrants who moved from village homes to city apartments tended to create their own functional spaces within the built environment. Part of the adjustment to an urban situation was accomplished through assigning spaces to suit the family composition. This might mean using the living room for sleeping, providing a sleeping space in the kitchen or rearranging the bedrooms so that opposite-sex children would not have to sleep in the same room. Personal privacy was reduced from that originally planned by designers because of the functions assigned to different rooms.

Flexibility in the use of space was achieved by movable furniture. Diurnal/nocturnal differences in the use of spaces for different functions, such as using the living room or kitchen for different purposes during the day and at night, also contributed to flexibility in fitting the family to the space available. Table 7.1 summarizes the most important changes discussed in this chapter.

The consequences of family cultural accommodations to apartment building "ideology" were unintended. People strove to preserve some of the traditional

Table 7.1 Domestic Space Before and After Urbanization in Serbia

The organization of domestic space before and after urbanization:

BEFORE:	AFTER:
• Few enclosed spaces in the house.	• More compartmentalization of domestic space.
• Kitchen and living room in the same space.	• Kitchen separate with no dining area.
• Guest room used only for celebrations.	• Living room used for celebrations.
• Few rooms for sleeping only.	• Bedrooms strictly separate.
• Free-standing out-buildings for food preparation/storage.	• Pantry (for storage only) incorporated in apartment.

The impacts of changes in the organization of domestic space:

BEFORE:	AFTER:
• Little division of public and private space.	• Public and private spaces separated.
• Age/sex division of space.	• Individualism in use of space.
• High level of sociability.	• Sociability reduced.

social values associated with the use of domestic space at the same time that they coped with the highly structured legal constraints governing urban housing in Serbia and former Yugoslavia.

Acknowledgements

The authors would like to thank Donna Birdwell-Pheasant and Denise Lawrence-Zúñiga, organizers of the symposium "Houses: Material Dimensions of the Family in Europe" for allowing us to participate, and for their helpful comments while we prepared for this volume. We would also like to thank Mary Kay Gilliland-Olsen for her detailed comments. Greg Guldin, Bisenija and Adrian Kisovec, Andre Simić, and Predrag Stevanović provided advice and support.

Notes

1. Stevanović and Ilić lived much of their lives in Beograd and are familiar with the housing situation as participants. Both are from families that lived in *zadruga*s. Stevanović's great-grandmother was born into an 80-member *zadruga*; she married into a family where the brothers lived as separate households, but with more than two generations living together; her sons lived the same way; her grandson and Stevanović's father moved into the same apartment building in Beograd after the Second World War. Ilić's father grew up in a *zadruga* in eastern Serbia. Rasson worked in former Yugoslavia

frequently from 1968 to 1982. All of the authors have spent time in villages and towns as well as the large cities, which lends some comparative depth to the picture.

2. Pronunciation of Serbo-Croatian places the stress near the front of the word. Vowels are pronounced similarly to those of French or Spanish; consonants are similar to those in English with some exceptions: c sounds like the ts in cats; g is hard, as in the first letter of garage; j sounds like y in you; the lj consonant cluster sounds like the li in million; the nj consonant cluster sounds like the ny in canyon; r is somewhat like a trilled r in Spanish. Some letters that do not occur in English are: č and ć, pronounced like the first and last ch of church, respectively; dj pronounced like the j in just; dž pronounced somewhat like an emphatic j in jam; š pronounced like the sh in shoe; and ž pronounced like the s in treasure. Although Serbo-Croatian is a tonal language, the tones are not indicated in the orthography.

3. Among Balkan populations, the social organization and customary law of the Slavs were studied extensively in the nineteenth century. Although not uniquely Serbian or Yugoslav or even Slavic, the *zadruga* type of household was heavily researched in Serbia during the first half of the twentieth century. The household or zadruga has continued to be an object of particular ethnographic inquiry (Stahl 1986; Hammel and Laslett 1974; Hammel 1984; Djordjević 1984; Hammel *et al.* 1982; Cvijić 1987 [1921–2]).

4. In the vicinity of Čačak (central Serbia) in the nineteenth century, a homeowner installed one plaque that read: "Stevan Stojanović made this house with his endeavors, 1874" and installed another that commemorated the contractor (*majstor*) "Cost 80 ducats, the *majstor* was Milenko Stojanović." After the turn of the century, another homeowner in the Čačak area inscribed: "Dimitrije Belić himself and his sons built this house, March 20, 1921. *Majstor*: Muntimir Stojanović" (Stojanović is a common surname) (Pavičević-Popović 1975: 266).

5. In older Romanian homes, sacred and profane spaces in the main room were demarcated by a ceiling beam. A table, usually with an icon, was placed in a corner of the sacred area, although icons could also be used elsewhere in the house (Joel Marrant, personal communication 1995; Dăncuş 1986: 133).

6. Observed in Smederevska Palanka, Serbia.

7. The floorplan was drawn from memory in 1993 by his daughter.

8. They still make *ajvar* and *kiseli kupus*, but they are more likely now to buy jam and much more likely to buy canned fruit. *Slatko* is important to hospitality because of the custom of offering guests a spoonful of preserved fruit as a prelude to coffee. Young urban professionals are less likely to follow the custom of offering *slatko*, but other urban dwellers may do it, especially if they can get *slatko* made by a grandmother. It is still a common village practice to offer *slatko* to guests.

9. This is probably more common around small cities than around Beograd itself. This behavior pattern seems to be a response to both inflation and uncertainties about food supplies. For the informants observed in this activity, it drew on knowledge carried from village life. Another side of this behavior, not talked about so much, is its restfulness; people do it to get away, but they don't have to raise food for a living.

References

Arandjelović, Svetislav T. 1967. *Štambena Svojina u Jugoslaviji* [Residential Property in Yugoslavia]. Belgrade: Centar za Istraživanje Društvenih Odnosa, Institut Društvenih Nauka.

Balikci, Asen. 1965. "Quarrels in a Balkan Village." *American Anthropologist* 67: 1456–69.

Bojanić, D. 1986. "Krupanj i Radjevina u XVII i XVIII veku [Krupanj and Radjevina in the Seventeenth and Eighteenth Centuries]." In *Radjevina u Prošlosti* [Radjevina in the Past], ed. D. Bojanić. Belgrade.

Burić, Olivera. 1976. "The Zadruga and the Contemporary Family in Yugoslavia." In *The Zadruga: Essays by Philip E. Mosely and Essays in His Honor*, ed. Robert F. Byrnes, pp. 117–38. Notre Dame, IN: University of Notre Dame Press.

Burić-Čuković, Olivera. 1968. *Promene u Porodičnom životu Nastale pod Uticajem ženine Zaposlenosti* [Changes in Family Life Brought About by Women's Employment]. Belgrade: Centar za Istraživanje Društvenih Odnosa, Institut Društvenih Nauka [French.]

Cvijić, J. 1987 [1921–22]. *Antropogeografski Spisi* [Writings on Human Geography]. Belgrade: Serbian Academy of Sciences and Arts.

Dăncuş, Mihai. 1986. *Zona Etnografica, Maramure*. Bucharest: Editura Sport-Turism.

Deroko, Aleksandar. 1964. *Narodna Arhitektura*, Vol. 2. *Folklorna Arhitektura u Jugoslaviji* [Folk Architecture in Yugoslavia]. Belgrade: University of Belgrade.

——. 1968. *Narodno Neimarstvo* [Folk Architecture], Spomenik 118. Belgrade: Serbian Academy of Sciences.

Djordjević. 1984. *Naš Narodni život* [Our Folk Life]. Belgrade: Prosveta.

Djurović, Tihomir Dragoljub (ed.). 1966. *Yugoslavia, 1941–1965*. Belgrade: Mladost.

Durham, Edith. 1910. *High Albania and Its Customs in 1908*. London: Royal Anthropological Institute.

Erlich, Vera St. 1966. *Family in Transition: A Study of 300 Yugoslav Villages*. Princeton, NJ: Princeton University Press.

Evans, Arthur. 1867. *Bosnia and Herzegovina on Foot*. London: Longmans, Green and Company.

Findrik, Ranko. 1980. "Prilozi Poznavanju Krovnih Pokrivaće od Drvene Gradje u Našem Narodnom Graditeljstvu [Contributions Toward Recognizing Wooden Roof Coverings in our Folk Construction Methods]." *Raška Baština* 2: 215–31. Kraljevo, Yugoslavia: Zavod Za Zaštitu Spomenika Cultura.

Gilliland-Olsen, Mary Kay. 1989. "Authority and Conflict in Slavonian Households: The Effect of Social Environment on Intra-household Processes." In *The Household Economy: Reconsidering the Domestic Mode of Production*, ed. Richard R. Wilk, pp. 149–69. Boulder, CO: Westview Press.

Gropius, Walter. 1925–26. "Where Artists and Technicians Meet." *Die Form (New Series)* 1: 117–20.

Halpern, Joel M. 1958. *A Serbian Village*. New York: Columbia University Press.

——. 1963. "Yugoslav Peasant Society in Transition – Stability in Change." *Anthropological Quarterly* 36: 156–82.

——. 1965. "Peasant Culture and Urbanization." *Human Organization* 24: 162–74.

——. 1967. "The Process of Modernization as Reflected in Yugoslav Peasant Biographies." In *Essays in Balkan Ethnology*, Kroeber Anthropological Society, pp. 109–26. Berkeley, CA: University of California Press.

——, and Barbara Kerewsky Halpern. 1972. *A Serbian Village in Historical Perspective*. New York: Holt, Rinehart and Winston.

Hammel, Eugene. 1967. "The Jewish Mother in Serbia or *les structures alimentaires de la parenté*." In *Essays in Balkan Ethnology*, Kroeber Anthropological Society, Special Publication No. 1, pp. 55–62. Berkeley, CA: University of California Press.

——. 1968. *Alternative Social Structures and Ritual Relations in the Balkans*. Englewood Cliffs, NJ: Prentice-Hall.

——. 1969a. "Economic Change, Social Mobility, and Kinship in Serbia." *Southwestern Journal of Anthropology* 125: 188–97.

——. 1969b. *The Pink Yo-yo*, Institute of International Studies, Research Series. Berkeley, CA: University of California.

——. 1980. "Sensitivity Analysis of Household Structure in Medieval Serbian Censuses." *Historical Methods* 13: 105–18.

——. 1984. "On the *** of Investigating Household Form and Function." In *Households: Comparative and Historical Studies of the Domestic Group*, ed. R. Netting, R. Wilk, and E. Arnould, pp. 29–43. Berkeley, CA: University of California Press.

——, Robert Ehrich, R. Fabijanić-Filipović, Joel Halpern, and Albert Lord, (eds). 1982. *Among the People: Native Yugoslav Ethnology. Selected Writing of Milenko S. Filipović*. Ann Arbor, MI: University of Michigan Press.

——, and Peter Laslett. 1974. "Comparing Household Structure Over Time and Between Cultures." *Comparative Studies in Society and History* 16: 73–109.

Kojić, Branislav. 1979. *Društveni Uslovi Razvitka Arhitektonske Struke u Beogradu*

1920–1940 [Social Conditions for the Development of the Architecture Profession in Beograd, 1920–1940]. Posebna Izdanja 516, Odelenje Društvenih Nauka. Belgrade: Serbian Academy of Sciences and Arts, Social Science Section.

Krunić, Jovan. 1980. "O Poreklu i Razvoju Tipa Gradske Kuće Centralnog Balkana u XIX Veku [On the Origin and Development of the Central Balkan Town House in the Nineteenth Century]." *Raška Baština* 2: 203–14. Kraljevo, Yugoslavia: Zavod za Zaštitu Spomeniku Kulture. [French.]

Laveleye, Emile de. 1886. *La Péninsule Des Balkans*. Paris.

Lockwood, William. 1975. *European Moslems: Economy and Ethnicity in Western Bosnia*. New York: Academic Press.

Lodge, Olive. 1941. *Peasant Life in Jugoslavia*. London: Seeley, Service, and Co.

Mladenović, Tanasije. 1958. "The Soil and the Peasant." *Jugoslavia (Belgrade)* 15: 134–41.

Modell, John, and Tamara K. Hareven. 1978. "Transitions: Patterns of Timing." In *Transitions: The Family and the Life Course in Historical Perspective*, ed. Tamara K. Hareven, pp. 245–69. New York: Academic Press.

Mosely, Philip E. 1976 [1940]. "The Peasant Family: The Zadruga, or Communal Joint-family in the Balkans, and Its Recent Evolution." In *The Zadruga: Essays by Philip E. Mosley and Essays in His Honor*, ed. Robert F. Byrnes, pp. 19–30. Notre Dame, IN: University of Notre Dame Press.

Nenadović, Slobodan. 1975. "Seoska Arhitektura Koja Nestaje: Zabileške iz Sela Grača [Disappearing Village Architecture: Notes from the Village of Grača]." *Raška Baština* 1: 213–28. Kraljevo, Yugoslavia: Zavod za Zastitu Spomenika Kulture. [French.]

Nikolić-Stojančević, V. 1989. Porodica u Sistemu Tradicionalnih i Savremenih Ustanova u Društveno-Običajnom Životu Radjevaca. [*The Family in the System of Traditional and Modern Institutions Regarding the Social Customs of the People of Radjevac*]. Belgrade: Ethnographic Institute, Serbian Academy of Sciences and Arts.

Pavićević-Popović, Radmila. 1975. "Natpisi na Seoskim Kućama u Okolini Čačka i Gornjeg Milanovca [Inscriptions on Village Houses in the Region of Čačak and Gornji Milanovac]." *Raška Baština* 1: 263–7. Kraljevo, Yugoslavia: Zavod za Zaštitu Spomenika Kulture. [French.]

Roth, Leland M. 1993. *Understanding Architecture: Its Elements, History and Meaning*. New York: Harper Collins (Icon Editions).

Simić, Andre. 1973. *Peasant-urbanites: A Study of Rural–Urban Mobility in Serbia*. New York: Seminar Press.

——. 1988. "Bogdan's Story: The Adaptation of a Rural Family to Yugoslavian Urban Life." In *Urban Life: Readings in Urban Anthropology*, ed. George

Gmelch and Walter P. Zenner, pp. 189–98. Prospect Heights, IL: Waveland Press.

——, and Les Blank. 1989. *Živeli: Medicine for the Heart*. [Film.] Berkeley, CA: Flower Films.

Stahl, P. H. 1986. *Household, Village and Village Confederation in Southeastern Europe*, East European Monographs. New York: Columbia University Press.

Šabanović, H. 1982. *Bosanski Pašaluk*. Sarajevo, Yugoslavia.

Trouton, Ruth. 1952. *Peasant Renaissance in Yugoslavia, 1900–1950*. London: Routledge and Kegan Paul.

Yanagisako, S. J. 1979. "Family and Household: The Analysis of Domestic Groups." *Annual Review of Anthropology* 8: 161–205.

8

Use of House and Space: Public and Private Family Interaction on Chios, Greece
Alice V. James and *Loukas Kalisperis*

Four generations of women in a Greek family sit on the front step and up an exterior staircase discussing the house they inhabit together and their intertwined lives. Later they will invite me into their formal parlor (*saloni*) to drink coffee, and much later, into the kitchen. Talk in families often turns to the house, and their comments reflect the centrality of the house in everyday lives:

> My house will be my great-granddaughter's when I die. Of course, my daughter and her husband will have the right to use it as long as they live, but to avoid the taxes I will leave it to my great-granddaughter. The upstairs [a separate apartment] was part of the dowry of my granddaughter. She lives there now with her family. My children and their children were born in this house, and I will die here (Artemis).

The importance of the house and house life for Greek families has been noted by many students of modern Greek culture over the last thirty years. No ethnography of Greece is complete without a description of local house forms, simply because the house itself is so central to family life. Activities of primary social and economic importance are centered on the household. The ordering of house life defines important dimensions of life in general, especially along the critical continuum of public life/private life.

Friedl (1962) discusses the different areas of the house (kitchen, *saloni*, terrace) and the importance of obvious expenditure of women's time and energy in giving the house the appearance of cleanliness and order. Du Boulay (1974) points out the synonymous and interchangeable nature of the terms for "house" and "family." In the mountain village where she studied, co-residence in a house, even more than closeness of kinship, determined solidarity. This loyalty was particularly important in that before 1950 most houses in that village consisted of only one room, shared by people and animals, and it was impossible to keep secrets from co-residents. Recently, an additional room, a *saloni*, had been added to many houses in the village for the formal entertainment of visitors. Du Boulay reports that the house is seen as more than a place to sleep and eat; it is a sanctuary from the outside world (1974: 38). Hirschon (1981, 1985) has particularly detailed descriptions of the physical setting and uses of the interior and exterior of houses in an urban area near Athens, and also deals with issues of territoriality as they relate to the home (Hirschon and Gold 1982). As she points out (1978: 80), women of virtue are described as being "of the house," while immoral women are "of the road." Dubisch (1986) also discusses the distinction between the inside of the family dwelling and the outside, and points out that women can be viewed as the controllers of pollution that may potentially enter the house. Women prevent the contamination of the outside world from entering the house through their alteration of natural products. Dubisch discusses the courtyard (*avli*) as an important area for boundary maintenance.

In another study, Pavlides and Hesser (1989) report on the ritual use of the house on Lesbos. Not only do houses always include an *eikonostasi*, a place for sacred Orthodox icons; they often also include objects placed in the house and courtyard against the evil eye. Rituals are performed at the household entrance to mark "the threshold between the sanctuary of the home and the dangers of the external world" (1989: 276). The ritual use of the house distinguishes it from the profane outside space.

Recently, Pavlides and Sutton (1995) edited a volume on form and process in Greek architecture. Of particular interest in our analysis of house and space in Chios is Pavlides' (1995) study of the expression of social stratification, religion, allegiance to the Greek state, and support for political parties through house form and decoration. Residents in the villages he studied were able to interpret social and cultural information embedded in the architectural environment. Pavlides shows how the family house embodies membership in a cohesive community.

Greek language has made a distinction between public and private (*demios* vs. *idios*) at least since Homer, with women traditionally occupying the private space of the house. In *Politics*, Aristotle mentions officials whose duty it was to supervise wealthy women and children, keeping them within the confines of the family property and out of the streets. Aristotle asks, "How is it possible to prevent the wives of the poor from going out of doors?" (cited in Moore 1984: 135). Obviously, it was not possible, as poor women had to work outside the home. Xenophon stated that it was wives who took care of indoor tasks (Moore 1984: 136). In fifth-century BC Athens, women were not permitted to enter the *agora*, the central public gathering place of the city (Franck and Paxon 1989). Descriptions of the domestic realm of women continue up to the current day (see, among others, Danforth 1982 for description of restrictions on bereaved women, and articles in Loizos and Papataxiarchis 1991; Herzfeld 1991; Sutton, this volume, Chapter 3).

The anthropological literature on Greece has often analyzed the concept of the house as the private space of the family – especially of women – versus the public space of strangers. This public/private formulation has been useful in discussing Greek society; however, household space is best understood as a continuum of use. There is a gradual transition from completely public (the street fronting the house) to very private (sleeping areas). Use of house space in Greek society is complex and multidimensional, reflecting as it does the social relations within the family and of the family with others. In this chapter, we will examine the house as a set of thresholds that express social meaning in terms of materiality or even of void space. As Chambers and Low (1989) aptly point out, houses have meanings that transcend their physical boundaries.

The House on Chios

The four women sitting and talking on the front stairs live in a small fishing village, and although they must work hard in order to earn a living, they were willing to spend many hours discussing their lives and families. The village is on the island of Chios in the eastern Aegean, the locale of this investigation into the relationship between the architecture of the house and the meanings with which the use of space along the interior/exterior continuum is imbued by Greek families.

House Form: Internal Life

The traditional architecture of Chios reveals that it has long been exposed to foreign influences through invasion and occupation, as well as through commerce and intellectual contacts (Smith 1962; Tyrwhitt 1966). While Byzantine occupation is not much in evidence in the traditional house architecture, one of the finest examples of Byzantine monastic architecture can be found on Chios at Nea Moni. The Genoese period (mid-fourteenth to mid-sixteenth centuries) is more in evidence; many stone towers and some walled villages remain from this time. Great prosperity came to the island with Ottoman rule, which began in 1566. An island agricultural product, mastic (a resin used for flavoring food and for varnish), was highly valued by the Turks, and the island had special protection both as a mastic and citrus production center and as a center for the transshipment of goods in the eastern Aegean. This prosperity had an impact on both rural and urban architecture. Large houses remain from this period, although architectural form does not reflect the almost four centuries of Ottoman occupation to any large extent; the only remnants are a defunct mosque in the capital and a few overhanging alcoves, typical of Turkish architecture.

Prosperity ended with the Massacre of Chios in 1822. In retribution for an uprising supporting the Greek Independence Movement against the Ottoman Empire, 25,000 Chians were killed, 5,000 were enslaved, and most of the remainder of the original population of 120,000 scattered as refugees. Although many refugees later returned and the island was liberated in 1912, the population has only reached one-half of its previous size and has not regained its former wealth.

As has been described for other areas of Greece, the kitchen is the center of household activity (see especially "Culture Enters through the Kitchen," Dubisch 1986, for a description of the importance of food preparation). On Chios the kitchen is not only a place for preparing food (which actually often takes place outdoors), but is also the center of activity in the house, the spatial heart of the family, the locus of its interaction. Traditionally, as his wife finishes preparing the evening meal, the husband will sit in the kitchen to talk over family matters and catch up on local affairs. A wife will usually be more knowledgeable about these topics, as she has had more time during the day to talk to the children and neighbors. Close family friends are also allowed to sit in the kitchen or in an informal area open to the kitchen, signifying their privileged relationship with the family. Older houses on Chios sometimes do not have a separate room for the kitchen. In these older houses the kitchen area occupies one wall of a larger main room (see Figure 8.1). But even if, as in these cases, no physical divider exists between the kitchen area and a more formal sitting area, in the empty circulation space an unmarked threshold is present that creates the "other side," serving as the in-between space; only the family and close friends may sit in the kitchen area.

More divisive than empty space, but not as prohibitive as walls, physical entities such as tables or dividers may create an implicit kitchen threshold with visual separation. A larger house will have a separate kitchen, but it will serve many other purposes besides cooking, which on Chios is a lengthy and open activity. Food preparation is not confined to the kitchen unless the facilities needed are only available there. Snapping beans, cleaning fish, and other tasks are often carried out in the area in front of the house – on the front steps in the case of Artemis, the great-grandmother mentioned earlier. In that family, the great-grandmother controls the kitchen by cooking the family meals and also by sleeping there. She sleeps in the kitchen, which is warm in the winter, in order to avoid sharing a bedroom with her married daughter (see Pavlides and Hesser 1986, among others, on the multiple use of rooms). By her position, she exerts influence on the family activities. The day begins when she gets up to make coffee, and activity stops when she goes to bed. When she expresses a desire to sleep, everyone must leave the kitchen.

Although women (Artemis and her daughter Smaragda included) publicly defer to men (in this case the daughter's husband, as Artemis' husband is dead), their relationship is, in reality, more complex. Men and women in the family are mutually dependent on each other. Of course, idiosyncratic differences between families exist, but in general the power is shared between the sexes, with age being the most important determining factor. In Artemis' family, Smaragda's husband, Antonis, fishes and sells fish to provide income for the family. Artemis and Smaragda farm to provide produce for the house and care for their mastic trees, the gum of which is sold. Antonis turns his money over to his wife to run the household, and does not question how it is spent. Artemis' granddaughter, Theano,

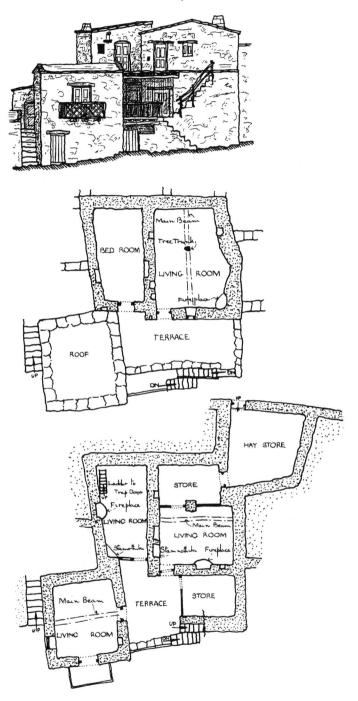

Figure 8.1 Typical older Chian house with no separate kitchen area. Source: Smith 1962.

and her husband, a schoolteacher, live in a separate apartment upstairs and are somewhat independent, although Artemis and Smaragda often care for Theano's daughter when Theano must be away from home. The oldest woman in the household cares for the *eikonostasi*, the religious center of the house (cf. Pavlides and Hesser 1989). The notion of separate bedrooms for each child does not exist in most Chian families, especially the more traditional ones with many children. Children do not take their friends into the bedroom area to play; rather they spend time in the kitchen area or in part of the house open to the kitchen. More usually, they play outside. Often the house is too small for children to play with their friends inside, as with one family with sixteen children that lives in a four-room house.

Adult visitors to the house can be entertained in the kitchen, but only if they are relatives or intimate friends. Revered guests will always be placed in the *saloni*. Chian *salonia* are similar to those found in other parts of Greece (for a detailed description of *salonia* in Piraeus, see Hirschon 1981). How far visitors are allowed to penetrate the house indicates their social standing with the family. Outsiders are not invited into the kitchen area. Even in houses on Chios with one large main room with the kitchen along one wall, outsiders are led to a corner away from the kitchen area. Chians prefer to have a formal area, separated from the family living area by walls and doors, in which to entertain guests and strangers. Even if the separation cannot physically exist, a significant invisible threshold of empty space creates the symbolic separation.

The back area of the house is very private. Adult visitors are invited into a bedroom only on the occasion of "dressing the bed," a celebration that involves the making of the marital bed and throwing money on it the Friday night before the wedding. Another very private area in some Chian houses is an exterior space opening off the kitchen, used as an extension of the kitchen. Laundry may be hung here (as well as on the roof), and other private household tasks are carried out in this area. Some Chian houses, especially in the area of mastic-producing medieval walled villages, *Mastichochoria*, have an area open to the outside on the second floor of the house. Most of the houses in the walled villages have ground-floor stables in the house, because all available land inside the walls has been built upon, and in the past it was unsafe to leave the animals outside the walls. There is often room for storage of hay and agricultural produce on the ground floor as well. Living quarters for the family are one floor up. For defensive purposes, no house exceeds two stories in height, and for the same reason there is access to other houses via the flat roof and connecting vaults (see Figure 8.2).

House and Street: Threshold Behavior

Houses address the street in a dynamic rather than a static manner. To reflect its attitude towards visitors, the family will change the appearance of the house.

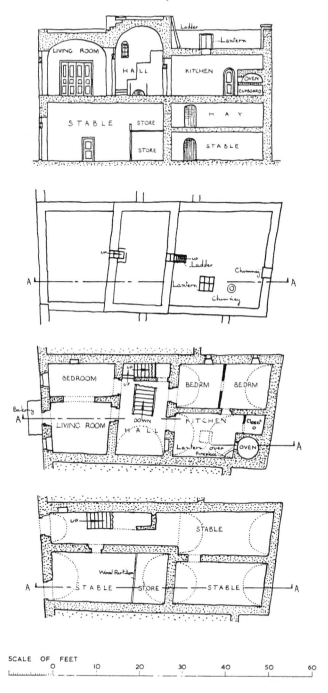

Figure 8.2 Floor plan of a typical house of the Mastichochoria area with ground-floor stables. Source: Smith 1962.

Shutters on windows, which function as protection from the elements, are also indicators of the degree of openness of the family. Closed or almost closed shutters suggest that the family does not wish to be disturbed. Only by prearrangement would a guest disturb such a house. Open shutters (and windows, weather permitting) indicate passively that the family is available for social visits. If the occupants of the house position themselves on the *avli* (fenced courtyard), passers-by understand that the family is actively seeking social interaction. Normally, the *avli* is separated from the street by steps, a wall with a gate, or both. The gate is a symbolic marker; its physical position – open or closed – indicates whether passers-by are welcome to enter. Even if the gate is open, visitors will usually wait to be invited before entering the *avli*. If there is no gate, steps can act as a threshold. People pause at the steps or lean across the wall without entering, signifying they mean to stop only for a short while. If visitors come up the steps or through the gate and enter the *avli*, they may be invited to sit down.

That the entrance to the *avli* provides a symbolically important threshold rather than a functional barrier can be seen by the fact that most gates cannot be locked. They are not used to secure the house. Many times the step into the *avli* is not necessary to facilitate movement. It is a weak physical manifestation of a strong social meaning and, as such, symbolizes the social interaction between the house and the street. Walls that separate the Greek house from the street are not as massive as those seen in Moslem architecture, in which the walls actually protect the house physically and create an internal domain within which open space is very privately simulated by a courtyard. The Greek walls that separate the house from the street are short and often ornamented with ironwork to create a show of separation. On Chios, high walls actually create true separation in only one area – in Kampos, a very wealthy citrus-growing area, where aristocratic families wish to separate themselves from casual social interaction with passers-by. A survey of the Kampos area reveals the differences in house form that make explicit the manner in which the residents view the outside world; the threshold between exterior and interior is a functional barrier – gates can be locked and high walls prevent intrusion, even visual intrusion (see Figure 8.3).

Settlement in the Kampos area dates back at least to the Genoese era (fourteenth century), when wealthy families began building large fortified houses and planting groves of lemon, tangerine, and bitter orange trees. Later, during the Ottoman Empire (eighteenth century), the area flourished; the elite of the island built large expensive villas. Often the original Genoese buildings were modified, and it is possible to see where the rough, early stonework has been incorporated into the later luxurious red sandstone and marble villas.

A majority of these villas were abandoned after the Massacre of 1822. But some families returned, and many of the estates have been subdivided among the descendants. Since the Second World War, Chians who became wealthy from

Figure 8.3 High walls and gate typical of the Kampos area (Photo credit Alice James).

establishing shipping lines have bought estates in Kampos, and it continues to be the residential area of choice for the very wealthy. The settlement area is five kilometers long and two kilometers wide, with an intricate mesh of narrow streets. High stone walls split property into private groves. One side of each house lines the road; however, houses are oriented inward, and access to the house is not directly from the road, but rather up a monumental stairway from a large flagstone courtyard. Access to the courtyard from the road is through a large gateway in the high stone wall enclosing the property. The design of the house and gate heightens the prestige of the family and serves the functional needs of outdoor life. The open-air courtyard always has a well and a cistern, as well as a large trellis with vines to provide a shady seating area. The height of the house (two or three stories) allows a view over the expanse of orange groves (see Figure 8.4). The physical existence of high walls abutting the street does not necessarily in itself disrupt the interior/exterior continuum.

A close look at house styles in another area of Chios in which walls directly abut the street reveals that it is behavior, not form, that creates a continuum, rather than a sharp division, from interior to exterior. In the Mastichochoria (the area of walled mastic villages), high stone walls directly adjoin the street. However, in this area people actively extend the house into the street to encourage socializing. Hirschon (1985) has described how women in an urban setting near Piraeus, the port of Athens, mark an area exterior to their houses with whitewash in order

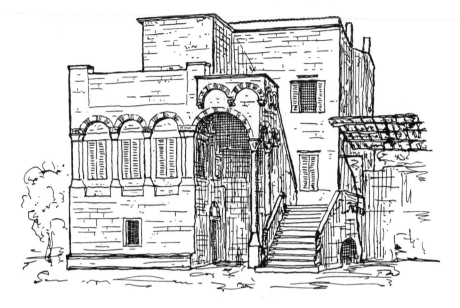

Figure 8.4 A large house of the Kampos area of Chios. Source: Smith 1962.

to indicate a street area under the domain of that house. While Chians in the Mastichochoria do not use whitewash, they do consider the area of the street directly exterior to their house as their own.

Within the usual *avli* is the veranda – the actual sitting place – one step further along the continuum of entry into the private area than the space just inside the *avli* wall. Once visitors are sitting on the veranda, they will be offered something to drink. Usually this offer will be of coffee, a soft drink, beer, or wine, but if the family is poor, the offer may be only cold water. If visitors accept a drink, they are indicating their intention to remain for a lengthy visit.

Villages in the Mastichochoria have very limited space owing to the heavy fortifications. In these villages families create the functional equivalent of the *avli* and veranda on the street. In front of their ground-floor stables, they set chairs near the house. By bringing items of indoor furniture to the outside, the domestic area is extended into the public arena (see Figure 8.5). As Hirschon so aptly states, "The house enters the street" (1993: 83). The surrounding street thus becomes an *avli*. Passers-by proceed through exactly the same social process as described before. They walk by and see how open the house is; if the homeowners are about, visitors pause at a distance, cross the unmarked "threshold" into the *avli* area, and talk; if invited, then visitors may sit down and accept a drink if they wish to linger. If at this point a visitor is invited inside "to talk privately," the invitation would indicate an even greater intimacy with the family, unless of course the visitor were taken into the *saloni*, indicating the status of honored guest.

Figure 8.5 The house enters the street in the Mastichochoria – the street becomes an *avli* (Photo credit Alice James).

Hirschon (1993) has described a similar situation in the poor urban area built in 1928 for refugees from Asia Minor just north of Piraeus where she carried out her research. These inhabitants also treated the street as the *avli*. Although its history is very different from that of the medieval walled villages on Chios, which were reputedly founded just after the Trojan war, this refugee area shares with these Chian villages a severe circumscription of territory.

From Streets to Public Life

People treat the street outside their houses as an extension of the house and view "their street" as an extension of the household's exterior area. Streets provide a series of connections to other houses in the village, the *plateia* or promenade, and ultimately, to the outside world (Figure 8.6). The *plateia* or promenade is the center of village social interaction. Friends and neighbors meet in these open public spaces. In the inland villages, built in a circular settlement pattern, a central square forms the *plateia*. Maritime villages have a shoreline promenade, rather than a *plateia*, as their central meeting area. *Plateies* and promenades have open areas for walking, cafes, and at least one *kafeneio*, where women are not allowed. In the *kafeneio*, men drink coffee, ouzo, or beer, play *tavli* or cards, and discuss politics. Women on Chios do not have the same severe restrictions on their movements as Hirschon (1993) and Pavlides and Hesser (1986) describe for other areas of Greece (Figure 8.7). However, while women may meet their friends while passing through the *plateia* on their way to and from shopping or gardening, they may not sit at the *kafeneio*.

The *plateia* provides connections to many different roads – to work, to fields, to friends, to stores. It is the hub, a focal point for transportation. During the day the *plateia* has an informal character, but at night it becomes a more formal space. In fact, it is the most formal space a family can use to entertain visitors, as well as the most public. Just as a stranger would be entertained in the formal area of the house, a stranger would be also entertained in a *taverna* or cafe in the *plateia*. Chians view the *plateia* as an extension of the formal space in their house. To be taken to the *plateia* and entertained there indicates the social status of the guest; it is a sign of respect.

Chians approach friends seated at a cafe or *taverna* in the *plateia* in a manner very similar to that described for approaching the *avli*. People promenade in the evening in the *plateia* to meet friends at a time slightly later than that for sitting and talking on the *avli*. Men socialize in the *plateia* or promenade in the evening at a less formal level than women, especially at the *kafeneio*. The presence of women among the group signifies that a family is present. At least one *kafeneio* is always set aside as a males-only meeting place for men to pass time. On Chios, this *kafeneio* is usually off to the side, adjacent to the *plateia*, but not central to it.

The amount of time and space a family devotes to public socializing depends on the wealth of the family in particular and the village in general. In Artemis' village, Kataraktis, most people are poor. Kataraktis has no dock, and the promenade has few restaurants, cafes, or *kafeneia*. A small village, its economy depends mostly on fishing and gardening. Only a few men are highly paid captains or skilled sailors. The promenade is rarely busy, and few villagers bring chairs outside to sit and socialize in the evening. A group of older men sit at the *kafeneio*, and a

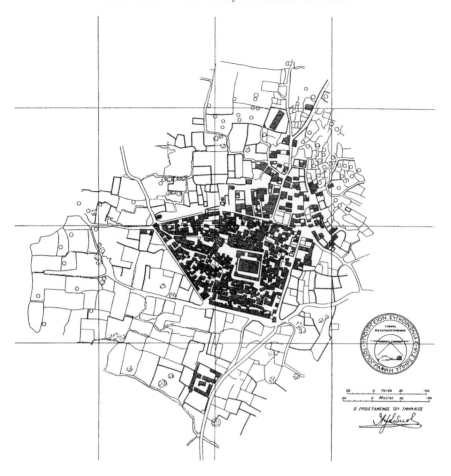

Figure 8.6 Plan of a walled medieval village with a central *platia.* Source: Smith 1962.

few older women sit in groups at the side of the street, doing hand work, not just socializing. People may also meet their friends and exchange the news of the day at the local grocery store, but in this poor village, where people say, "We merely survive," very little of the evening is spent in conversation and promenade. Although this village is not circumscribed, few houses have a large outside social area for entertainment. Artemis uses the small space of her front steps and an exterior flight of stairs for seating visitors. Only the few wealthiest families have verandas where people can sit outside to enjoy the evening. In this village, social-izing begins late and lasts only a short while. Often the people will exchange a few words with their friends as they visit the small local store in the evening to make a quick purchase. They do not have ground-floor stables and, thus, the front of the house on the street would seem to be more appealing; but people do not sit

Figure 8.7 A central *platia* with an older woman walking through the *kafeneion* area (Photo credit Alice James).

in chairs in front of their houses. If a village is wealthy, like the Mastichochoria village discussed earlier, families have more time to socialize in the evening and so create the spaces to do so, even where no obvious space exists. In villages that have both household wealth and adequate open spaces, *avles* and verandas can be found. In wealthy villages that are circumscribed by fortifications, the street *avles* are created by social behavior.

Conclusions

People modify their environment to suit their social needs, but in Chios most people occupy a house that existed before their birth, and alteration is expensive and difficult. In the Mastichochoria region, villages are built entirely of stone, each house abutting the others in a continuous line, surrounded entirely by a double-thick wall that is the exterior of the outside houses. Barrel vaults across the two-to three-meter-wide streets connect houses on opposite sides of the street. The central *plateia* has the only open ground remaining inside the village. In these walled villages, even wealthy families cannot build onto their house – there is no land. People create an implied *avli* by occupying and entertaining on the street.

In less constricted areas, such as Artemis' village, wealthy people with time to sit out in the evening sometimes do permanently transform their physical environment by building a veranda and a corresponding *avli*. Other families may expand the house they have inherited by adding another story (as a separate apartment) for the dowry of a daughter. In both cases the families have not accepted the house "as is" and simply dwelt there, but rather have appropriated the house and made it their own, by actively changing it. Chian houses are not only physical loci, but also symbolic constructs with social meaning. The house is maintained as a part of the flow from the past to the future, and is transformed in the process.

Acknowledgements

The research described here was funded by NSF grant No. BNS-9103886.

References

Chambers, Erve, and Setha M. Low. 1989. "Introduction." In *Housing, Culture and Design: A Comparative Perspective*, ed. Setha M. Low and Erve Chambers pp. 3–9. Philadelphia, PA: University of Pennsylvania Press.

Danforth, Loring. 1982. *Death Rituals of Rural Greece*. Princeton: Princeton University Press.

Dubisch, Jill. 1986. "Culture Enters Through the Kitchen: Women, Food, and Social Boundaries in Rural Greece." In *Gender and Power in Rural Greece*, ed. Jill Dubisch, pp. 195–214. Princeton, NJ: Princeton University Press.

du Boulay, Juliet. 1974. *Portrait of a Greek Mountain Village*. Oxford: Clarendon Press.

Franck, Karen A., and Lynn Paxon. 1989. "Women and Urban Public Space." In *Public Places and Spaces*, ed. I. Altman and E. H. Zube, pp. 121–46. New York: Plenum Press.

Friedl, Ernestine. 1962. *Vasilika: A Village in Modern Greece*. New York: Holt, Rinehart and Winston.

Herzfeld, Michael. 1991. "Silence, Submission, and Subversion: Toward a Poetics of Womanhood." In *Contested Identities: Gender and Kinship in Modern Greece*, ed. P. Loizos and E. Papataxiarchis, pp. 79–87. Princeton, NJ: Princeton University Press.

Hirschon, Renée. 1978. "Open Body, Closed Space: The Transformation of Female Sexuality." In *Defining Females: The Nature of Women in Society*, ed. Shirley Ardener. London: Croom Helm.

——. 1981. "Essential Objects and the Sacred: Interior and Exterior Space in an Urban Greek Locale." In *Women and Space: Ground Rules and Social Maps*, ed. Shirley Ardener pp. 72–88. London: Croom Helm.

——. 1985. "The Woman–Environment Relationship: Greek Cultural Values in an Urban Community." *Ekistics* 52: 15–21.

——. 1993. "Open Body/Closed Space: The Transformation of Female Sexuality." In *Defining Females: The Nature of Women in Society*, (2nd edn), ed. Shirley Ardener pp. 51–72. Oxford: Berg.

Hirschon, Renée, and J. R. Gold. 1982. "Territoriality and the Home Environment in a Greek Urban Community." *Anthropological Quarterly* 55(2): 63–73.

Loizos, Peter, and Evthymios Papataxiarchis (eds). 1991. *Contested Identities: Gender and Kinship in Modern Greece*. Princeton, NJ: Princeton University Press.

Moore, Barrington. 1984. *Privacy: Studies in Social and Cultural History*. Armonk, NY: M. E. Sharpe.

Pavlides, Eleftherios. 1995. "The Expression of Institutional Meaning in Greek Domestic Architecture." In *Constructed Meaning: Form and Process in Greek Architecture*, Modern Greek Studies Yearbook, ed. Eleftherios Pavlides and Susan Buck Sutton pp. 345–88. Minneapolis, MN: University of Minnesota.

——, and Jana E. Hesser. 1986. "Women's Roles and House Form and Decoration in Eressos, Greece." In *Gender and Power in Rural Greece*, ed. Jill Dubisch, pp. 68–96. Princeton, NJ: Princeton University Press.

——, and ——. 1989. "Vernacular Architecture as an Expression of Its Social Context in Eressos, Greece." In *Housing, Culture and Design: A Comparative Perspective*, ed. Setha M. Low and Erve Chambers, pp. 357–74. Philadelphia, PA: University of Pennsylvania Press.

——, and Susan Buck Sutton (eds). 1995. *Constructed Meaning: Form and Process in Greek Architecture*, Modern Greek Studies Yearbook. Minneapolis, MN: University of Minnesota.

Smith, Alfred C. 1962. *The Architecture of Chios*. London: A. Tiranti.

Tyrwhitt, J. 1966. "Order Out of Chios." *The Architectural Review* 139(832): 475–8.

Part III:
House and Symbol –
The Power of Constructions

−9−

Re-entering the West Room:
On the Power of Domestic Spaces
Lawrence J. Taylor

In the rural west of Ireland, Arensberg and Kimball found that every farm house was possessed of a *west room* . . .

> behind the hearth in the kitchen . . . [where] all the objects of sentimental value . . . are always kept: the religious pictures, the ceremonial objects brought in by the bride at marriage, and the bric-a-brac associated with the past members of the household. Where there is only one couple in the house, this room is reserved as a sort of parlor into which none but distinguished visitors are admitted. The family heirlooms are there, and, lining the walls along with religious pictures, there appear the photographs of the members of the family, especially the familiar daguerreo-types of the last century. Whatever 'fine' pieces of furniture there may be, such as highboys, cabinets, brass candlesticks, are kept there, as are all the religious objects used when mass is celebrated in the house. All these objects are inalienable in the sense that the family parts with them only when it must. They descend from father to son with the house and the farm on which it stands (1940: 129).

Arensberg and Kimball's *Family and Community in Rural Ireland* is most often remembered as a paradigmatic functionalist account of the small farmers of County Clare, in the West of Ireland. However, in a manner unusual for that genre and period, they allowed an intriguingly important role for domestic spaces. In particular, the west room in the small farmer's cottage was not, by their account, only a backdrop, nor even simply a repository of valued objects, but a room that played a crucial role in the drama of domestic life at the moment when the household social system reproduced itself.

Though but a small portion of their text, Arensberg and Kimball's discussion of the west room sticks in our collective memory not only as an exercise in functionalist explanation, but also as a vivid detail in their portrait of rural Irish domesticity. The space, objects, and social drama of the west room serve to reinforce the centrality of household and "stem" family – for the inhabitants and for the readers. The room itself embodies structure and authority and brings these forces to aid in the process of social reproduction.

But consider the following passage, from Frank O'Connor's novel - also published in 1940 – *Dutch Interior*:

> The rain had come in under the back door and there were some rags there to sop it up. The lamp was lowered, the fire covered, the clocks ticked loudly and he sweated profusely as he untied his laces; and for some reason the dim, airless kitchen, its walls crowded with pictures, the noisy clocks, the ornaments, the bolted doors, his mother's whispers, all combined to give him the feeling that he had been shut off from life and was being physically suffocated, and it seemed to him that murderers must feel like this before they were driven to a crime; a claustrophobia which only violence could shatter. (O'Connor 1940: 99)

Here we have the dark side of domesticity, where the meaning of social and cultural constraint seems to owe more to Freud than to Durkheim. Patricide is here – as elsewhere in Irish literature – a lurking possibility, and in fact symbolically realized in the subsequent pages of the novel.

On the one hand, the novelist and the anthropologists seem to agree not only on the particular force of domesticity in Irish culture, but on the actual power of rooms. Both accounts raise the possibility that domestic spaces may be more than tableaux for the expression of cultural values, that some rooms have transformative power, of the sort we commonly associate with rites of passage. On the other hand, the respective authors reach very different conclusions about the precise character of the rooms they examine, and the psychological dynamic through which such power is exercised. In Arensberg and Kimball, the retiring Irish couple are materially aided in their role transition by the locus and objects that define their new dwelling space. There is at least the appearance of great stability. O'Connor's novel, furthermore, portrays not only the life cycle of a number of individuals, but also, if more subtly, the historical changes in the definition of class and the criteria of membership. In this realm too, rooms have a special power, but O'Connor's characters are more self-conscious, insecure, and/or troubled about the role of such places and things in the process of self-definition.

Are we dealing with a difference between literature and ethnography, authors' perspectives, or the rooms themselves – and hence their respective formations?

This speculative and exploratory essay was provoked by the consonance and dissonance of these two versions of Irish domesticity, as well as my own fieldwork experience in that country over two decades. The limited agreement of anthropologist and novelist suggests a consideration of the general proposition that rooms have power – as both a cultural and a theoretical belief. That task requires a reflexive intellectual and cultural history that examines the roots of our assumptions about the power of rooms and objects, and some attention to the divergence of literature and ethnography as modes of exploring and representing culture. On the other hand, the specific contrast between Arensberg and Kimball's and O'Connor's rooms suggests an empirical question about rooms in 1930s Ireland. Here too, a historical approach may be necessary – one that notes the role of rooms in cultural change as well as in cultural reproduction. Any features of the dynamic identified in the Irish context, however, may well prove relevant outside that island.

Rooms, Objects, and Power

The world of advertising clearly operates on the assumption that consumers believe that their selves are both expressed and formed through domestic spaces (as well as through their clothing and cars). Anthropology, however, has only recently explored this perspective. Thus Lawrence and Low posit the questions, among others: "How does society produce forms and the forms reproduce society? What roles do history and social institutions play in generating the built environment? What is the relationship between space and power?" (1990: 455). Amid this new flurry of interest in such questions (spurred at least in part by the character of postmodern architecture and discourse – and the influence of Foucault) it is perhaps worth asking why, despite Arensberg and Kimball's intriguing if brief glimpse, there was (and perhaps still is) so much truth in Amos Rapoport's complaint that "ethnographers have generally written relatively little about the built environment although they have probably observed much" (1976: 13)? I would say that the same is true for the "assembled environment," by which I refer to the objects with which domestic spaces are furnished or decorated.

In seeking the roots of this inattention, I am led to an important strain of the general dialectic in Western thought concerning the power of the built and assembled environment, which took its most obvious shape within a religious context. The rise of Catholicism as a system of belief and an institution through the Middle Ages was – on one level – based on the belief in (and hence reality of) the power of settings and things, from relics to cathedrals. This is particularly clear through the history of pilgrimage, beginning with the visits to saints' graves (see Brown 1981) and, later on, in the development – for example – of the series of Romanesque cathedrals, such as Vézelay in France, through which pilgrims passed on their way to Santiago de Compostela. There was a self-conscious notion of the power of ecclesiastical architecture not just to express devotion and faith, but to structure it. So too with the myriad religious objects – from relics and their containers, to the countless two- and three-dimensional images of holy personages and events.

All such images were instructional, but also understood to be powerful in their own right, exercising a direct effect on those who stood in faith before them. Even reactions to the abundance and richness of such architecture and objects – whether returns to simplicity or virulent iconoclasm – implicitly acknowledged the power of that which they rejected. This consciousness is evident, for example, in the Cistercian reaction to Cluny: the resulting stark simplicity of the "built environment" of Fontenay was meant to impose an order and a sort of reflection on those who dwelt within. This dialectic continued through the ensuing centuries and became a central issue in the Protestant Reformation.

That Reformation (itself of course devised from subversive strands of Catholic thought), in its more radical forms, not only devalued ritual but, concomitantly, a belief in the transformative power of settings and objects. Further, this disenchantment of the material seemed to accentuate the power of reasoned discourse. Yet, as with earlier, Catholic, reactions, one wonders whether the rejection of the material was not also, in some measure, an acknowledgement of its power. Certainly, the self-conscious creators of the starkly simple hoped that a division of space and decoration would construct a social and psychological world. This is patently the case in the ecclesiastical architecture of many churches and sects, for example the Quakers, Baptists, or Presbyterians, but went further, extending into the mundane domestic environment with such groups as the Shakers, Amish, or Moravians. I have lived in Bethlehem, Pennsylvania, a Moravian town in which the shape, function, and spatial relations of buildings erected to house the mid-eighteenth-century colony were believed to play an absolutely vital role in shaping comportment, social relations, and values. As in monastic settlements like Fontenay, the belief of the inmates that this was so perhaps had the character of a self-fulfilling prophecy. At least it would take an uncommonly inattentive or resistant individual to miss the builders' intentions and to disregard the *regulation* that the buildings were meant to impose.

Secular enlightenment philosophy, developing from these Protestant roots that stressed empowered discourse, sought rational models for understanding and sometimes utilizing the ways in which the built environment – along with external stimuli generally – acted upon the individual. Hume (1962) and Hartley (1775), for example, were among the early authors of theories of "association" that specified a connection between individual mental process and the surrounding material world (see Abrams 1953). Certainly the rational/discourse model of architecture was taken furthest by the French architect Ledoux, whose royal salt works village in France amounts to an enlightenment monastery, and whose unrealized models – barrel-shaped barrel factories and so on – were rather extreme expressions of a developing philosophy of architectural power: *l'architecture parlante* (Ledoux 1983).

In the guise of what is now seen as "British early Romanticism" – in many ways a subtle shift rather than a radical departure from existing sensibilities – the same period (first half of the eighteenth century) also saw the development of a number of more popular theories that assumed that the built environment in particular not only provided the general framework for a sense of self, but actually manipulated that consciousness through "associations": ". . . the associational and the picturesque. Both were developed by theorists of the eighteenth century [Romantic Revival]. A building is clothed in the garb of a special style, because of the meditations which that style will rouse" (Pevsner 1968: 352).

This associational quality was mainly attributed to "important" architecture – ecclesiastical and other public buildings, and the homes and gardens of the very wealthy. In such contexts, the viewer was supposed to undergo a directed series of associations, a triggering of memory – or, as we might now add, a *construction* or *invention* of memory. But all this was understood to work mainly on the cognitive and conscious level. Over the ensuing decades, notions of the power of architecture followed the general shifts in the Romantic era toward an emphasis on the role of the emotions or *feelings*, rather than *ideas*, and drifted toward a notion of the unconscious. Memories and associations were, in this model, "evoked."[1] In this way, Romantics like Coleridge gendered their epistemology, following the stock opposition of "male instruction" versus "female influence." It was a pervasive discourse, which, on the popular level, was increasingly concerned with the domestic.

> By the 1830s, discussions of domesticity and society also were infused with a second strain of deterministic thought that assigned to the house's physical setting and details the power to shape human character. Fully articulated by the 1830s, this 'domestic environmentalism' conflated moral guidance with the actual appearance and physical layout of the house and its contents (Grier 1988: 5).

This developing "theory" or world view was also particularly associated with the newly expanding and increasingly culturally dominant "middling classes" – themselves the experiencers of transition. Thus, while aristocrats probably did not think that the bourgeois could or should be transformed by entering their domestic spaces (more likely, they were to be put or kept in their place by the experience of disconnection), the middle class salon or parlor was typically expected to domesticate and civilize two sorts of savage: children and members of the working classes. Beyond the domestic, architecture in general was given a conscious role in both "improving" and controlling – once again, a gendered opposition. In private spaces, the role of such new rooms as the parlor (like the woman who presided over it) was to influence through the expression of an attractive world of values and decorum into which the initiate would be drawn and transformed. In public space, the role of such decidedly masculine structures as Egyptian revival prisons was to enclose and restrain, and of their symbols to distance and frighten.

Grier (1988) has provided a particularly penetrating and precise view of the ways in which this cultural formation operated in the United States, where the focus was emphatically domestic. That is, the particular "built environment" that was given the task of producing and reproducing the culture was the middle-class parlor – which always existed in implicit opposition to its opposite, the working-class hovel and/or barroom. Just as the properly accoutred middle-class parlor was meant to "civilize" both children and the working class, so too would improper working-class domestic environments – where dirt and disorder reigned – encourage uncivilized social behavior. Accordingly, reformists wished to build the former and dismantle the latter. Thus, in addition to what Norbert Elias (1978, 1982) called the "Civilizing Process" (inherent in the building of new rooms), we have a "Civilizing Offensive" (Verrips 1987), which amounts to a cultural attack of one class on another, in this case via their domestic spaces. Not coincidentally, "environmentalism" as one aspect of this self-conscious plan of social control and transformation went along with the temperance movement in America (see, for example, Gusfield 1963; Johnson 1978): the attack on the saloon was not only because drink was served there, but because of the social disorder that automatically accompanied such built environments.

The cult of domesticity and the belief in the power of rooms to produce and reproduce middle-class civility no doubt reached a zenith in the cultural formation we call Victorian. In this period, domestic spaces and objects multiplied not only in numbers but in function. Activity-specific rooms and furniture (for example) served as physical templates for behavior. There were music rooms and sewing rooms, each with the right sort of tables, chairs, and comportment. Decoration also proliferated. In addition to their belief in the power of the rooms to make a middle class, the bourgeoisie may have been interested in the material objects as creators of a family and class memory that they lacked. Accordingly, a new parlor was filled with memory-evoking objects.

To return to the Catholic/Protestant contention on these matters, it is interesting to note the manner in which even such strongly Protestant areas as New England took to the use of "relics" like the ubiquitous floral collages rendered from the hair of the dear departed. More and more, the parlor became a sacred space – and by that token a powerful field for the "evocation of associations."

The resemblance of all this to contemporary anthropological views of symbolism is more than coincidental. In all this, the Victorians – who most elaborated these theories – were structuralists and hermeneuticists both, and indeed verging toward a psychoanalytic perspective as well. Briefly, meaning was to be found both in structural opposition (nature/culture, female/male, soft/hard, etc.) and in the interpretive layers of personal and cultural associations inherent in generic and specific items – from Father's favorite chair to the floral piece woven of the dear departed's hair. Such meaning was transmitted through both conceptual and emotional paths, unconsciously as well as consciously. Finally, the recipient open to such "influence" was literally transformed by enough exposure. This theory –

in both its academic and popular varieties – can be found, explicitly and implicitly, throughout the nineteenth century and on both sides of the Atlantic. We find it in the promoters of new public (garden cemeteries, parks) and private (gothic revival cottages) spaces. The laboring classes would be civilized and domesticated if their little dwellings could be properly laid out with a simple but decorated parlor and kept clean, and if the inmates could further imbibe not liquor but the softening effects of a stroll through the park.

This is not to say that the Victorian middle class invented this perspective. Many of the same oppositions and even associations can be found in European (and of course other) folk traditions. But the Victorians – both within the academy and then in popular discourse – consciously organized these notions into a theory of domestic power that could at once account for, authorize, and validate their own experience of cultural transformation, and, at the same time, provide a way of shaping and controlling the lower classes.

Such popular perspectives were also implicated in the development of social science in this period. As Elias argues (1982), the development of Romanticism in Germany can be understood as rooted in the particular position of the middle classes there, as can the notion of *Kultur*, which has occupied center stage in German social thought and, through its emigrants, American anthropology. It was not surprising that neither Marx nor Freud was ready to relinquish rooms and objects to the antiquarian. Whether as symbol or fetish, both allowed for a key (if sometimes undesirable) role of empowered objects in the life of the individual and the culture.

Ironically, however, social science in England and America developed in disregard of things (and bodies). As noted, the popular cult of domesticity there was very strong, and indeed both the Gothic revival and the theory of associations were first promulgated there. However, though the literati certainly retained a notion of the importance of rooms as emblems and producers of specific class behavior, developing social scientific thought seems to have been far more rooted in eighteenth-century rationalist, enlightenment, notions of mentality than nineteenth-century romantic ones.[2] Buildings, rooms, and objects were ignored in favor of an internalist and rationalist model of behavior. Malinowski's *mittel-Europa* concern with objects and experience seems only to have spawned descriptive accounts of material culture among his students rather than explorations of their possible role in cultural and social reproduction. The dominant paradigm of the middle decades of the twentieth century, Radcliffe-Brownian structural func-tionalism, with which Arensberg's work is generally (if inadequately) associated, was based largely on Durkheimian notions of how social systems operated. In general, functionalist ethnographies of the 1930s through 1960s did not assign either the built or the assembled environment a critical role in the social processes with which they were concerned. Behavior was produced by rules and values, which, in turn, were internalized either mysteriously or by the effects of social action itself. The relegation of the material world to insignificance was not, however, a necessary element in the *Année Sociologique* program.

Maurice Halbwachs, a particularly gifted student of Durkheim, elaborated a general theoretical framework that might have supplied the basis for an ethnography of the built and assembled environment. Halbwachs' posthumously published *La Mémoire collective* (1950; translated into English as *The Collective Memory*, 1980) accorded a vital function to the built environment, in effect attempting to extend the Durkheimian program into the philosophic discourse on self – to show (in response to his other teacher, Bergson) that even the apparently internal and private realms of memory and identity were socially constructed. Halbwachs noted, in fact, that he was not the first to assign the material world a critical (we might say mediatory) function in the social construction of self: "Auguste Comte remarked that mental equilibrium was, first and foremost, due to the fact that the physical objects of our daily contact change little or not at all, providing us with an image of permanence and stability" (Halbwachs 1980: 129).

According to Halbwachs, social groups make spaces and buildings and arrange objects that serve not only to express cultural values but also to constitute the groups as such through time – not so much by means of the patterns of behavior learned in such settings (if only because this was not a central concern of a book treating collective memory) as through a series of collective representations of the group(s) as such – with each social group representing itself in its own material world (household, neighborhood, etc.). The later domination of Lévi-Strauss' mentalist model of culture no doubt stifled the further development of this perspective in France.

In England, subsequent analyses of social dramas – curiously enough, considering the source of the metaphor – paid relatively little attention to "setting" unless (as most notably in the case of Turner) the action was explicitly religious ritual. Halbwachs' work, and indeed the interpretive/symbolic side of the *Année* project, is otherwise detectable in England (before the 1960s) principally in the work of Evans-Pritchard, and later Mary Douglas, who developed experiential and structural approaches to the construction of meaning. Within this new discourse – at first of only limited impact on their compatriots – spaces and objects assumed real significance as symbols, and Romantic assumptions about the power of spaces and objects re-emerged, under the guise of novel anthropological theory.[3]

Yet the rise of interpretive anthropology still brought attention to objects mainly in the guise of religious symbols or things that worked like religious symbols – for example, political symbols. The mundane world of secular space and objects did receive occasional attention through the last several decades, but mainly as a three-dimensional semiotic restatement of an unchanging world view and social structure – Hicks' (1976) discussion of the Tetum house, for example, or Bourdieu's

(1977) famous account of the Kabyle dwelling. In such semiotic decodings there is little to suggest, however, that such spaces and objects – unless they are specific-ally religious – have the transforming power routinely ascribed to ritual. There is in the anthropological approach a curious symmetry with Victorian thought as discussed above. Protestant Victorians were willing to ascribe power to spaces and objects in secular settings – and less so in overtly religious contexts, where the dissonance between Catholic and Protestant assumptions about how religion worked was more obvious. Latter-day anthropologists, on the other hand, are happy to accord mysterious powers to religious things, but – until quite recently – less so to secular objects or spaces (Fernandez's (1986) and Gilsenan's (1982) work, for example, are important exceptions).

As for literature, I have neither the space nor the expertise to explore here the differences among and development of novels through the nineteenth and twentieth centuries. It can be noted, however, that attention to rooms as class and, increas-ingly, psychological indices was perhaps an earmark of the nineteenth-century novel in the west. Rooms, and objects within them, are critical actors in the works of Balzac, Dickens, or Henry James. Even where they are critical of the material manifestation of class identity, such authors often assume that the individual – like Balzac's Père Goriot, who fails to create himself by these means – reveals himself in the process. Which is to say that these novelists were working within the dominant world view of their time and class.

The Anglo-Irish writers of the period were no exception. In that tradition, the role of the house and room in the construction and maintenance of class behavior and identity – or its loss through material decay – is a central feature of what is typically called "the big house novel," as it is of the caricatures of the Irish peasantry, always pictured in a chaotic squalor that violates Victorian categories and sensibilities. In a phrase: "The pig in the parlor." As for the middle classes (slower to emerge and achieve dominance there than elsewhere in western Europe) Kate O'Brien's suggestively titled novel, *The Ante-Room*, opened up that territory.

Irish Rooms

Which brings us back to the scenes of Irish domesticity with which we began this exploration. O'Connor's version of Irish life has much in common with Arensberg and Kimball's. While the novelist's account is of working- and lower-middle-class urban Cork rather than rural Clare, both works depict Irish society as consisting of a series of domestic boxes that contain, in all senses of the term, the people who live in them. Particular rooms achieve a palpable power as the material embodiments of the Father through the evocation of memories and emotions.

But the difference in the sentiments associated with that domesticity are striking. Arensberg and Kimball's characters seem to stick around from choice, while

O'Connor's – when as young men and women they attempt the Cork version of the *passagera* – are driven back by the force of gossip and the constant rain. Some of this difference can be attributed to the perspectives of the authors, not only as individuals, but as anthropologists and novelist respectively.

Even though they discuss historical transformations, Arensberg and Kimball's Ireland seems the very model of a stable, self-reproducing family and community social system. In that world, the "west room" seems to embody authority and status, and thus to find its ritual role in reproducing the social relations of what was apparently a stable social formation. In symbolic aid of this task, the important attributes of the room are its position (behind the hearth in the west end of the house) and the sacred and valued objects that decorate it. Here we have the nub of both a structural and a hermeneutical appreciation of the source of the power of the west room. The movement into the room can be taken as a ritual moment, whose sense and power derive from binary oppositions (east/west, etc.) and the trains of conscious, pre-conscious, and unconscious associations of the sacred objects. It is enough to make both Mary Douglas and Victor Turner, as well as all their Victorian forebears, happy.

But this nascent interpretive stance, potentially akin to O'Connor's literary perspective through a common ancestry in Romantic and Victorian culture, is still held captive to among the least 'novelistic' of social science theories, for in so far as dramatic narratives thrive on conflict, there was no more undramatic anthropological form than structural functionalism. Arensberg had learned it well, and so when he saw the potential for or the reality of "basic" conflict, he put it in its cyclic, holistic place: "Freud might illuminate us about the sort of conflicts such a human structure engenders, but he has little to say of the far more important, more apparent balance of emotional forces which it entails." (Arensberg 1959: 59–60). Not surprisingly, while there are many "psychoanalytic" novels, there must be few structural-functionalist ones. As for O'Connor, one of his most famous stories was entitled, "My Oedipus Complex." The same contrast can be drawn on the issue of class. For Arensberg and Kimball, the differences between large farmers, small farmers, and others amounted to another balanced system producing more harmony than conflict. For O'Connor, as for many other writers of social fiction, the same differences engendered internal as well as external conflict – born of insecurity and instability as much as of antagonism.

It might of course be argued, however, that the difference is simply one of rooms. That is to say, that the differences in class-consciousness and stability between rural west Clare and urban Cork gave rooms different roles and potentials in the two contexts. But was the family and community structure depicted in the ethnography as thoroughly and stably domestic as the authors implied? Arensberg and Kimball's description concentrates on the domestic setting – farm and farmhouse. Even communal gatherings are located there, whether in the collective labor of cooring at harvest, or the meetings of the old men in *cúaird*. My own experience does not contradict this picture. I would, in fact, extend it by observing that the public institution most often visited and least described by Arensberg – the pub – is also curiously domestic in Ireland.

Contrary to foreign stereotypes, perhaps, most rural pubs are very quiet places, where men enter and leave for social visits with publican and patrons much as they do each other's homes. When referring to such "visits," locals will use the same idiom used for visiting one another, "Which house were you in last night?" No matter what the official name of a pub, it is only referred to by that of the proprietor. Even when weekend musical entertainment brings larger and livelier crowds, comportment will follow a decorum developed in the good-natured competitive structure of the *oiche mór* – "big night" – in anyone's kitchen. Patrons treat one another as "guests" who need to be cajoled into performing.

Yet older descriptions and accounts of rural Ireland reveal a less isolated and contained and much less domesticated round of rural life. Only a few generations before Arensberg and Kimball's arrival, the predominant settlement pattern in the west was the *clachán*, a cluster of cottages with surrounding fragmented fields held in "rundale" tenure. Pilgrimage and pattern were frequent social holidays marked by revelry and conflict, where the crossroads was a frequent place of entertainment.

Through the course of the nineteenth century, two forces – the Protestant ascendancy in the guise of landlord or government, and the Catholic Church represented by Bishop and parish priest – conspired to drive all this social life inside, and into the separate boxes (houses or church) that defined the character of the activity in question. Whatever the religious difference between these two powerful regimes, they shared a belief in the Victorian cult of domesticity, in the civilizing and domesticating power of rooms.[4]

For the Protestant, "improving" landlord, the *clachán* or "cluster" of houses without clear and consolidated holdings were not only economically irrational, they were the seed of all social evil. Indeed, not surprisingly, landlord and British government rhetoric was reminiscent of the domestic moralism of the temperance movement in the United States. Both believed that the evils of drink were part and parcel of a specific type of sociability shaped by the "promiscuous confusion" of dwelling and settlement. By the mid-nineteenth century most *clacháns* had been dispersed and, helped along by the depredations of famine and immigration, had vacated the human landscape described by Arensberg and Kimball.

The Catholic Church, for its part, aimed its domesticating efforts at the wild social life beyond the home (see Taylor 1995). Outdoor religion was either eliminated or greatly reduced and controlled, and the church became the principal site of access to the divine. Beyond the church, the house was increasingly used as an extension of clerical control – and in the rural institution of "stations" was the occasional site of a Mass performed for the household and neighbors. Drinking and associated behavior was also increasingly driven indoors – into the kitchens of *airneal* houses (local gathering spots) or finally into licensed public "houses" – the pubs. These changes came as the result of both inducement and threat. A certain domesticity was certainly held up as emblematic of civility, and achievable through the proper division and decoration of space and performance of associated activity. But if the warm glow of the domestic hearth attracted, it is also the case that a stiff offensive against outdoor and non-domesticated social life was promulgated. Like the ever-present downpour in O'Connor's novel, the forces of social control drove the rural and urban Irishman and woman into their homes.

It is in this context that we need to view the power of the west room in the Irish home. If apparently stable, the social formation described by the anthropologists was in crucial respects quite recent, and the symbolic power of the west room – as the authors themselves imply – was not just evidence of the hold of traditional cultural symbols and values, but rather the product of the conjuncture of Victorian domestic civility and religiosity (embodied in many of the decorative objects kept there) and more ancient, chthonic notions of a charismatic landscape. Interestingly, given these symbolic emblems, this room was "behind the hearth" – a private space, whereas the values and relations of the egalitarian community were in the public kitchen. But this arrangement was not to last, for if the west room was a civilizing of sacred fairy space within the home, then the parlor was its eventual replacement for the true middle class – rural or urban – interposing itself between the private kitchen and the public outside.

Which brings us back to the lower-middle-class denizens of Cork described by O'Connor, who seem acutely conscious of the instability of their world and of their respective positions in it. In this more obviously fluctuating scene, house, rooms, and decor become crucial ways not only of displaying, but also of achieving class position. Consequently there is a self-conscious and thoroughly ambivalent attitude toward these elements of material culture: a lack of self-confidence in some cases, and a great sense of oppression in others. The more powerfully emblematic such rooms became, the more poignant was the failure to achieve them in their proper form. What kind of a parlor could you afford to make?

We can end with another suggestive image from O'Connor's *Dutch Interior*, in the same home described above. The domineering but finally ineffectual father knows how to make a kitchen – the first room described above. But the parlor he knows he must have is beyond his ken. In it one son has contracted consumption and died, and the other, from whom we heard at the beginning of this chapter, has withdrawn from the very domesticity of which it should be emblematic:

> It was a square, cold, damp box of a room papered in yellow with floral designs in red and green. On the mantelpiece one of his father's favourite clocks tick-tocked noisily.

There were two high-backed armchairs upholstered in black leather – purchased second-hand – at either side of the fireplace, and a round, one-legged table with two dining-room chairs. There was a cheap red carpet, and in a bookcase along one wall were Ned's books . . . Before settling down in this cold, lonesome room, Stevie put the candle behind him and looked out from under the blind (1940: xx).

The emotional power of the domestic space in this passage, as in those social science theories rooted in romanticism, is a function of self-consciousness. As Grier remarks in relation to the American version, "they must perceive the possibility of economic and social mobility to be real – that society is fluid, to some degree, without the restraints of ironclad castes" (Grier 1988: 20).

Perhaps the old couple moving into the west room were as aware as their counterparts in urban Cork of the power and insecurity of rooms and objects in a volatile world colored by class and familial conflict. For the tensions between father and son – and daughter – are perhaps even more characteristic of rural Irish literature. For a recent, and penetrating example I would cite the writing of John McGahern (see especially "The Gold Watch").

In all the literary cases, the authors are depicting a world of which they have personal experience. Though it might be pointed out that their form of "representation" required the presence of conflict as much as functionalism required its absence, one cannot help but suspect that a sensitivity to both historical and personal context would have taken Arensberg and Kimball's observations on the power of rooms further. My own experience – in the Irish field and elsewhere as well – convinces me that it is precisely those whom history – personal and /or collective – has made aware of change and conflict that most feel the power of rooms and their objects as anchors of memory and identity. Perhaps there is an element of the self-fulfilling prophecy in all that. Those who believe they are in a drama will learn their roles, and if the set is in the script, then it too will be expected to play its part.

Notes

1. Abrams (1953) has an interesting discussion of the movement from Hartley and Hume to Mill and Coleridge. In the latter, "feelings" replace "ideas" as the key to memory association.
2. This is no doubt related to a certain lack of confidence in the romantic world view often detectable in Protestant England and America. In their writings on the transformative power of architecture or cemeteries, for example, English and American authors seemed to feel the need to include discursive instructions on just how the symbols were going to act on you, the visitor.
3. Could it be a coincidence that Turner, Evans-Pritchard, and Douglas were

Catholics – and two of them converts? One must wonder about the depth of the cultural character of the Catholicism involved – at least as compared to traditions in Catholic countries. From the Oxford movement through Turner, we still encounter the convert's need for explicit instructions.
4. The "institutionalization" of rural Ireland through asylums and poor houses played a critical role as well (see Saris 1996).

References

Abrams, M. H. 1953. *The Mirror and the Lamp: Romantic Theory and the Critical Tradition*. New York: Norton.

Arensberg, Conrad M. 1959 [1937]. *The Irish Countryman*. Gloucester, MA: Peter Smith.

——, and Solon T. Kimball. 1940. *Family and Community in Rural Ireland*. Cambridge, MA: Harvard University Press.

Bourdieu, Pierre. 1977 [1972]. *Outline of a Theory of Practice*, transl. Richard Nice. Cambridge, UK: Cambridge University Press.

Brown, Peter R. L. 1981. *The Cult of the Saints: Its Rise and Function in Latin Christianity*. Chicago: University of Chicago Press.

Elias, Norbert. 1978. *The Civilizing Process*, Vol. I, transl. Edmund Jephcott. New York: Pantheon Books.

——. 1982. *The Civilizing Process*, Vol. II, transl. Edmund Jephcott. New York: Pantheon Books.

Fernandez, James. 1986. *Persuasions and Performances: The Play of Tropes in Culture*. Bloomington, IN: University of Indiana Press.

Gilsenan, Michael. 1982. *Recognizing Islam: An Anthropologist's Introduction*. London: Croom Helm.

Grier, Katherin C. 1988. *Culture and Comfort: People, Parlors, and Upholstery 1850–1930*. Rochester, NY: The Strong Museum and University of Massachusetts Press.

Gusfield, Joseph. 1963. *Symbolic Crusade: Status Politics and the American Temperance Movement*. Urbana, IL: University of Illinois Press.

Halbwachs, Maurice. 1980 [1950]. *The Collective Memory*. New York: Harper and Row.

Hartley, David. 1775. *Hartley's Theory of the Human Mind, on the Principle of the Association of Ideas: With Essays Relating to the Subject of It*. London: J. Johnston.

Hicks, David. 1976. *Tetum Ghosts and Kin*. Palo Alto, CA: Mayfield Publishing Co.

Hume, David. 1962. *Hume on Human Nature and the Understanding*. New York: Collier Books.

Johnson, Paul. 1978. *A Shopkeeper's Millenium*. New York: Hill and Wang.

Lawrence, Denise L., and Setha M. Low. 1990. "The Built Environment and Spatial Form." *Annual Review of Anthropology* 19: 453–505.

Ledoux, Claude Nicolaus. 1983. *Architecture Considérée Sous le Rapport de L'art, Des Moeurs et de la Législation*, Avery Architecture and Fine Arts Library, Columbia University. Princeton, NJ: Princeton Architectural Press.

McGahern, John. 1993. "The Gold Watch." In *The Collected Stories, John McGahern*. New York: Alfred A. Knopf.

O'Connor, Frank. 1940. *Dutch Interior*. New York: Alfred A. Knopf.

Pevsner, Nikolaus. 1968 [1943]. *An Outline of European Architecture*. Harmondsworth: Penguin Books.

Rapoport, Amos. 1976. "Socio-cultural Aspects of Man–Environment Studies." In *The Mutual Interaction of People and Their Built Environment*, ed. Amos Rapoport, pp. 7–35. The Hague, Netherlands: Mouton.

Saris, A. Jamie. 1996. "Mad Kings Proper Houses, and an Asylum in Rural Ireland." *American Anthropologist* 98(3): 539–54.

Taylor, Lawrence. 1995. *Occasions of Faith: An Anthropology of Irish Catholics*. Dublin: Lilliput Press and Philadelphia, PA: University of Pennsylvania Press.

Verrips, Kitty. 1987. "Noblemen, Farmers, and Laborers: A Civilizing Offensive in a Dutch Village." *Netherlands Journal of Sociology* 23(1): 3–16.

–10–

The Memory House: Time and Place in Jewish Immigrant Culture in France
Joëlle Bahloul

The concept of "house," Collomb suggests, has two distinct but collaborative meanings in European cultures (1983: 81). It designates the house as edifice or the house as family. Collomb explores this semantic combination in seventeenth-century Provençal culture, which established a confusion between these two "levels" of signification, symbolically associating the social concept to the image of the edifice. This process is specific neither to Mediterranean societies, nor to European ones in general. It constitutes a native social taxonomy whose symbolic operation is the identification of a genealogical or kinship unit with a built structure. It consists of metaphorical terminology establishing an analogy between people and place in individual and collective identity through place-naming, rules of residence and inheritance, and the symbolic representation of the family as a built structure (Fernandez 1977, 1988). Thus, in Southern European societies, for example, the presence of the taxon *oustal* designates "a farm in the sense of a conjunction between a specific named place and the family line associated with it" (Rogers 1991: 68). This metaphorical procedure has been treated in anthropological theory by the Lévi-Straussian concept of *société à maison* ("house-based society"), in which the house is conceived of as an organizing principle operating at both the material and the non-material levels (Lamaison 1987; Lévi-Strauss 1987). The concept of "house" is thus not limited in scope to its mere social and practical meaning. Rather, it seems to determine the configuration of a key symbolic structure, as several recent ethnographic studies have demonstrated, in the footsteps of and beyond Lévi-Strauss's theoretical premises (Carsten and Hugh-Jones 1995).

Recent theoretical developments in anthropology tend to emphasize this level of meaning of the "house" terminology, and decipher the house as a system of signs. In Bourdieu's approach, the Kabyle house is analyzed as a social and cosmological classifier combining dimensions of both space and time (Bourdieu 1989). Augé follows a similar perspective when he deciphers real estate ads in major French magazines that nurture the modern mythology and imagery of the countryside "abode," a symbolic repository of family memory and bourgeois ideology (Augé 1989). Dwelling fashions and representations are then analyzed in a manner similar to Barthes's treatment of clothing fashions; the built structure is approached as a semantic system of social and cultural identity. The following presentation of migrants' remembrances of the original house will pursue a similar perspective, though it will have to address a specific theoretical problem.[1]

In effect, what the taxon "house" seems to signify primarily is the highly territorial nature of the "house-based society," as if the kin group that it designates was inscribed – if not transcribed – on the ground. The process becomes more complex in the culture of migrants whose historical contingency has dissociated them from their territorial referent. In addition, a cultural process characteristic of these migrant cultures is their being "trans-cultural" (Fischer 1986), transformed into an organized patchwork of cultural traits assembled through a history of multiple migrations. Because the native concept of "house" is in all cases tightly related to the structure and folk conceptualization of kinship, designating either a specific group of relatives or the "family" as an "imagined" reality, migrants necessarily modify their symbolic construction of the "house" in the migration process, while modifying their cultural, political, and economic characteristics. Moreover, not only the contents and construction of the concept of the house are modified in the migration process, but also its social usage. Now the sturdy and fixed image of the original edifice functions as a locus for the crystallization of the imagined past, and for the symbolic strengthening of the kin group shattered in the displacement. Social memory plays a pivotal role in this process. As Lévi-Strauss has analyzed it, wherever it applies, the concept of "house" is elaborated by complex forms and the structure of collective memory (1983: 177). Thus, he suggests that social anthropologists use historical and ethno-historical analysis in their exploration of the folk concept of "house" (1983: 174).

Immigrants from former French colonies of the Maghreb who are now established in France offer an archetypical illustration of this trans-cultural reality in European society, one that consists of the formation of a deterritorialized culture by the continuous crossing of cultural boundaries, in this case the French and the Maghrebian ones. On both shores of the Mediterranean, these immigrants have evolved within different types of "house-based societies." And yet, beyond migration, uprootedness, and transplantation into post-industrial urban communities, the native category of "house" seems to remain operative in identifying people historically and within their present networks of socialization. The questions thus remaining are: how has the native concept of "house" survived these symbolic and geographical movements in migrants' culture? How is the concept of "house" as a social, practical, and symbolic classifier manipulated by deterritorialized groups when the material embodiment of the concept has been lost?

I have explored the answer to these questions in the collective memory of a group of French Jewish families who shared a multi-family house in Sétif, Eastern

Algeria, until 1962. My analysis follows their emigration to France, and the independence of the Algerian nation.

The Historical Background

Like other Jewish communities in North Africa, these Jews inscribe their domestic memories in a long history of trans-cultural experiences. The onset of the colonial era, in the early nineteenth century, had put an end to the eleven-centuries-old Muslim regime of the *dhimma*, and marked the beginning of a long and profound process of cultural Westernization and socio-economic emancipation that peaked in 1870, when Algerian Jews collectively acquired French citizenship. For these Jews, colonial Westernization meant voluntary and frantic Frenchification, principally by their entry into the French school system, with consequent progressive dissociation from their native Arabic culture and language. Since the turn of the twentieth century, Sétif's tiny Jewish community experienced these historical upheavals while vigorously clinging, until the 1950s, to its traditional patrilineal, patriarchal and patrilocal rules. The progressive entrance of Jewish women into the French secular education system from the early years of the twentieth century introduced major changes and tensions in domestic life. The process was completed when most Maghrebian Jews emigrated *en masse* to France, Israel and the Americas between the mid-1950s and the late 1960s. Thus the experience of migration has underlined changes in the kinship system that had already been initiated before these Jews left the Maghreb through the effects of rationalized Europeanization and social advancement.

The largest segment of the Algerian community – about 150,000 persons – went to France, where, like other formerly colonized groups that had been incorporated into the colonizer's society, they are now striving to blend into the dominant French social and cultural landscape, while maintaining clear-cut social and cultural boundaries through the elaboration of narrative and ritual strategies of ethnic memory. The following discussion is an attempt to analyze these forms of collective memory, as they rationalize the process of migration itself, and its effects on the folk concept of "house." I start with the narrative strategies.

The House as it is Told: The Edifying Past

The narrators are a group of about ten families – making up around 80 to 90 individuals – most of whom now live in Marseilles (southern France), although some are in the Parisian and Lyons metropolitan regions. Some of these families are related by past alliances. They all share the experience of having cohabited in the same named house in Sétif, between the early 1930s and 1962. The kin-related part of this group gathers today more frequently than that which is not related.

But they all maintain some kind of communication, through correspondence and invitations to family life-cycle rituals or to rituals of the religious calendar, as well as through circumstantial visits.

My informants' ethnohistorical evocation of their genealogical structures is a significant rendition of the historical tensions developed above. It evolves as an epic narrative describing a domestic group in its original house, its past social organization in Algeria, its peregrinations and dispersion, and finally its settlement in French society. At the center of this epic, the house and its internal courtyard appear as the centripetal principle of the mnemonic narrative. The house is referred to as "Dar-Refayil," (the "house of Refayil" in Arabic), and is named after a former male owner, a sort of eponymous and unrelated founder of the domestic community, designating the domestic unit as a male-oriented entity.[2] The house was a two-story building sheltering several families in individual rooms set around a square open-air courtyard, a space inhabited by both Jewish and Muslim families since the early 1940s. A marked patriarchal group, Dar-Refayil was also a bi-religious one. In the narrators' remembrances, the house is the frequent topic of many nostalgic and joyous family reunions wherein their former neighbors and domestic experiences are evoked with a host of detail on particular domestic places and events. These evocations usually emerge during celebrations of life-cycle rituals and other religious ceremonies.

The taxon "house" is articulated here in specific symbolic procedures that transform it into a mnemonic device (Halbwachs 1992). This specific art of memory – describing the past by shaping it along architectonic lines – is ancient in European and Mediterranean popular and scholarly thought (Yates 1966; Spence 1984). In ancient Greek rhetoric, the orator remembers discursive structures in rebuilding places, and his discourse becomes a speech edifice. Similarly, the metaphor of the house is a key literary trope in Maghrebian culture, as evidenced in the contemporary francophone north African novel (Dib 1952; Boudjedra 1969).

In this spirit, Dar-Refayil's memoirs are dominated by what Bachelard calls a "topo-analysis" (1969). Remembrance of the house unfolds as a narrative interpreting the past and providing ethics for the future. Here the past is a house, and the house a moral locus (Fischer 1986: 197). The structure of this mnemonic narrative follows, in my view, three discursive principles: first, the symbolic tension between the female and the male sexual identity of the house; second, the moral function of the narrative representation of the past house; and third, the constant shift from the private to the universal dimension of domestic life.

A Mother-House or the House of the Father?

The tension in the sexual identity of the domestic group is represented in the narration of its foundation. Domestic memory is here organized along mythological structures, isolating one particular family experience as the nucleus for the unfolding of domestic history. At first the narrative logic is one of procreation: a male character emerges out of a family shattering, travels, settles down in a city and encounters a female character with whom he founds a family. After another family shattering with the death of the mother, the original male character joins a house community, founds another family and has more children.

Moushi Senoussi was born in 1898 in Bordj-Bou-Arreridj, a rural borough located some 70 kilometers west of Sétif. His parents were wealthy farmers who raised cattle and sheep and developed extensive economic and cultural relationships with their Muslim neighbors. After the First World War, the farm was sold and the family wealth split among Moushi's eleven siblings. Moushi established himself in Sétif, like many other Jewish and Muslim rural migrants at this time, and started a small butchery business. Soon after his arrival he married Sarah, an educated young woman with determined aspirations for cultural advancement. Sarah and Moushi had five children between 1923 and 1935. A dedicated mother, Sarah went through seven pregnancies during these twelve years, two of which ended in miscarriage. In 1936, she decided to end her eighth pregnancy with the help of a neighbor who attempted a sloppy abortion, from which Sarah died after a severe infection. Her death was a major tragedy for the Senoussi family and for the entire Jewish community, which had recently suffered from an epidemic of typhus that killed two of Sarah's younger sisters. At that time, the Senoussis lived in an apartment building in the middle-class section of Sétif. After the tragedy, Moushi's mother suggested that her son leave the apartment where Sarah had died, because "a house where death had occurred was cursed." She also suggested that Moushi remarry and that the family move to Dar-Refayil, where some of their relatives were already established and which was located in a working-class Judeo-Arabic neighborhood. With the rabbi's help, Moushi married Gilda, a "little cousin" (distant relative), about three months after Sarah's death, and moved with his children and his new wife to Dar-Refayil by the end of 1936.

This episode has been memorized as the drama of motherhood, which first failed in Sarah's destiny and was then rehabilitated with Moushi's second marriage, a way of "bringing a mother back to the family," as women repeatedly say. For the vulnerable Jewish demography of Sétif, motherhood was the locus of its most threatening challenges. Family fertility was strongly encouraged, yet emancipated women were increasingly uneasy in the stiff patriarchal family. Jewish women's work and income were often necessary to the economic survival of these large families. Yet, although the family's move to Dar-Refayil is definitely interpreted as a social regression (fewer commodities, communal domesticity viewed as primitive, as opposed to the previous individual household, viewed as socially "advanced"), Dar-Refayil is described as a house that salvages the stability of the family. The narrative unfolds as if Moushi had encountered a house as his true second wife, as if he had impregnated her; Gilda is withdrawn from the narrative's core; none of her children and step-children ever portrays her as the ultimate mother that replaced Sarah. It is Dar-Refayil, the house as a "moral person" (Lévi-Strauss 1983: 174) that the narrative emphasizes as the real mother, thus making it a female relative, if not the female founder of the domestic community.

The house is characterized as a mother-house, with its courtyard described as a womb, a domestic environment that, in a sense, replaced the deceased mother with the collectivity found around the courtyard in 1936. The house is a female "body" and a feminine figure giving birth to a community. Yet Moushi has been transformed by memory into a hero of patriarchal resistance. He is evoked as the charismatic leader of the domestic community, he who adamantly insisted that his sons remain by his side and take over his butchery business. The remembered story of Dar-Refayil is a complete reversal of the ideal patrilineal scenario: Moushi's sons did form their own households in Dar-Refayil, but after a period of progressive financial scarcity, they dissociated from their father's authority and left the house and Sétif to find their happiness in Algiers. While the mnemonic epic started with the recovery of motherhood, it ends as a patriarchal failure, epitomized by Moushi's death in 1960 and the subsequent dismantling of the Jewish part of the domestic group. Yet the dispersed former Dar-Refayil residents get together in 1962 and migrate to Marseilles, where most of them are established today in the same neighborhood. After their establishment in Marseilles, Moushi's sons get together again and open their corporate butchery business, and together they take care of their siblings' families. One of their younger sisters, Yvette, who had lost her husband in 1961 in the Algerian war, shares the responsibility and becomes the head of the household composed of Gilda and her four children. Yvette is the one who financially and socially supported the remainder of Moushi's family in France, the one who married off all her younger siblings (offspring of Moushi's second marriage), and has developed a vibrant authority over the entire extended family in the few decades following its immigration into France.

The tension between male and female characters, between patriarchal/patrilineal rules and female authority that emerged before the Second World War in Sétif's Jewish community, has persisted in Dar-Refayil's community exiled in France. We find here a typical ethnographic illustration of what Lévi-Strauss had underlined in the organization of the folk concept of "house": a kinship institution that "combines together a series of opposing principles or social forms such as filiation/residence, patri-/matrilineal descent," thus "reunit(ing) or transcend(ing) these incompatible principles" (Lévi-Strauss 1983: 187, as cited in Carsten and Hugh-Jones 1995: 8). The house is used to resolve or to manipulate the structural and contingent conflicts born in the rules of kinship and in their historical destiny.

The House as Communal Ethic

Related to the narrative tension in the gender structures of the domestic memory is the *evocation of openings*, namely doors and windows, or the metaphorical tension between the inside and the outside. In Dar-Refayil, most rooms had windows and doors overlooking only the courtyard space. The opening of the rooms to the street is defined in domestic memory as a sign of social and economic distinction. In effect, the wealthier part of the domestic community, the owner's family, occupied the only apartment on the façade, with openings towards the street and the outside world. For Jewish women in particular, having access to the street side meant social advancement and emancipation, as opposed to the status of Muslim women, who were still secluded within patriarchal households. In contrast with the lack of openings toward the *outside* world, *inside* doors, the doors of each room and household, were constantly open, women say. Every neighbor could come in at any time to sip a cup of coffee, to chat or to exchange some service. The open doors epitomize the solidarity and conviviality that are said to be the rule inside Dar-Refayil:

> We never closed the doors, one woman says. If a neighbor needed anything, she came, she didn't need to knock the door. *Here* [in France], doors are closed, but *there* they were always open. At night, we just closed with a little bolt. One could open the door with a finger. That's why we lived as a family. We were not neighbors, we were a family. And we had a beautiful life.

The recurrence of the theme of the inside open doors, as opposed to the enclosure of the house to the outside world, signifies what Bachelard characterizes as a form of *topophilia* (1969). The open doors constitute the core of a semantic articulation that tends to express the idea that although the house was lacking comfort because it was an enclosed universe, it also was, inside, a harmonious community, which the narrators identify as a kinship community. In effect, Dar-Refayil's topophile chronotope above all conveys the idea of the strength of the family and of kinship ties that were threatened by the initial mother's death. They are a family epic and a family ethic, as if the family, in the various misadventures it undergoes, were constructed like a building and imagined with symbolic steadiness. In fact, the Jewish branch in Dar-Refayil was almost entirely related by the end of the 1950s: religious endogamy was practiced within the domestic group, and one of Moushi's sons recounts delightedly how he married his neighbor, how he just had to cross the courtyard to find a wife. Here again, the house functions as a symbolic and discursive resolution of the changes that kinship was undergoing during the inter-war period in Algeria. The house is an illusory institution transfixing an unstable kinship reality "to which it lends (symbolic) solidity" (Lévi-Strauss 1987: 155).

The Courtyard as Historical Center

The narrative of domestic memories overall conveys an optical feeling of centripetal construction, and one gets a sense of the enclosure of the narrative within the limits of the courtyard as the described lives are portrayed. But this is an effect of the narrative illusion specific to the autobiographical genre. In fact, Dar-Refayil's memoirs do not confine their protagonists' experiences to the limits of the courtyard. They also tell how the domestic group went through the Second World War, the war of independence, and the conflictual relationships between Jews and Arabs. Sétif was a plural urban community, yet this colonial society was traversed by triangular lines of ethnic and religious distinction. There were the Christian Europeans in the city's northern section and the native Muslims and Jews in its southern section. And although the Jews had been French citizens since 1870 and were educated in the French school system, they were still deeply immersed in Arabic culture. Local Jews started to distinguish themselves from the Muslims after the Algerian war of independence began in 1954. In Dar-Refayil, they strove to remain closer to the Muslims, because their political emancipation was never followed by a process of social elevation and of complete integration into the French community. "We were all the same class," said Bu-Slimo, whom I interviewed in Sétif in 1980, "That's why we got along with respect and without animosity." On the other hand, the separation from the French Christian community was pronounced. Anti-Semitism was virulent until the Second World War, and then continued silent but sturdy. No Jew could enter a Christian bar; Jewish youngsters could not entertain themselves in Christian ballrooms. "It always ended in fights," says Eddy Senoussi, one of Moushi's sons. More than two decades later, Dar-Refayil is remembered as a social microcosm representing *from within* the most decisive events that unfolded *outside*. The pattern was mutual respect. Interreligious respect is time and again represented through a material metaphor: when Jews celebrated their weddings in the courtyard, they say they hung a curtain across the courtyard that would protect the privacy of Muslim families, especially women. The curtain, a "symbolic" form of separation, epitomizes respect – distinction but not segregation. Dar-Refayil's memoirs report on domestic life through integrating it into general history, as if the materiality of this cramped dwelling were enlarged, "magnified," in being universalized. It is as if remembrance were shifting constantly from the intimate and private structure of the courtyard to the universal and general pattern of regional and international conflicts, from the particular to the universal.

What this optical effect reveals, first and foremost, is a tension characteristic of domestic memory: one between its practical and symbolic dimensions. Dar-Refayil's memoirs are sealed in the concreteness of domestic gestures, objects, places and interactions. They evolve as embodied memory (Connerton 1989). Yet past practices are evoked in a manner that turns them into the symbolic texture of the practice of memory. The former house is a material support for remembrance as it strengthens family cohesion; but, at the same time, the performance and discursive construction of memory strive to erase this contingency when they aim to convey the sense of Dar-Refayil's universality. In his *Remembrance of Things Past*, Proust constructs the poetics of remembrance through the literary elaboration of body remembrance: the taste of the *madeleine*, odors of the country landscape, etc. In Dar-Refayil's memoirs, reminiscence emerges with narrative re-enactment of physical contact with walls, doors, and windows. This process transforms the physicality of past experiences into intangible and irreversibly symbolic ones in the present. It is a discursive strategy whereby displaced ethnicity aims to restore its shattered geography.

Domestic Ritual and Domestic Memory

Narrative might appear as a logical discursive procedure for the unfolding of collective memory, by which images of physical and material objects and loci are crystallized and experienced through words. Another powerful expression of the memory of the past house is developed through gestures of a ritual nature. These gestures unfold as an archival film in which people re-enact their past physical relation to places and people, though the latter no longer exist. In Dar-Refayil's memoirs, this dimension is necessarily associated with the family gathering of a ritual nature, i.e. during the celebration of life-cycle rituals or rituals of the religious calendar. The performance of memories of the house allows the illusory reconstitution of family stability. In addition, remembering in family gatherings accentuates the moralization of the past house as a kinship construct. The emergence of spontaneous recollections is almost exclusively articulated in family and home ritual settings, and is associated with the dramatic reunion of dispersed relatives and former neighbors gathered for family and religious holidays. The recounting of Dar-Refayil memoirs, by older relatives to younger ones around a festive table, is a verbal operation of kin communion. Those who recount are related to those who listen, and all are related to the characters evoked in the narrations. Telling memories of the past family house unfolds as the transmission of genealogical knowledge; it is a timeless and symbolic communication between generations in the same speech event. The permanence of the taxon "house" reveals a symbolic form of "historical inversion" (Bakhtin 1986).

   This last ethnographic datum gives me the opportunity to attempt an answer to my initial question concerning the destiny of the concept of "house" in a migrant population, and through the migration process. It appears that the imagined house is a mobile concept. As it allows broad flexibility to dramatic changes and conflicts that the family and kinship system undergoes, it also shows great capacity for adjustment to geographical mobility, dispersal of the members of the household, and major changes in gender roles and in domestic economy. After their settlement in France, Dar-Refayil's members now relate to each other through circumstantial events rather than in daily exchanges. Does this mean that Dar-Refayil has survived and will survive, as a house community, the many turmoils generated by migration, economic stress, and political conflicts within the domestic group? It is doubtful. What will remain is the concept of the house itself, which has so deeply shaped the rationalizations of kinship relations, of all individual experiences, and the reconstruction of family history.

Notes

1. A more extensive presentation of this research will be found in Bahloul's *The Architecture of Memory*, Cambridge and New York: Cambridge University Press, 1996.
2. The actual names employed by the narrators have been changed for the sake of anonymity. I have selected this particular name among a series of first names commonly assigned to male individuals among North African Jews.

References

Augé, Marc. 1989. *Domaines et Châteaux*. Paris: Editions Du Seuil.

Bachelard, Gaston. 1969. *The Poetics of Space*. Boston: Beacon Press.

Bakhtin, Mikhail. 1986. *Speech Genres and Other Late Essays*. Austin: University of Texas Press.

Boudjedra, Rachid. 1969. *La Répudiation*. Paris: Denoël.

Bourdieu, Pierre. 1989. *The Logic of Practice*. Stanford, CA: Stanford University Press.

Carsten, Janet, and Stephen Hugh-Jones (eds). 1995. *About the House: Lévi-Strauss and Beyond*. Cambridge, UK: Cambridge University Press.

Collomb, Alain. 1983. *La Maison Du Père: Famille et Village en Haute-Provence Aux XVIIè et XVIIIè Siècles*. Paris: Presses Universitaires de France.

Connerton, Paul. 1989. *How Societies Remember*. Cambridge: New Cambridge University Press.

Dib, Mohammed. 1952. *La Grande Maison*. Paris: Seuil.

Fernandez, James W. 1977. *Fang Architectonics*. Philadelphia: Institute for Studies in Humanities Issues.

——. 1988. "Andalusia on Our Minds: Two Contrasting Places in Spain as Seen in a Vernacular Poetic Duel of the Late Century." *Cultural Anthropology* 3: 21–35.

Fischer, Michael. 1986. "Ethnicity and the Post-modern Arts of Memory." In *Writing Culture: The Poetics and Politics of Ethnography*, ed. J. Clifford and G. E. Marcus, pp. 194–233. Berkeley: University of California Press.

Halbwachs, Maurice. 1992. *On Collective Memory*. Chicago: University of Chicago Press.

Lamaison, Pierre. 1987. "La Notion de Maison: Entretien avec Claude Lévi-Strauss." *Terrain* 9: 34–9.

Lévi-Strauss, Claude. 1983. *The Way of the Masks*. London: Jonathan Cape.

——. 1987. *Anthropology and Myth: Lectures 1951–1982*. Oxford: Blackwell.

Rogers, Susan Carol. 1991. *Shaping Modern Times in Rural France: The Transformation and Reproduction of an Aveyronnais Community*. Princeton, NJ: Princeton University Press.

Spence, Jonathan. 1984. *The Memory Palace of Matteo Ricci*. New York: Penguin Books.

Yates, Frances. 1966. *The Art of Memory*. Chicago: University of Chicago Press.

Author Index

Author Index

Illić, Ivan, 9

James, Alice, x, 11, 13–14, 16–18, 164, 205
Johnson, Matthew, 10, 16, 19
Johnson, Paul, 228
Just, Roger, 76

Kalisperis, Loukas, x, 11, 13–14, 16–18, 164, 205
Karakasidou, Anastasia, 77, 92n2
Kayser, Bernard, 93n8, 96n42
Kelly, Fergus, 106, 108
Kenna, Margaret, 76
Kennedy, Robert E., 118
Kent, Susan, 1, 5, 16, 28n1
Kertzer, David I., 91
Khambatta, Ismet, 26
Kimball, Solon T., 15, 18, 223–5, 231–3, 235, 112
Knodel, John, 96n41
Kojić, Branislav, 191
Kolodny, Emile, 93n8
Kordosis, Michail, 93n10
Korosec-Serfaty, Perla, 159
Kousoulos, Konstantinos, 75, 78–80
Kremmydas, Vasilis, 76
Krunić, Jovan, 178

Lagopoulos, Alexandros, 96n45
Laiou-Thomadakis, Angeliki, 77, 92n7, 95n27
Lamaison, Pierre, 239
Lambrinidos, Michail G., 78
Laslett, Peter, 3, 8, 12, 91, 200n3
Laveleye, Emile de, 185
Lawrence, Roderick J., 6, 158
Lawrence-Zúñiga, Denise L., x, 5, 11–12, 18–19, 21, 23, 40, 87, 157, 225
Ledoux, Claude Nicolaus, 226
Leontis, Artemis, 91
Lévi-Strauss, Claude, 7–8, 28n5, 29n9, 230, 239–40, 244–5
Lockwood, William, 178
Lodge, Olive, 178, 183, 185–7
Lofgren, Orvar, 23, 159
Loizos, Peter, 76, 206
Low, Setha M., 5, 12, 40, 207, 225
Lowenthal, David, 87, 91

Lumley, Henry de, 1
Lumley, Robert, 143

McCourt, Desmond, 108
Macdonald, C., 7
Macfarlane, Alan, 7, 91, 96n41, 115
McGrew, William, 78, 93n8, 94n15
McGuire, R. H., 12, 14
Mack Smith, Denis, 154n6
Maclachlan, Morgan, 73
McNeill, William, 76–7
Malinowski, Bronislaw, 2, 229
Mansolas, Alexandros, 75, 78
Mantzourani, Eleni, 74, 77, 92n2
Megas, Georgios, 74
Milazzo, Adalgisa, 75, 78–9
Miliarakis, Antonios, 78, 79
Mladenović, Tanasije, 190
Modell, John, 179
Moore, Barrington, 206
Moore, Henrietta, 68
Moore, Roland, 76, 90
Moore, Sarah, 122
Morgan, Lewis Henry, 2
Mosely, Philip E, 181
Moustaka, Calliope, 84
Mouzelis, Nicos, 76

Nenadović, Slobodan, 178, 182
Netting, Robert McC., 2, 73
Nikolić-Stojančević, V., 179, 198
Nouhakis, Ioannis Emm, 75, 79

O'Connor, Bertie, 119, 125n15, 125n16
O'Connor, Frank, 18, 224–5, 231–5 passim
Oliver, Paul, 1, 5, 135
O'Neill, Brian, 70n10
O'Neill, Kevin, 117
O'Tuama, Séan, 107
Oppo, Anna, 67

Panayiotopoulos, Vasilis, 75, 77, 93n8
Papataxiarchis, Evthymios, 76, 206
Papayiannakis, Lefteris, 79
Pardailhe-Galabrun, Annik, 87
Parkin, Robert, 2, 6, 8
Patterson, Nerys Thomas, 106–9, 123n4, 125n17

Subject Index

DATE DUE

DEMCO, INC. 38-2931